STUDY GUIDE
to accompany

THEORY AND PRACTICE

SIXTH EDITION

PATRICK J. WELCH
St. Louis University

GERRY F. WELCH
St. Louis Community College at Meramec

John Wiley & Sons, Inc

This book is printed on acid free paper. ∞

Library of Congress Cataloging-in-Publication Data
Welch, Patrick J.
    Study guide to acccompany economics theory and practice / Patrick J. Welch, Gerry F.
Welch.—6th ed.
        p.   cm.
    ISBN 0-470-00440-1
    1. Study Guide.   I. Welch, Gerry F.   II. Title

Printed in the United States of America

10   9   8   7   6   5   4   3

TABLE OF CONTENTS

PREFACE

To the Student

This study guide has been written for you. It is the result of working with students to understand the types of instructional aids that will lead to student success in comprehending economic concepts, organizing and reenforcing material, and studying for examinations.

In this study guide there are six learning aids for each chapter of *Economics: Theory & Practice*, sixth edition: chapter objectives, key terms and concepts, a study organizer, a chapter review, exercises, and sample examination questions. How do you use each of these?

The **chapter objectives** are those found at the beginning of each chapter in the textbook. These provide a summary of what you can expect to learn in each chapter. Use them as a preview or a summary.

The **key terms and concepts** and the **study organizer** provide two excellent lists for organizing the subject matter in each chapter and for reviewing your knowledge of terms, concepts, and other important material. You should be able to define each key term and concept and to explain each item in the study organizer list before taking an examination. Space is provided for you to write the definitions of key terms and concepts.

The **chapter review** is a detailed review of each chapter. It allows you to write missing words and numbers into the spaces provided and then check your entries against a column of correct answers. This review can help you evaluate your understanding of each chapter. You should read the chapter before attempting this review.

Exercises are included to enable you to apply the tools and concepts developed in the text, and especially to reenforce your skill at using graphs and numbers to explain economic relationships. Some of the exercises require computations and/or the completion of tables, some involve the location of data and should familiarize you with your library, and some involve graphing. The correct answers to the exercises are given at the end of this study guide.

Finally, there are twenty **sample examination questions** included for each chapter. These provide some indication of the types of multiple-choice questions that might be asked in a course using this textbook. The answers to these questions are found at the end of the study guide.

Good luck! We hope that you enjoy your study of economics and this course!

Patrick J. Welch
Gerry F. Welch
September 1997

Chapter 1
Introduction to Economics

To the Student: Take a few minutes to read the Preface to this **Study Guide.** *It provides you with valuable tips to use the* **Study Guide** *more effectively and improve your understanding of the material in the text.*

▣ CHAPTER OBJECTIVES

- To define economics and introduce the scarcity problem, which underlies economics.
- To understand the relationship between scarcity and choice.
- To define opportunity cost.
- To explore how efficiency and equity are related to the problem of scarcity.
- To identify the four factors of production and the income return to each type of factor.
- To differentiate between economic theory and economic policy.
- To introduce the tools economists use to express theories and policies.
- To show through a production possibilities example how the tools of economics can be used to illustrate and explain the basic problem of scarcity.
- To differentiate between macroeconomics and microeconomics.
- To explain (in an appendix) how to construct a graph and interpret the illustrated relationship.

▣ KEY TERMS AND CONCEPTS

Economics

Scarcity

Tradeoff

Value judgment

Opportunity cost

Efficiency

Equity

Resources (factors of production)

Labor

Capital

Land

Entrepreneurship

Wages

Interest

Rent

Profit

Economic theory

Econometrics

Assumptions

Economic policy

Graph

Direct relationship

Inverse relationship

Model

Production possibilities table (or curve)

Unemployment

Economic growth

Capital goods

Consumer goods

Macroeconomics

Microeconomics

1.   Understand the nature and basis of the scarcity problem, and how scarcity is related to the definition of economics.

2.   Recognize the decisions that must be made by individuals, businesses, and societies because of scarcity.

3.   Know the role of value judgments in economic decision making.

4.   Understand and give examples of opportunity costs.

5.   Distinguish between efficiency and equity, and understand the relationship of each to scarcity.

6.   Identify the four factors of production and the income return to each factor.

7.   Understand why economists say resources are scarce when so many resources are available in large numbers.

8.   Distinguish between economic theory and economic policy.

9.   Identify and explain the importance of each of the four elements that are the framework for building an economic model.

10. Explain the role of value judgments in economic policy.

11. Construct and read a graph, and differentiate between a direct and inverse relationship, illustrating each graphically.

12. Understand how models are used to develop economic theories.

13. Graph and interpret the meaning of a production possibilities curve.

14. Illustrate unemployment and economic growth on a production possibilities curve.

15. Distinguish between macroeconomics and microeconomics.

Appendix

16. Know how to assign numbers to the axes of a graph, and plot data points.

17. Understand how the choice of spacing for numbers on an axis can affect the appearance of data in a graph.

scarce,
  limited
unlimited

1. Economics is the study of how _____, or _____, resources are used to satisfy people's _____ material wants and needs.

resources

a. Since there are not enough _____ to produce everything necessary to satisfy individual, business, and society wants for material things, there is a

scarcity

_____ of goods and services.

choices

tradeoffs

b. If individuals, businesses, and societies cannot have everything, they must make _____, or _____, between what they will consume and what they will forgo.

value

c. These choices are influenced by the _____ judgments of the decision makers.

opportunity

d. Tradeoffs carry _____ costs, which means that the cost of a decision, purchase, or such, is

alternative

measured by the best _____ forgone.

efficiently

lowest

largest

e.   The problem of scarcity can be lessened if resources are used _____, which occurs when goods and services are produced at the _____ possible cost, or the _____ attainable output is produced from a given set of resources.

equity

f.   A major issue resulting from scarcity is the determination of a fair distribution of goods and services, or the issue of _____.

resources, factors production

2.   Items used in the production of goods and services are called _____, or _____ of _____.

labor

wages

a.   Human effort going into the production of goods and services is classified as _____, and the income from this resource is called _____.

land

rent

b.   Inputs used in production that originate in nature are classified as _____, and the income from these resources is called _____.

capital

c.   Trucks, warehouses and other goods that are used to produce goods and services are classified as _____,

interest

organizing
risk
profit

scarce

theory

why
policy

model

variables

assumptions

and the income their owners receive is called
_____.

d. Entrepreneurship is the factor of production that performs the functions of _____ economic activity and bearing the _____ of a venture's success or failure. The entrepreneur's income is called _____.

e. While resources are abundant in an absolute sense, they are _____ when compared to the wants and needs their production must satisfy.

3. An economic _____ is a cause-and-effect interpretation of a set of events or relationship; it is a formal explanation as to _____ something happens. An economic _____ is an action taken to change an economic condition.

a. The setting within which an economic theory is presented is an economic _____.

b. The framework for a model includes: the selection of two _____ that will be explored; the determination of the conditions held to be true, or the _____; the collection and analysis of

6

data

relationship

_____; and the conclusion which gives the resulting

_____ between the variables.

c. A theory is proven by showing that it is mathematically

valid

or logically _____. The data in an economic model

may be analyzed using statistical techniques called

econometrics

_____.

d. The choice of a particular economic policy action is

value judgments

influenced by the _____ _____ of the decision

maker.

4. Economic theories and policies can be expressed verbally,

graphs

visually through _____, or through mathematical

equations

_____.

a. In Figure 1.1a, as the value of X increases, the value of

increases
    direct

Y _____. This is referred to as a _____

relationship, and is graphed as a line that slopes

upward

_____. In Figure 1.1b, as the value of X

decreases

increases, the value of Y _____. This is referred

inverse

to as an _____ relationship, and is graphed as a

downward

line that slopes _____.

Figure 1.1

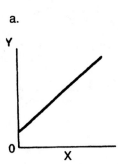
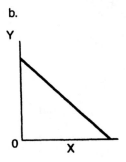

300

b.   According to the equation, "Pounds of Tea Demanded = 500 - 100(Price of Tea)," at a price of $2.00 per pound, _____ pounds would be demanded.

5.   A production possibilities table or curve shows that when resources and technology are held constant and an economy is

full

another

operating at _____ employment, more of one good or service can be produced only by giving up some of _____ good or service.

production
  possibilities

a.   The _____ _____ curve in Figure 1.2 is based on a model of a hypothetical economy that produces two goods, Good A and Good B. These goods

variables

are the _____ in the model.

Figure 1.2

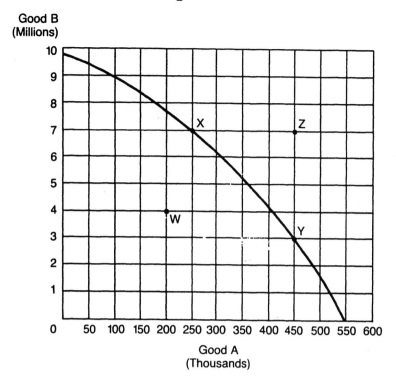

Good B
(Millions)

Good A
(Thousands)

b.   Currently, it would be impossible for the economy shown in Figure 1.2 to produce the combination of goods A and B shown by point _____.

Z

c.   If the economy shown in Figure 1.2 were operating at less than full employment, it might produce the combination of goods A and B shown by point _____.

W

d.   If the economy in Figure 1.2 were operating at full employment, it might produce the combination of goods A and B shown by point _____ or _____.

X, Y

A

B

450,000, 4, B

7, 200,000, A

right

economic growth

macroeconomics

microeconomics

e.   By going from point X to point Y, the economy would produce a larger amount of good _____, and a smaller amount of good _____.

f.   In moving from point X to point Y, the opportunity cost of increasing the quantity of good A from 250,000 to _____ is _____ million units of good ___. In moving from point Y to point X, the opportunity cost of increasing the quantity of good B from 3 million to _____ million is _____ units of good ___.

g.   If technological change or more available resources allowed an increase in the production of both goods A and B, the production possibilities curve would shift to the _____, and the economy would experience _____ _____.

6.   The study of the operation of the economy as a whole is called _____, and the study of the behavior of individual households, businesses, and specific products and markets is called _____.

Chapter Appendix

relationship

horizontal

vertical

zero

up

equal

combination

points

direct

inverse

axis

1. A graph illustrates the _____ between two variables, one measured along the _____ axis and the other along the _____ axis of the graph.

    a. When numbering the axes of a graph, one should place a _____ at the origin of the graph where the axes meet, work _____ the number scale when measuring along each axis, and assign _____ spaces for equal amounts when measuring along an axis.

    b. A point on a graph represents a particular _____ of the two variables under consideration, and a line on a graph is a series of connected _____.

    c. An upward-sloping line results from a _____ relationship between the variables; a downward-sloping line results from an _____ relationship.

    d. The impression one gets from observing a line on a graph can be influenced by the spacing used for the numbers along an _____. Changing the numbering along one of the axes causes the appearance of the line on the graph to become more or less steep.

Graphing

1. Assume that the following table gives the average number of tickets that would be sold per showing if a movie theater charged the various prices listed below.

Price per Movie	Average Number of Tickets Sold
$2	1650
3	1350
4	1050
5	750
6	450
7	150
8	50
9	0

The grid in Figure 1.3 will be used to graph the above information. Answer questions a through d based on this information.

Figure 1.3

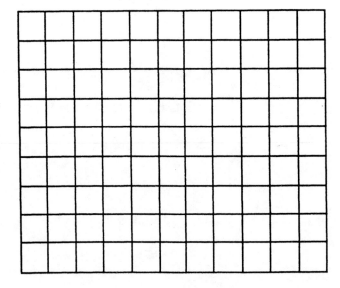

a. Label and number the vertical and horizontal axes of the graph, remembering that it is conventional to list price on the vertical axis. (Hint: The horizontal axis should be numbered in series of 150.)

b. Plot the various price-average number of tickets sold combinations on the graph, and connect the plotted points to form a line.

c. Does the line on the graph indicate a direct or inverse relationship between the variables? Why?

2. On each of the following graphs in Figure 1.4, draw a line to illustrate the relationship between the variables given in examples a through f below. Be sure to label the axes for each graph.

a. Show the relationship between pounds overweight and exercise.

b. Because of a government-guaranteed pricing program, the price of a bushel of wheat is the same regardless of the amount sold. Graph this price-amount relationship.

c. Statistics indicate that the efficiency at which an automobile operates decreases at high speeds. Graph the relationship between miles per hour at high speeds and miles per gallon.

d. Illustrate the relationship between household income and the number of new-model cars per household.

e. Show that the amount of satisfaction received from each additional slice of pizza increases, and then decreases, as more slices are eaten.

f. The attendance at baseball games is related to the number of games the team has won during the season. Graph this relationship.

Figure 1.4

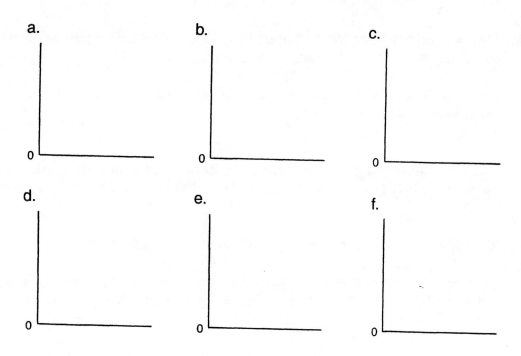

a.   b.   c.

d.   e.   f.

Production Possibilities

1.   Assume that with full employment and no changes in resources or technology, an economy can produce the following combinations of capital goods (those, such as machinery, that are used to produce other goods) and consumer goods (those, such as food, that directly satisfy a consumer).

Capital Goods (thousands of units)	Consumer Goods (thousands of units)
100	0
90	25
70	50
40	75
0	100

a.   Plot the above combinations in Figure 1.5 on the next page and connect the points.

b.   What would be the effect of operating at point A or B?

c.   At what point on this curve should this economy produce? Why?

14

Figure 1.5

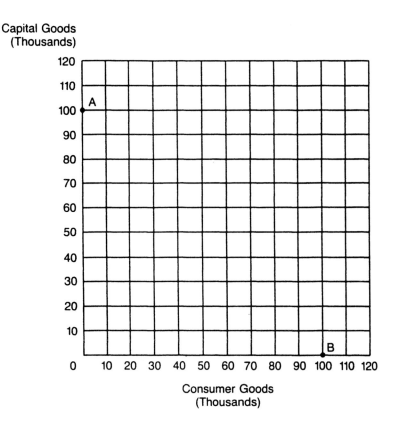

Capital Goods
(Thousands)

Consumer Goods
(Thousands)

d. Plot a point labeled U on Figure 1.5 to indicate that the economy is experiencing some unemployment. Plot another point labeled U1 to indicate more serious unemployment than at point U.

e. Show graphically the effect on the production possibilities curve of economic growth arising from new technology that influences the production of both capital goods and consumer goods.

f. Illustrate by a dashed line the effect of technological advances that improve the production of capital goods, but not consumer goods.

g. The opportunity cost of increasing the production of consumer goods from 25 thousand units to 75 thousand units is _____; the opportunity cost of increasing the production of consumer goods from 75 thousand units to 100 thousand units is _____; the opportunity cost of increasing the production of capital goods from 0 to 40 thousand units is _____; and the opportunity cost of increasing the production of capital goods from 40 thousand units to 100 thousand units is _____.

Indicate the best answer to each question.

1.   Economics is about how people use:
     a.   limited resources to satisfy limited material wants and needs.
     b.   unlimited resources to satisfy limited material wants and needs.
     c.   limited resources to satisfy unlimited material wants and needs.
     d.   unlimited resources to satisfy unlimited material wants and needs.

2.   Which of the following statements is FALSE?
     a.   Scarcity is the basic reason for studying economics.
     b.   Scarcity forces people to make decisions about how to best satisfy their material wants and needs.
     c.   The study of economics is simplified because value judgments are eliminated from making choices.
     d.   People must make tradeoffs, or give up one thing for something else, because of scarcity.

3.   The opportunity cost of an item purchased is:
     a.   the tax paid on the item.
     b.   the time required to make a decision about the purchase.
     c.   the dissatisfaction experienced by the buyer when the item is no longer desired.
     d.   the alternative purchase that is forgone to acquire the item.

4.   Efficiency and equity refer to, respectively:
     a.   producing at the lowest possible cost, and producing the largest attainable output.
     b.   producing the largest possible output from a given set of resources, and fairness in the distribution of goods and services.
     c.   paying people based on what they contribute to output, and based on what they need.
     d.   economies that face a scarcity problem, and those that do not.

5.   Entrepreneurship involves:
     a.   taking the risk for the success or failure of a business venture.
     b.   organizing factors of production to produce goods and services.
     c.   human effort not included in the factor of production category called labor.
     d.   all of the above

6. John receives a wage, Carol receives profit, and Sandy receives interest. John's, Carol's, and Sandy's incomes are from, respectively:
    a. land, labor, and entrepreneurship.
    b. entrepreneurship, land, and capital.
    c. labor, capital, and entrepreneurship.
    d. labor, entrepreneurship, and capital.

7. Resources, or factors of production, are scarce:
    a. both in an absolute sense and relative to the wants and needs they must satisfy.
    b. in an absolute sense, but not relative to the wants and needs they must satisfy.
    c. relative to the wants and needs they must satisfy, but some are abundant in an absolute sense.
    d. only because of inefficiency; if we produced efficiently scarcity would disappear.

8. Which of the following statements concerning economic theories is <u>FALSE</u>?
    a. A model is a setting within which an economic theory is presented.
    b. Any time a hypothetical situation is created in a model or in a theory, the model or theory becomes invalid.
    c. Theories are generalized explanations of the relationships between economic variables.
    d. Since a graph illustrates a relationship between variables, a graph could portray an economic theory.

9. Which of the following is NOT a basic element of a model?
    a. Assumptions, which are conditions held to be true in developing economic theories.
    b. Two variables that are explored for a relationship.
    c. Data collection and analysis
    d. Recommendations for action based on the resulting relationship between the variables.

10. Which of the following is an example of an economic policy?
    a. A tax cut passed by Congress to reduce unemployment.
    b. Statistics indicating the rate of unemployment for the mid-1990s.
    c. An explanation as to why a tax cut might reduce unemployment.
    d. The relationship between changes in taxes and rates of unemployment.

11. If A decreases as B increases, then A and B are:
    a. directly related, and the line showing their relationship slopes upward on a graph.
    b. directly related, and the line showing their relationship slopes downward on a graph.

c.   inversely related, and the line showing their relationship slopes upward on a graph.
d.   inversely related, and the line showing their relationship slopes downward on a graph.

12.   How much of good X would be demanded at a price of $30.00 if the relationship between the price of good X and the quantity demanded were shown by the equation: quantity demanded = 1000 - 25 (price of good X)?
a.   50 units.
b.   250 units.
c.   750 units.
d.   950 units.

13.   A point inside, or to the left of, a production possibilities curve indicates that:
a.   some of the economy's resources are unemployed.
b.   the economy is operating at full employment.
c.   the economy is growing.
d.   more of one good can be produced only by giving up some of another good.

14.   Which of the following is an example of a capital good?
a.   In-line skates.
b.   Frozen yogurt.
c.   A cash register.
d.   Food donated to flood victims.

Answer questions 15 through 18 on the basis of the following production possibilities curve.

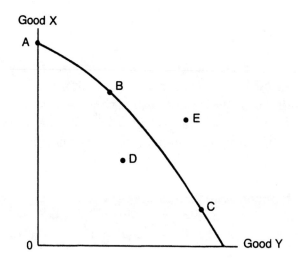

15. Currently, it would be impossible for this economy to produce the combination of goods X and Y shown by point:
    a. A.
    b. B.
    c. D.
    d. E.

16. A move from point B to point D would occur if the economy:
    a. experienced economic growth.
    b. began to experience some unemployment.
    c. went from unemployment to full employment.
    d. none of the above.

17. Which of the following statements is true?
    a. There is no opportunity cost when going from point B to point C.
    b. The economy cannot go from point B to point C because it is at full employment at point B.
    c. The opportunity cost of going from point B to point C is the amount of good Y that must be given up.
    d. The opportunity cost of going from point B to point C is the amount of good X that must be given up.

18. If the economy were growing, the production possibilities curve would:
    a. remain in its current position.
    b. shift inward to the left.
    c. shift outward to the right.
    d. become perfectly horizontal.

19. The study of the U.S. economy as a whole, and how all households in the economy interact with all businesses and the government is:
    a. macroeconomics.
    b. megaeconomics.
    c. metaoeconomics.
    d. microeconomics.

20. (*appendix*) Which of the following steps in constructing a graph would result in a faulty graph?
    a. Use a zero at the origin where the vertical and horizontal axes meet.
    b. When assigning numbers, use equal spaces for equal amounts.

c. When assigning numbers to the horizontal axis, work from right to left along the axis so that the largest number is at the origin.

d. Plot data points that reflect a specific combination of the two variables, and connect the points.

NOTE: Correct answers to the Exercises and the Sample Examination Questions can be found at the end of the Study Guide.

Chapter 2
Economic Decision Making and Economic Systems

■ CHAPTER OBJECTIVES

- To introduce the basic economic choices that must be made in every society because of scarcity.
- To differentiate between a market and a planned economy, and to introduce the manner in which the basic economic choices are made in different economic systems.
- To explain the structure and operation of a market economy.
- To explain why, where, and how government intervenes in decision making in a mixed economy.
- To distinguish among capitalism, mixed capitalism, and socialism, and to discuss the restructuring of the economies of Eastern Europe and the former Soviet Union.
- To explore the British foundations and the historical highlights of the development of the U.S. economy.

■ KEY TERMS AND CONCEPTS

Basic economic decisions

Economic system

Market economy

Price system

Circular flow model

Output markets (product markets)

Input markets (resource markets)

Least-cost (efficient) method of production

Planned economy (command economy)

Mixed economy

Market failure

Planning failure

Capitalism

Free enterprise

Property rights

Mixed capitalism

Socialism

Privatization

Laissez-faire capitalism

Mercantilism

Invisible hand doctrine

Industrial Revolution

Muckrakers

New Deal

Employment Act of 1946

1. Identify the three basic economic decisions that must be made in every society.

2. Differentiate among market, planned, and mixed economies.

3. Explain and illustrate the operation of the circular flow model, including real and money flows, and input and output markets.

4. Explain, using the circular flow model, how the three basic economic decisions are made in a market economy.

5. Understand how economic decisions are made in a planned economy.

6. Identify some strengths and weaknesses of market and planned economies.

7. Identify where, and give some examples of how, government intervenes in a mixed economy.

8. Differentiate among capitalism, socialism, and mixed capitalism.

9. Understand the changes that have occurred in the economies of Eastern Europe and the former Soviet Union, and the problems that have accompanied those changes.

10. Identify and explain the British foundations of U.S. capitalism.

11. Recognize the importance of Adam Smith and *The Wealth of Nations* in the development of capitalism.

12. Appreciate the positive and negative aspects of the British Industrial Revolution.

13. Identify the historical turning points in the movement of the U.S. economy away from laissez-faire capitalism toward a mixed system.

14. Understand the roles of the U.S. industrial boom, the New Deal, the Employment Act of 1946, and more recent regulatory and federal budget developments in bringing U.S. capitalism to its present form.

1. Scarcity, or the fact that no economy can fully satisfy all of its members' material wants and needs, imposes three basic economic choices, or decisions, on every society: _____ and how many goods and services are to be produced; _____ those goods and services are to be produced; and _____ is to receive those goods and services.

what

how

who

    a.   The way in which these decisions are made depends upon a society's economic _____.

system

    b.   Basically, economies can be classified into three types: a _____ economy, a planned economy, or a _____ economy.

market, mixed

2. In a market economy, the basic economic decisions are made by _____ and _____ interacting in markets. A market economy is also called a _____ system because of the way in which market communication occurs.

buyers
  sellers
price

    a.   Households are buyers and businesses are sellers of goods and services in _____, or _____, markets.

output, product

input

resource

Businesses are buyers and households are sellers of land, labor, capital, and entrepreneurship in _____, or _____, markets.

b. A good or service will be produced in a market economy if enough buyers demand the item at a _____ that allows sellers to produce it at a _____.

price

profit

c. How goods and services are produced in a market economy is decided by _____ through their choices of the _____-cost, or most _____, method of production. This method allows a business to maximize its _____ from the sale of a good or service.

businesses

least
   efficient

profit

d. In a market economy, goods and services go to those who can _____ them. What and how much individuals can afford to buy in output markets depends largely on what they receive in _____ markets.

afford (pay for)

input

e. The relationships between businesses and households, and the roles of output and input markets in a market economy can be illustrated in a _____ _____ model.

circular flow

efficiency

incentives

buyers

sellers

value
  judgments

protection

resources

dominated

harm

planners

plan

f.   Advantages of a market economy include the _____ that results from profit and income _____ and from information passing directly between _____ and _____ rather than through a central planning authority; and that production and distribution decisions reflect the _____ _____ of buyers and sellers rather than planners.

g.   Problems with a market economy include no _____ for people lacking adequate knowledge to make informed market decisions or for people lacking adequate _____ to buy the goods and services they need; the possibility of markets becoming _____ by one or a few sellers; and production decisions that result in _____ to the environment.

3.   In a planned, or command, economy, the basic economic decisions are made by _____, who operate with stated objectives to be accomplished in a specific time period, or according to a _____.

a. In a planned economy, what goods and services are produced is decided by planners, how goods and services are produced is determined primarily by the types and amounts of _____ planners make available to producers, and planners determine to _____ goods and services go.

resources

whom

b. A planned economy may experience problems due to differences in the goods and services that planners and _____ consider important, _____ difficulties caused by the complexities of planning, _____ product quality due to a lack of _____, and damage to the _____.

consumers
  production
poor
  (inferior)
incentives

environment

c. Advantages of planning include quicker achievement of some _____ and greater ease in controlling _____ and the _____ of goods and services.

goals

unemployment
distribution

4. In a mixed economy, the three basic economic choices are made through some combination of _____ and _____ decision making.

market
  centralized

27

market
failure

planning
failure

markets

government

monopolizing
(dominating)
information

least-cost

discrimination

production

a. A mixed economy may result from _____ _____,
which occurs when a market system creates a problem or
cannot achieve its goals, or from_____ _____,
which occurs when there are problems or unachievable
goals arising in a planned economy.

b. While all economies are "mixed," the term is most often
associated with economies that depend primarily on
individual decision making in _____, but also
exhibit some centralized decision making through
_____ intervention.

c. Some types of market failure leading to government
intervention include: the _____ of a market by
one or a few sellers; lack of good _____ to make
decisions; problems, such as pollution, created because
businesses seek to produce using the _____-_____
method; unequal treatment of workers due to
_____; and failure to provide goods and services
to those who cannot contribute to _____.

output
  input
businesses
  households

d. Government can affect economic relationships by influencing _____ markets, _____ markets, _____ and/or_____ .

legal

regulation

workers

income

e. Some ways in which government intervenes to make the U.S. economy a mixed economy include establishing the _____ framework within which businesses and households operate, _____ of specific industries or problems, protection of _____ , taxing and spending, and _____ support programs.

resources
  capitalism
capitalism
  socialism

5. A second method for classifying economies is to group them according to the ownership of _____ , or as _____ , mixed _____ , and _____ .

privately

free enterprise

profit

decisions

a. With capitalism, property rights to the factors of production are _____ held, and businesses are operated on a _____ _____ basis, which means businesses are free to operate with a _____ motive and to make their own _____ regarding price, quantity of output, and other considerations.

29

b.   Mixed capitalism retains some of the basic features of

_____, including a dependence on _____

for decision making, but also has some _____

intervention.

c.   In socialism, many factors of production are owned by

_____, and there is some effort to _____

the distribution of income.

d.   Some disadvantages of classifying economies as capitalist or

socialist are that these terms are less _____

neutral than market and planned; they do not focus on how

societies make the basic economic _____ caused by

_____; and they are not helpful for sorting economies

according to how they combine _____ and

_____ decisions when making the basic economic

choices.

6.   Major changes have occurred in the countries of Eastern Europe

and the former Soviet Union as they have moved from planned

economies toward _____ systems.

capitalism
markets
government

society
equalize

ideologically

decisions

scarcity

individual

collective

market

a. An important element in the transition from a planned to a market economy is _____, or the granting to individuals of _____ rights to resources that were previously _____ owned, or owned by the state.

privatization

property

collectively

b. For some countries the transition from a planned to market economy has been complicated by opposition to _____ and institutions that are not compatible with _____; a _____ of professionals and inadequate _____ to carry the transition forward; and inflation and _____.

change

privatization
shortage
laws

unemployment

7. The character of the U.S. economy has been influenced by developments in both the United States and Britain.

a. The British developments, which occurred during the eighteenth and nineteenth centuries, were: the decline of the economic system known as _____, in which the interests of the state dominated; the rise of a philosophy of _____ and the justification of that philosophy in writings such as *The Wealth of Nations* by _____ _____; and the technological and social

mercantilism

individualism

Adam Smith

Industrial Revolution	changes of the British _____ _____, which transformed England into a modern economy.
laissez-faire	b. Adam Smith advocated _____-_____ capitalism, an economic system based on individual decision making and
government invisible hand	minimal _____intervention, and developed the _____ _____ doctrine, the argument that the interests of society
self	are best served by producers acting in their own _____-
interest	_____ to provide buyers what they want.
	c. Important events in U.S. history that helped shape the U.S. economy include: the industrial boom following the Civil War when large corporations grew, working conditions deteriorated, and government passed antitrust legislation to
competition	protect _____ and regulations to protect consumers
workers	and _____; the economic programs and legislative
New Deal	reforms of the 1930s known as the _____ _____; the
Employment	period following World War II when the _____
Act	_____ of 1946 was passed giving the federal government increased responsibility for economic activity; and changes
regulation	in government _____ and the size of the
debt	federal _____ from the 1960s through the 1990s.

The Circular Flow Model

1.　In Figure 2.1, label the
   a.　household and business sectors.
   b.　input and output markets.
   c.　real flows of resources and goods and services.
   d.　money and income flows for goods and services and resources.

Figure 2.1

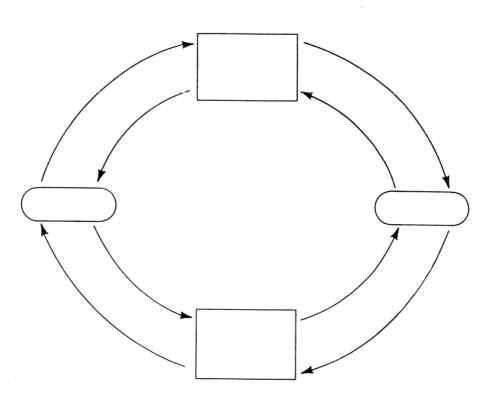

U.S. Economic Development

1.　Application 2.3, "The Factory Girl's Last Day," and the excerpt from Upton Sinclair's *The Jungle* (text pages 66-69) make statements about working conditions during the industrializations of Britain and the United States. Locate another poem, drawing, cartoon, or book that illustrates the dark side of the British Industrial Revolution or the U.S. industrial boom. What kind of statement is the author or artist of your work making? Locate the work of an author or artist who is favorably impressed by these industrial changes and describe the statement that he or she makes in that work.

Indicate the best answer to each question.

1.   Which of the following is NOT one of the three basic economic decisions?
   a.   Who will receive goods and services.
   b.   How goods and services will be produced.
   c.   When and where goods and services will be produced.
   d.   What and how many goods and services will be produced.

2.   Markets are important in economies where decisions are made:
   a.   collectively.
   b.   by planners.
   c.   by individuals.
   d.   by the government.

3.   In a pure market economy, buyers and sellers communicate their intentions to one another through:
   a.   individuals elected to public office.
   b.   negotiations overseen by government agencies.
   c.   planners.
   d.   prices paid or charged.

4.   In a pure market economy:
   a.   goods and services are distributed to those who can afford them.
   b.   goods and services are produced using the smallest total number of resources.
   c.   households buy and businesses sell resources.
   d.   what is produced is based on what businesses think is best for society.

5.   Which of the following occurs in a pure market economy?
   a.   Businesses are guaranteed a profit.
   b.   Government has an important role in the circular flow model.
   c.   Households are sellers and businesses are buyers in resource markets.
   d.   Collective decision making is valued more highly than individual decision making.

Answer questions 6 through 8 on the basis of the following circular flow model.

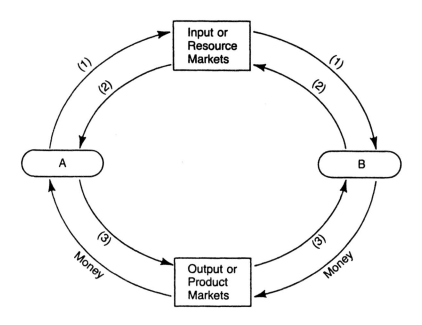

6. If this were a pure market economy, households would be shown by:
    a. box A.
    b. box B.
    c. lines (1) and (2).
    d. none of the above.

7. Line (3) illustrates the flow of:
    a. factors of production.
    b. goods and services to their final users.
    c. payments to owners of factors of production.
    d. payments for the purchase of goods and services.

8. The flow of resources to businesses is shown by:
    a. line (1).
    b. line (2).
    c. line (3).
    d. lines (2) and (3).

9. Which of the following statements is <u>FALSE</u>?
   a. In a market economy, goods and services are produced using least-cost production techniques.
   b. In a market economy, the basic economic questions are answered through the interaction of buyers and sellers.
   c. In a planned economy, how goods and services are produced is determined largely by the resources made available to producers.
   d. In most economies, the basic economic decisions are made either entirely by private individuals, or entirely by centralized authorities.

10. The economic system in which all of the basic decisions are made through a centralized authority, such as a government agency, is termed a:
    a. capitalistic economy.
    b. market socialist economy.
    c. mixed economy.
    d. planned economy.

11. A lack of incentives to protect the environment when producing goods and services is a weakness of:
    a. a pure market economy.
    b. a pure planned economy.
    c. both a pure market economy and a pure planned economy.
    d. neither a pure market economy nor a pure planned economy.

12. Free enterprise exists where:
    a. resources are publicly owned and available free to anyone who wants to produce goods and services.
    b. businesses can make their own decisions and seek profits.
    c. the government provides free goods and services to the needy.
    d. limits are set on how much government can tax.

13. The economic system where private individuals own the factors of production is:
    a. a people's republic
    b. capitalism.
    c. collectivism.
    d. socialism.

14. After studying the various economic systems, it is clear that:
    a. the U.S. has a pure market economy.
    b. an economy based on collective decision making needs markets to function.

c.   the economies of the world can be differentiated from one another by how they mix individual and collective decision making.

d.   all of the above.

15.   Since the mid-1990s, the economies of Eastern Europe and the former Soviet Union have depended:

a.   completely on central planning.

b.   completely on individual decision making.

c.   less on individual decision making than before.

d.   more on individual decision making than before.

16.   The economic system, important in Britain in the 17th and 18th centuries, in which national economic interests outweighed individuals' economic interests, was:

a.   a free enterprise system.

b.   laissez-faire capitalism.

c.   market socialism.

d.   mercantilism.

17.   Which of the following statements about the U.S. economy is true?

a.   A major current concern is over the size of the federal debt.

b.   The Sherman Act was passed to ensure there would be full employment.

c.   The New Deal programs decreased government's role in the economy during the 1930s.

d.   The Employment Act of 1946 was passed to control poor working conditions.

18.   The economic programs and legislative reforms developed in the U.S. during the Great Depression were named:

a.   the New Deal.

b.   the Employment Act.

c.   Free Enterprise Reforms.

d.   none of the above.

Answer questions 19 and 20 on the basis of the following figure.

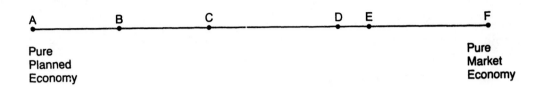

19. The type of economy advocated by Adam Smith in *The Wealth of Nations* would operate at or near point:
     a. A.
     b. C.
     c. D.
     d. F.

20. The change in the U.S. economy following the Employment Act of 1946 might best be illustrated by a movement from point:
     a. B to point A.
     b. E to point D.
     c. F to point D.
     d. F to point A.

NOTE: *Correct answers to the Exercises and the Sample Examination Questions can be found at the end of the* Study Guide.

Chapter 3
Demand, Supply, and the Determination of Price

- To define demand, Law of Demand, supply, and Law of Supply.
- To explain demand and supply through schedules and graphs.
- To show how price is determined in a market through the interaction of demand and supply.
- To define and illustrate equilibrium price, equilibrium quantity, and shortages and surpluses in a market.
- To explain the reasons for a change in demand or a change in supply.
- To distinguish between a change in demand or supply, and a change in quantity demanded or quantity supplied.
- To explain how changes in demand and changes in supply affect equilibrium price and quantity in a market.
- To illustrate how government-imposed price ceilings and price floors influence market conditions.
- To introduce the concept and calculation of price elasticity, which measures buyers' and sellers' sensitivities to price changes.

■ KEY TERMS AND CONCEPTS

Demand

Demand schedule

Law of Demand

Demand curve

Supply

Supply schedule

Law of Supply

Supply curve

39

Market

Market demand and market supply

Shortage

Surplus

Equilibrium price and equilibrium quantity

Market clearing price

Change in quantity demanded and quantity supplied

Nonprice factors influencing demand

Nonprice factors influencing supply

Change in demand and change in supply

Increase (decrease) in demand and supply

Change in quantity demanded and quantity
    supplied versus change in demand and supply

Price ceiling (upper price limit)

Usury laws

Price floor (lower price limit)

Price elasticity

Price elastic

Price inelastic

Elasticity coefficient

Unitary price elastic

1. Know the Law of Demand, the Law of Supply, and the reasons for each relationship.

2. Graphically illustrate a demand curve and a supply curve.

3. Define market demand and market supply, and explain how price is determined in a competitive market.

4. Identify equilibrium price and equilibrium quantity on a schedule and a graph.

5. Define surplus and shortage, explain why each occurs, and measure the size of each graphically.

6. Explain how surpluses and shortages move the market price to its equilibrium level.

7. Explain how a change in price causes quantity demanded and quantity supplied to change, and how this is represented graphically.

8. Identify some major nonprice factors that influence demand and influence supply.

9. Explain the relationship between changes in nonprice factors and changes in demand and supply.

10. Graphically illustrate increases and decreases in demand and in supply.

11. Understand the difference between a change in quantity demanded or quantity supplied, and a change in demand or supply.

12. Determine the changes in equilibrium price and equilibrium quantity that result from changes in demand and in supply.

13. Understand when government-imposed price ceilings and price floors take effect, and how they can create shortages and surpluses.

14. Understand the concept of price elasticity.

15. Distinguish among an elastic, an inelastic, and a unitary elastic response to a price change.

16. Calculate an elasticity coefficient and interpret the resulting number.

17. Identify the causes of elastic and inelastic responses to price changes for demand and for supply.

nonprice
demand

1. The different amounts of a good or service that a buyer would purchase at different prices in a defined time period with all _____ factors held constant is the buyer's _____ for that product.

schedule

a. In developing a demand _____ for a product, all nonprice factors that influence buyer demand are held _____ in order to highlight the relationship between the product's _____ and the amount of the product a buyer would purchase in a given time period.

constant

price

decreases

increases

inverse

b. The Law of Demand states that, as the price of a product increases, the quantity of that product demanded by a buyer _____, and as the price of a product decreases, the quantity demanded _____. In other words, according to the Law of Demand, there is an _____ relationship between price and quantity demanded.

income

substitutes

c. Buyers' reactions to price changes are based on scarcity and choice: that is, a buyer's _____ is limited, or scarce, and there may be _____ for a good or service available to a buyer.

d. A demand schedule may be illustrated as a demand curve in a graph. Typically, a demand curve is _____ sloping, illustrating the _____ relationship between price and quantity demanded.

downward

inverse

2. The different amounts of a good or service that a seller would make available for sale at different prices in a defined time period with all _____ factors held constant is the seller's _____ of that product.

nonprice

supply

a. In developing a supply schedule for a product, all nonprice factors that influence supply are held _____ in order to highlight the relationship between the product's _____ and the quantity of the product supplied in a given time period.

constant

price

b. The Law of Supply states that there is a _____ relationship between price and quantity supplied: as price increases, quantity supplied _____, and as price decreases, quantity supplied _____.

direct

increases

decreases

c. The basic reason for the Law of Supply is the seller's ability to cover costs and earn a _____.

profit

upward direct	d. When a supply schedule is illustrated graphically, a typical supply curve is _____ sloping, indicating a _____ relationship between price and quantity supplied.
market, market intersect equilibrium, equilibrium	3. When the demand and supply schedules or curves of all the individual buyers and sellers in a market are added together, _____ demand and _____ supply are determined. The price and quantity at which market demand equals market supply, or at which the market demand and market supply curves for a product _____, are called the product's _____ price and _____ quantity.
automatically change	a. Equilibrium is the point toward which a free market _____ moves, and at which there is no tendency for price and quantity to _____.
45 2000 clearing equals	b. In Figure 3.1, the equilibrium price is _____ cents per unit and the equilibrium quantity is _____ units. The equilibrium price is sometimes called the market _____ price because, at that price, the amount demanded by buyers _____ the amount supplied by sellers.

Figure 3.1

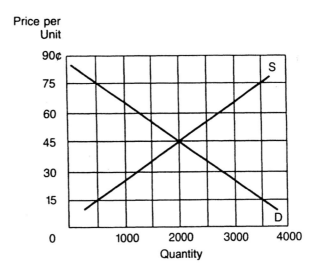

500

3500

surplus, 3000

c. If the price charged in Figure 3.1 were 75 cents per unit, the quantity demanded would be ____ units and the quantity supplied would be _____ units, or there would be a _____ of _____ units.

2750

1250

shortage, 1500

d. If the price charged in Figure 3.1 were 30 cents per unit, the quantity demanded would be _____ units and the quantity supplied would be _____ units, or there would be a _____ of _____ units.

along

4. A change in the quantity demanded or a change in the quantity supplied of a product is shown by a movement _____ the product's demand curve or supply curve from one price-quantity point to another. A change in quantity demanded or quantity

45

price

supplied results only from a change in the _____ of the product.

5. A change in a nonprice factor influencing the demand or supply of a product causes its demand or supply curve to _____ to the right or left. This is termed a _____ in demand or supply.

shift

change

a. When a change in a nonprice factor causes buyers to demand more or sellers to supply more of a product at each price, an _____ in the demand or an _____ in the supply of the product occurs, and the demand or supply curve shifts to the _____.

increase

increase

right

b. When a change in a nonprice factor causes buyers to demand less or sellers to supply less of a product at each price, a _____ in the demand or a _____ in the supply of the product occurs, and the demand or supply curve shifts to the _____.

decrease,
   decrease

left

c. Some major nonprice factors influencing demand include: _____ incomes; _____ about future incomes, prices, or availabilities; the _____ of related

buyers'
   expectations
prices

46

popularity	goods and services; the _____ of the good or
buyers	service; and the number of _____ in the market.
cost	d. Some major nonprice factors influencing supply include:
expectations	the _____ of producing the item; _____ of
prices	future market conditions; the _____ of other products
	that the seller could produce; and the number of
sellers	_____ in the market.
change	6. A _____ in the price of a product causes a change in the
quantity	_____ demanded or the _____ supplied of the
quantity	product and is illustrated graphically by a _____
movement	_____ the demand or supply curve. A _____ in a
along	nonprice factor influencing demand or supply causes a change
change	in the _____ or in the _____ of the product and is
demand, supply	illustrated graphically by a _____ of the demand or supply
shift	curve.
	7. When there is a change in the demand and/or supply of a
	product in a market, there is a change in the product's
equilibrium	_____ price and quantity.
	a. Based on Figure 3.2, an increase in demand with no
increase	change in supply would lead to an _____ in the

47

increase	equilibrium price and an _____ in the equilibrium quantity of the product; and an increase in supply with no
decrease	change in demand would lead to a _____ in the
increase	equilibrium price and an _____ in the equilibrium quantity of the product.

Figure 3.2

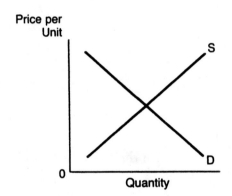

b. Based on Figure 3.2, a decrease in demand with no change

decrease	in supply would lead to a _____ in the equilibrium
decrease	price and a _____ in the equilibrium quantity of the product; and a decrease in supply with no change in
increase	demand would lead to an _____ in the equilibrium
decrease	price and a _____ in the equilibrium quantity of the product.

rising	8.	A price ceiling (upper price limit) keeps prices from _____ above a certain level, and a price floor (lower price limit) keeps
falling		prices from _____ below a certain level.

48

above	**a.** A price ceiling imposed on a market takes effect when the equilibrium price is _____ the ceiling. When a price ceiling takes effect the quantity demanded of the product is _____ than the quantity supplied, and a _____ develops.
greater	
shortage	
	b. A price floor imposed on a market takes effect when the equilibrium price is _____ the floor. When a price floor takes effect the quantity demanded of the product is _____ than the quantity supplied, and a _____ develops.
below	
less, surplus	
	c. Based on Figure 3.3, a ceiling price of $4 per unit would cause a _____ of ____ units to occur in this market; and a ceiling price of $10 per unit would keep the market at its _____ price, or the ceiling would ____ take effect.
shortage, 200	
equilibrium	
not	
	d. Based on Figure 3.3, a price floor of $4 per unit would keep the market at its _____ price; and a price floor of $10 per unit would result in a _____ of ____ units.
equilibrium	
surplus	
100	

Figure 3.3

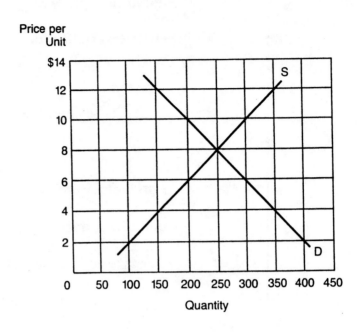

9. The measure of the strength of a buyer's or seller's response to a price change is referred to as price _____.

elasticity

a. If buyers or sellers react strongly to a price change, the response is said to be price _____. If buyers or sellers react weakly to a price change, the response is categorized as price _____.

elastic

inelastic

b. The formula for calculating an elasticity coefficient is: the absolute value of the _____ change in _____ divided by the _____ change in _____. The formula for determining the percentage change in quantity is: the change in Q

percentage

Q (quantity)
percentage
P (price)

base
Q (quantity)

base

P (price)

larger

greater

smaller

less

equal

one

30

120, 25

(quantity) divided by the _____ _____. The formula for determining the percentage change in price is: the change in P (price) divided by the _____ _____.

c. A response by either buyers or sellers to a price change is price elastic if a given percentage change in price leads to a _____ percentage change in quantity demanded or quantity supplied, or if the elasticity coefficient is _____ than one. A response to a price change is price inelastic if a given percentage change in price leads to a _____ percentage change in quantity demanded or quantity supplied, or if the elasticity coefficient is _____ than one. A response to a price change is unitary price elastic if a given percentage change in price leads to an _____ percentage change in quantity demanded or quantity supplied, or if the elasticity coefficient is _____.

d. If the price of bicycle helmets increases from $75 to $90 and the quantity of helmets demanded per month falls from 120 to 90 as a result, then the percentage change in quantity demanded equals _____ (change in Q) divided by _____ (base Q), or _____%, and the percentage change in

51

$15
  $75
20
  25
20, 1.25
 	
elastic
 	
luxury
 	
substitute
 	
income
 	
time
	price equals _____ (change in P) divided by _____ (base P), or _____%. The elasticity coefficient equals _____% divided by _____%, or _____. The response to the price change in this case is categorized as _____.
	
	e. The main factors determining the price elasticity of demand for a product are: whether the product is a _____ or a necessity; the ability of buyers to _____ other goods or services for the product; and the portion of a buyer's _____ that the product's price represents. The main factor determining price elasticity of supply is the amount of _____ a seller has to react to a price change.

Supply and Demand

1. The following are hypothetical market demand and supply schedules for ice cream sundaes in a resort town on an average summer day.

Price per Sundae	Sundaes Demanded per Day	Sundaes Supplied per Day
$1.00	3000	600
1.20	2800	1000
1.40	2600	1400
1.60	2400	1800
1.80	2200	2200
2.00	2000	2600
2.20	1800	3000
2.40	1600	3400
2.60	1400	3800
2.80	1200	4200

a. Plot the above demand and supply schedules on Figure 3.4 and label the curves D and S.

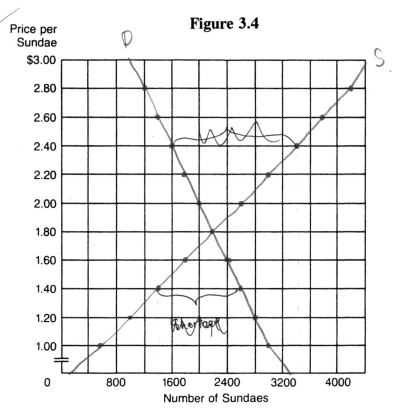

Figure 3.4

53

b. Both the schedule and the graph illustrate that as price falls, consumers will _increase_ the quantity demanded and suppliers will _decrease_ the quantity supplied; and as price rises, consumers will _decrease_ the quantity demanded and suppliers will _increase_ the quantity supplied.

c. In the above example, the equilibrium price is $1.80, and the quantity of sundaes sold at this price is _2200_.

d. Assume that the sellers of ice cream sundaes are not yet aware of the equilibrium price and are experimenting with their pricing. Would there be a shortage or a surplus if $1.40 per sundae were charged? _shortage_ How large would this shortage or surplus be? _1200_ Would there be a shortage or a surplus if $2.40 were charged? _surplus_ How large would this shortage or surplus be? _1800_ In this market, at every price above the equilibrium price a _surplus_ would occur, and at every price below the equilibrium price a _shortage_ would occur.

e. Assume that the local city council creates a Board for the Preservation of the Sweettooth that has as its charge the setting of prices on all ice cream, bakery, and candy items. This board initially sets a maximum price of $1.60 on all sundaes. What will happen as a result of this government-set price?

    shortage of 600

f. Since there are problems created by setting the maximum price of ice cream sundaes at $1.60, the board decides to raise the price ceiling to $2.60. What will happen in this case?

    Price ceiling doesn't take effect — the equilibrium price results.

g. During the winter months in this town, the equilibrium price of ice cream sundaes falls and fewer sundaes are sold. Identify some reasons for this change in equilibrium price and quantity, and illustrate graphically on Figure 3.4 what happens during the winter months.

    Since this is a resort town, there should be fewer buyers in the winter months. Also, ice cream is not as popular in the winter. Both of these cause the demand curve to shift to the left, which cause the equilibrium price & quantity to fall.

54

2. Given below are the demand and supply schedules--unlabeled--for a hypothetical market.

Price	Quantity
$ 4	100
8	200
12	300
16	400
20	500
24	600

Price	Quantity
$ 4	550
8	450
12	350
16	250
20	150
24	50

a. Plot these schedules in Figure 3.5 and correctly label each curve. Be sure to also label and number the axes of the graph.

b. The equilibrium price in this market is __$13.00__ and the equilibrium quantity is __325__.

c. Would there be a shortage or a surplus if the sellers charged $10? __shortage__ How much of a shortage or surplus would occur? __150__ Mark this on Figure 3.5. Would there be a shortage or a surplus if the sellers charged $22? __surplus__ How much of a shortage or surplus would occur? __450__ Mark this on Figure 3.5.

Figure 3.5

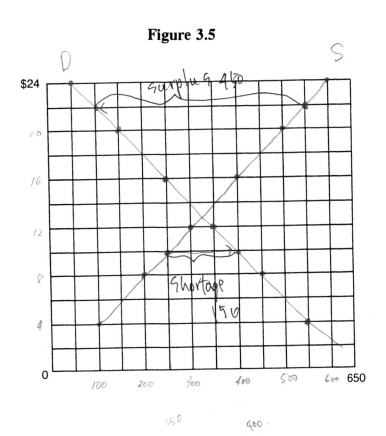

55

Changes in Demand, Supply, and Equilibrium Versus Changes in Quantity Demanded and Quantity Supplied

1. Each of the following gives an example that could change demand or supply, or change just the quantities demanded and supplied. Where applicable, illustrate the change in demand or supply graphically and note the effect on equilibrium price and equilibrium quantity.

EXAMPLE	GRAPHIC CHANGE	CHANGE IN EQUILIBRIUM PRICE AND EQUILIBRIUM QUANTITY
a. What is the effect in the market for aspirin when a major report says it is healthful to take one each day?		equilibrium price & equilibrium quantity increase
b. What happens in the market for compact discs by a recording group when its popularity fades?		equilibrium price & equilibrium quantity decrease
c. What happens in the market for quick, convenient oil changes when these businesses raise their prices?		no shifts & no change in equilibrium
d. What would be the effect of a severe drought on the market for popping corn?		equilibrium price increases equilibrium quantity decreases
e. What happens in the market for pasta when the cost of flour increases?		equilibrium price increases equilibrium quantity decreases

f. What will be the effect on the housing market now if buyers expect that the prices of new homes will increase significantly in the future?

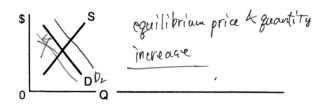

equilibrium price & quantity increase

g. What will be the effect in the market for home health care workers if the federal government establishes a minimum wage that is below the equilibrium wage rate?

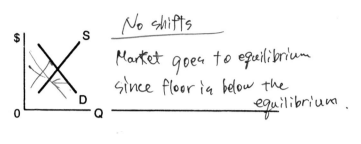

No shifts

Market goes to equilibrium since floor is below the equilibrium.

h. If movies shown in theaters and movies rented for home viewing are substitutes, what happens in the movie rental market when movie theaters raise their prices?

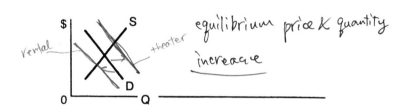

equilibrium price & quantity increase

i. What will happen in the market for copy services in a particular community when many new copy shops are opened? → S.

j. What effect would a decrease in the price of airline tickets have in the market for air travel?

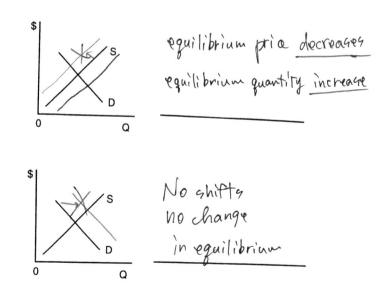

equilibrium price decreases
equilibrium quantity increase

No shifts
no change
in equilibrium

Price Ceilings and Floors

1.   Assume that the government sets a price ceiling of $1.20 in the market in Figure 3.6. What will result? What would happen if the price ceiling were set at $0.60?

2.   Assume that the government sets a price floor of $1.20 in the market in Figure 3.6. What will result? What would happen if the price floor were set at $0.60?

Figure 3.6

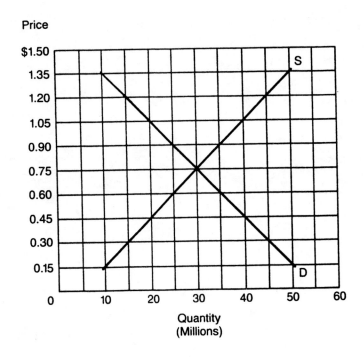

Elasticity

1.   A car dealership discovers the following information about the demand for auto accessories. Calculate the price elasticity coefficient for each example and determine whether the change is elastic or inelastic.

   a.   When the price of premium wheel covers is lowered by 20 percent, sales increase by 25 percent. The elasticity coefficient is _____ and the response to this price change is _____.

b.   When the price of car phones is increased by 30 percent, consumers buy 40 percent fewer car phones. The elasticity coefficient is _____ and the change is _____.

c.   When the price of leather interiors is raised by 30 percent, sales decrease by 20 percent. The elasticity coefficient is _____ and the change is _____.

d.   When the price of sunroofs is lowered by 20 percent, consumers buy 15 percent more sunroofs. The elasticity coefficient is _____ and the change is _____.

2.   Calculate the percentage change in quantity, the percentage change in price, and the elasticity coefficient for each of the following examples.

a.   When the price of macadamia nut turtles at Chocolate City is increased from $10 to $11 per pound, Chocolate City increases the quantity offered for sale from 200 to 250 pounds per week.

$$\frac{\% \text{ change in Q}}{\% \text{ change in P}} = \underline{\hspace{3cm}}$$

elasticity coefficient = _____

b.   When the price of home delivery of a newspaper falls from $24 to $21 a month, subscriptions increase from 16,000 to 18,000 subscriptions.

$$\frac{\% \text{ change in Q}}{\% \text{ change in P}} = \underline{\hspace{3cm}}$$

elasticity coefficient = _____

c.	When the average price of a condominium in a city drops from \$200,000 to \$190,000, builders decrease the number of units constructed per month from 100 to 97.

$$\frac{\%\ \text{change in Q}}{\%\ \text{change in P}} = \underline{\hspace{3cm}}$$

elasticity coefficient = \underline{\hspace{2.5cm}}

d.	When a tennis club increases its quarterly membership fee from \$120 to \$180, the number of memberships falls from 610 to 305.

$$\frac{\%\ \text{change in Q}}{\%\ \text{change in P}} = \underline{\hspace{3cm}}$$

elasticity coefficient = \underline{\hspace{2.5cm}}

e.	When wages rise from \$7 to \$8.05 per hour, the number of applicants for a job increases from 140 to 168.

$$\frac{\%\ \text{change in Q}}{\%\ \text{change in P}} = \underline{\hspace{3cm}}$$

elasticity coefficient = \underline{\hspace{2.5cm}}

Indicate the best answer to each question.

1.   The Law of Demand states that:
   a.   there is a direct relationship between a product's price and the quantity demanded.
   b.   the quantity demanded of a product will decrease when the product's price increases.
   c.   the demand curve for a product will shift to the left when the product's price increases.
   d.   consumers buy more of a product when its price is low because sellers supply more.

2.   When constructing a supply schedule for a product, nonprice factors affecting supply:
   a.   and the product's price are held constant.
   b.   and the product's price are allowed to change.
   c.   are held constant, but the product's price is allowed to change.
   d.   are allowed to change, but the product's price is held constant.

3.   If the equilibrium price of a product were $6 and the actual price charged in the market were $8, you would expect:
   a.   a shortage of this product at $6.
   b.   a surplus of this product at $8.
   c.   the equilibrium price to rise to $8.
   d.   the amount supplied to be equal to the amount demanded at $8.

4.   A surplus of a product in a market indicates that the quantity demanded:
   a.   exceeds the quantity supplied and that the equilibrium price is above the price charged.
   b.   exceeds the quantity supplied and that the equilibrium price is below the price charged.
   c.   is less than the quantity supplied and that the equilibrium price is above the price charged.
   d.   is less than the quantity supplied and that the equilibrium price is below the price charged.

5.   A change in the quantity supplied of a product:
   a.   causes the product supply curve to shift to the right or left.
   b.   is caused by a change in the price of the product.

c.   is caused by a change in the number of sellers in the market.
d.   means the entire supply schedule changes.

6.   The demand curve for a product would shift to the left if:
a.   buyers expected the product's price to be much higher in the future.
b.   the price of the product decreased.
ⓒ   the popularity of the product decreased.
d.   the number of sellers in the market decreased.

7.   Which of the following would cause an increase in the supply of a particular product?
a.   The product's price increases.
b.   The cost of producing the product increases.
c.   The profit on another product the seller produces increases.
ⓓ   None of the above.

Answer questions 8 through 11 on the basis of the following graph.

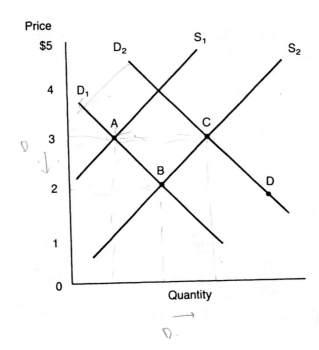

8.   An increase in the number of sellers in the market would cause a movement from:
ⓐ   S₁ to S₂.
b.   S₂ to S₁.
c.   D₁ to D₂.
ⓓ   D₂ to D₁.

S market competitive price

cheaper

62

9. The movement from point B to point C represents:
   a. a decrease in demand.
   b. a decrease in quantity demanded.
   c. an increase in supply.
   (d.) an increase in quantity supplied.

10. The movement from D_2 to D_1 represents:
    (a.) a decrease in demand.
    (b.) an increase in demand.
    c. a decrease in quantity demanded.
    d. an increase in quantity demanded.

11. There would be a surplus in this market if:
    a. the price were $2.00 and demand and supply were shown by D_2 and S_1.
    (b.) the price were $2.00 and demand and supply were shown by D_2 and S_2.
    c. the price were $3.00 and demand and supply were shown by D_2 and S_1.
    (d.) the price were $3.00 and demand and supply were shown by D_1 and S_2.

12. If there were an increase in the demand for a product and no change in supply, you would expect:
    (a.) an increase in the product's equilibrium price and equilibrium quantity.
    b. an increase in the product's equilibrium price and a decrease in its equilibrium quantity.
    (c.) a decrease in the product's equilibrium price and an increase in its equilibrium quantity.
    d. a decrease in the product's equilibrium price and equilibrium quantity.

13. A decrease in equilibrium price and quantity in a market would be caused by:
    (a.) a decrease in the number of buyers in the market.
    b. a decrease in the cost of producing the good sold in the market.
    (c.) an increase in the number of sellers in the market.
    d. an increase in the price of a good that competes with the good sold in the market.

14. If there were a decrease in the cost of producing a good sold in a market, you would expect the market's equilibrium price:
    a. and equilibrium quantity to decrease.
    b. and equilibrium quantity to increase.
    (c.) to decrease and equilibrium quantity to increase.
    (d.) to increase and equilibrium quantity to decrease.

15. If the price of a product is at its legally imposed ceiling rather than at equilibrium, then:
   a.   a surplus develops.
   b.   a shortage develops.
   c.   no surplus or shortage develops.
   d.   the ceiling price must be above the equilibrium price.

Answer questions 16 and 17 on the basis of the following figure.

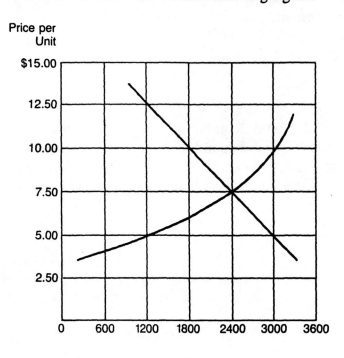

Price per Unit

Number of Units

16. If the government imposed a price floor of $5.00 in this market there would be:
   a.   a surplus of 1800 units.
   b.   a shortage of 1200 units.
   c.   a shortage of 1800 units.
   d.   none of the above.

17. If the government imposed a price ceiling of $5.00 in this market there would be:
   a.   a surplus of 1200 units.
   b.   a surplus of 1800 units.
   c.   a shortage of 1800 units.
   d.   none of the above.

18. Price elasticity of demand is equal to:

a. $\dfrac{\text{original quantity demanded}}{\text{original price}}$.

b. $\dfrac{\text{change in price}}{\text{change in quantity demanded}}$.

c. $\dfrac{\text{percentage change in quantity demanded}}{\text{percentage change in price}}$.

d. $\dfrac{\text{percentage change in price}}{\text{percentage change in quantity demanded}}$.

19. If the price elasticity of demand for a product were 0.8, buyers' demand for that product would be:
a. price elastic.
b. price inelastic.
c. unitary price elastic.
d. directly related to the product's price.

20. 100 units of a product were supplied by sellers at a price of $20 per unit, but only 70 units are supplied because the price fell to $16. The price elasticity of supply for this product is:
a. 0.67.
b. 1.0.
c. 1.5.
d. 3.0.

NOTE: Correct answers to the Exercises and the Sample Examination Questions can be found at the end of the Study Guide.

Chapter 4
Goals and Problems of the Macroeconomy: Employment, Prices, and Production

- To introduce the three fundamental areas on which macroeconomics focuses: employment, prices, and production.
- To define unemployment and explain its consequences.
- To identify different types of unemployment and to introduce measures and statistics on employment and unemployment.
- To discuss discouraged workers, regional differences in unemployment, and the pattern of job creation in the economy.
- To discuss full employment.
- To define inflation and explain its consequences.
- To identify the causes of inflationary pressure and to introduce measures and statistics on inflation.
- To distinguish between deflation and disinflation.
- To define full production and economic growth.
- To identify factors affecting economic growth and to introduce some costs associated with growth.
- To introduce GDP, the primary measure of production.
- To define productivity and discuss changes in U.S. productivity over the years.
- To highlight the policy problem that occurs when pursuing the goals of full employment, full production, and price stability simultaneously.

■ KEY TERMS AND CONCEPTS

Macroeconomics

Employment Act of 1946

Unemployment

Frictional unemployment

Full employment

Cyclical unemployment

Structural unemployment

Labor force

Participation rate

Unemployment rate

Discouraged workers

Underemployment

Natural rate of unemployment

Inflation

Hyperinflation

Money (nominal) income

Real income

Cost-of-living adjustment

Interest rate

Real rate of interest

Wealth

Demand-pull inflation

Cost-push inflation

Price index

Base year

Consumer price index (CPI)

Producer price index (PPI)

GDP chain-type price index

Deflation

Disinflation

Production

Full production

Economic growth

Technological change

Human capital investments

Gross domestic product (GDP)

Money (current) GDP

Real (constant) GDP

Underground economy

Productivity

■ STUDY ORGANIZER

1. Identify the three major problems and the three major goals of the macroeconomy.

2. Know the purpose of the Employment Act of 1946.

3. Understand the effects of unemployment on society and on unemployed individuals.

4. Differentiate among frictional, cyclical, and structural unemployment, and give some examples of each.

5. Explain what the labor force, unemployment rate, and participation rate measure.

6. Identify a group in the U.S. labor force with an increasing participation rate and some groups with higher than average unemployment rates.

7. Explain how the unemployment rate is determined.

8. Understand how discouraged workers, regional differences in unemployment rates, and differences in the types of jobs people hold create problems in interpreting unemployment statistics.

9. Understand the concept of full employment and the difference between the full employment rate of unemployment and the natural rate of unemployment.

10. Explain the effect of inflation on the purchasing power of money, persons living on fixed incomes or working under long-term contracts, savers and borrowers, and holders of wealth.

11. Differentiate between money income and real income, between income and wealth, and between a stated rate of interest and the real rate of interest.

12. Differentiate between demand-pull and cost-push inflation.

13. Construct and interpret a price index, and explain the role of the base year.

14. Distinguish among the consumer price index, producer price index, and GDP chain-type price index.

15. Differentiate between deflation and disinflation.

16. Understand the relationship between production and employment, the goals of full production and economic growth, and how economic growth is illustrated with a production possibilities curve.

17. Identify important factors for achieving economic growth, and some concerns about economic growth as a macroeconomic goal.

18. Know the difference between money GDP and real GDP, and calculate real GDP.

19. Understand the importance of using real GDP to evaluate economic activity.

20. Identify several types of production not included in GDP.

21. Explain the concept of productivity, and describe the trend in output per worker in the United States since 1970.

22. Understand the tradeoff between full employment and full production, and price stability, and the problem this creates.

price, full
 production
growth

1. The major macroeconomic goals of the U.S. economy are

_____ stability, _____ employment, and full _____

and economic _____.

Employment Act

a. Congress committed the federal government to providing

an environment to achieve these goals when it passed the

_____ _____ of 1946.

unemployed

fewer

scarcity

unemployed

2. A resource available for production but not being used is

_____. This is a matter of concern because unemployment

leads to the production of _____ goods and services than

would otherwise be the case, or it intensifies the basic economic

problem of _____. Unemployment is also a matter of

concern because of the hardships it imposes on _____

individuals and those around them.

frictionally

a. Persons voluntarily out of work and searching for another

job are classified as _____ unemployed.

cyclically

b. Persons laid off because the economy is in a recession and

the demand for the product they produce has decreased

are classified as _____ unemployed.

c. Persons who lose a job because the product they produce is no longer demanded, or because the product is produced in a way that no longer requires their skills, are classified as _____ unemployed.

structurally

d. While frictional unemployment is voluntary, cyclical and structural unemployment are _____.

involuntary

labor force
actively

3. The _____ _____ includes all persons 16 years of age and older who are working or _____ seeking work.

a. The percentage of some group that is in the labor force is indicated by that group's _____ rate. Over the years, the percentage of men in the labor force has _____ and the percentage of women in the labor force has _____.

participation

decreased

increased

b. The overall unemployment rate is the percentage of the _____ _____ that is _____ and actively seeking _____. The unemployment rates for various labor force subgroups differ: for married men it tends to be _____, and for teenagers it tends to be _____, than the overall rate for all workers.

labor force
  unemployed
work

lower

higher

c. Unemployment statistics are collected by surveying a

sample

any

_____ of households. A person is counted as employed if that person did _____ work during a survey week as a paid employee or in their own business.

d. The overall unemployment rate does not include

discouraged
workers
labor force

_____ _____, or persons who are unsuccessful in locating a job and drop out of the _____ _____.

regional

The overall unemployment rate also does not indicate _____ differences in unemployment since it is a national figure, and it provides no information about the

types

_____ of jobs held, the number of persons who are

full-time

working part-time but seeking a _____-_____ job, or

underemployed

the number of persons who are _____ because they are working below their skill level.

4. Full employment occurs when everyone in the labor force except

frictionally

the _____ unemployed is working.

a. There is not agreement on the rate of unemployment that represents full employment, and over the years this rate

changed

has _____. Determining this rate in the 1990s has been complicated by the substantial growth in involuntary

part-time

_____-_____ employment.

72

b. Some economists believe that an alternative goal to full employment is the natural rate of unemployment, which

cyclical

occurs when _____ unemployment is eliminated, or when the economy experiences only frictional and

structural

_____ unemployment.

5. An increase in the general level of prices is termed

inflation

_____. As the general level of prices goes up, the

falls

purchasing power of money _____. Extremely rapid

hyperinflation

inflation is called _____.

a. The amount of goods and services that can be purchased

real

with a particular amount of money income is _____

falls

income. Real income _____ if money income does not increase enough to compensate for inflation.

b. Inflation creates problems for some people. It is especially hard on persons, such as pensioners, who live on

fixed

_____ incomes; those working under contracts where

less

income increases _____ than the rate of inflation;

less

those who save or loan money at interest rates _____

real

than the inflation rate, or where the _____ rate of

inflation

interest (the nominal rate minus the _____ rate) is

wealth (assets)	negative; and persons who plan to acquire _____, such as homes, in the future.
	c. Winners from inflation include people whose incomes rise
faster	_____ than the inflation rate, borrowers who are paying
less	back loans at an interest rate _____ than the inflation
assets	rate, and owners of real _____.
	d. If prices are forced up because buyers' demands for goods and services are greater than the economy's ability to produce those goods and services, the economy is
demand-pull	experiencing _____-_____ inflation. This type of inflation tends to be associated with an economy operating
full	at or near _____ employment.
	e. Inflation coming from the sellers' side of the market is
cost-push	referred to as _____-_____ inflation. This is caused
production	by increases in the costs of _____ which lead to higher prices.
	f. Increases in prices can be caused by pressures coming from
buyers' sellers'	both the _____ and the _____ sides of the market, as well as by businesses' and households'
expectations	_____ of future economic conditions.

74

price index

base
100.0

25
higher

165, 150
110.0

consumer
energy

producer, GDP

6. The percentage scale used to measure changes in the price of an item or a collection of items is called a _____ _____.

a. In a price index, prices in different years are compared to the price in a specific year, called the _____ year. The price index number for the base year is _____.

b. If the price index number for a particular year is 125.0, this means that the price of the item(s) measured is _____ percent _____ in that year than in the base year.

c. If an item is priced at $150 in the base year and $165 in year 2, the price index number for year 2 is _____ / _____ x 100, or _____.

d. The price index that measures changes in the prices of goods and services ordinarily purchased by households is the _____ price index. Rapid increases in this index in the 1970s and early 1980s were caused by rising _____ prices. The price index that measures changes in the prices of materials and items purchased for further sale by businesses is the _____ price index. The _____ chain-type price index measures price changes for the entire economy.

75

decrease

inflation rate

full, full

economic growth

right

output, capita

grown

resources

efficiently

technological

human capital

7. Deflation occurs when there is a sustained _____ in the general level of prices, and disinflation occurs when there is a slowing of the _____ _____.

8. When an economy is producing at maximum output or capacity, it is operating at _____ production (and _____ employment). When an economy increases its full production level of output over time, it achieves _____ _____. This is illustrated by a shift of the economy's production possibilities curve to the _____. Economic growth is best measured by an increase in real _____ per _____ over time. In the United States, this measure has _____ over the decades.

a. Economic growth can be achieved by increasing the amount of _____ available for production, and/or by using resources more _____. The most important factor leading to economic growth is _____ change, or an increase in knowledge about production and its processes. Investments that increase the productivity of people, such as education, are called _____ _____ investments and are important to achieving growth.

demand

costs

environment

gross domestic

product

money

current

real, constant

production

production
 prices

real

b.	If economic growth is to be maintained, it is important to have a strong _____ for the additional goods and services the economy produces.

c.	Some people criticize the goal of economic growth because of the future _____ that may result, particularly with regard to the _____.

9.	The dollar value of all finished goods and services produced in an economy in one year is that economy's _____ _____ _____.

a.	The measure of an economy's output in prices during the year in which the output was produced is termed _____, or _____, GDP. The measure of an economy's output that has been adjusted to eliminate inflation is termed _____, or _____, GDP.

b.	Real GDP increases only when the level of _____ increases. Money GDP increases when the level of _____ or the level of _____ increases. When examining the level of activity in the economy it is better to use _____ GDP figures.

money GDP	c. Real GDP for a particular year is calculated by dividing _____ _____ for that year by the GDP price index
100	number for that year, and multiplying that answer by _____. For example, if money GDP is \$4.4 trillion for a particular year and the GDP price index number is 110.0,
\$4.4, 110.0, 100	then real GDP is _____ trillion divided by _____ times
\$4.0	_____, or _____ trillion.
greater	d. If the GDP price index number is less than 100.0 for a particular year, then real GDP is _____ than money GDP for that year. If the GDP price index number is greater than 100.0 for a particular year, then real GDP is
less	_____ than money GDP for that year.
market	e. GDP does not measure all production in the economy. Excluded is production that is not exchanged in a _____, and productive activity where payment was
reported underground economy	received but not _____. The term _____ _____ refers to productive activities not reported for
GDP	tax purposes and not included in _____.
productivity	10. Output per worker is a basic measure of the _____ of a nation's resources. The average annual growth rate in output
fallen	per worker has _____ from the 1970s through the 1990s.

	11.	An economy may have to make a tradeoff between full
employment production, price		_____ and _____ , and _____ stability.
demand-pull		This is because _____ - _____ inflationary pressure
full		tends to develop as an economy approaches _____
		employment, and reducing upward pressure on prices by curbing
unemployment		demand could lead to _____ .

■ EXERCISES

Unemployment, Inflation, and GDP Data

1. Given in Table 4.1 are the unemployment rates, consumer price index numbers, and money GDP figures from your text for selected years. Complete the table by locating and filling in the unemployment rate, consumer price index number, and money GDP for each year since 1996. (Hint: The annual *Economic Report of the President*, the annual *Statistical Abstract of the United States*, and the monthly *Survey of Current Business*, all government publications, are good sources for this information.)

Table 4.1

Year	Unemployment Rate	Consumer Price Index (1982-84 = 100)	Money GDP (Trillions)
1992	7.5%	140.3	$6.244
1993	6.9	144.5	6.553
1994	6.1	148.2	6.936
1995	5.6	152.4	7.254
1996	5.4	156.9	7.616[a]
1997			
1998			
1999			

[a]1996 figure is for the third quarter.

2. Calculate a price index for the hypothetical market basket of goods in Table 4.2, using 1996 as the base year.

Table 4.2

Year	Price of Market Basket	Price Index
1994	$ 175	
1995	180	
1996	200	
1997	240	
1998	260	
1999	270	

3. Given in Table 4.3 are the money GDP and the GDP price index for years 1 through 5 for a hypothetical economy. From this information, determine real GDP for each year.

Table 4.3

Year	Money GDP (Billions)	GDP Price Index	Real GDP (Billions)
1	$ 729	90.0	
2	800	100.0	
3	840	105.0	
4	990	120.0	
5	1,066	130.0	

4. Table 4.4 gives the annual output, measured in market baskets, of a hypothetical economy for years 1 through 5. Using the information given, complete the table.

Table 4.4

Year	Number of Market Baskets	Price per Market Basket	Money GDP	GDP Price Index	Real GDP
1	1,800	$135			
2	2,000	150		100.0	
3	2,000	180			
4	2,400	180			
5	2,300	195			

▣ SAMPLE EXAMINATION QUESTIONS

Indicate the best answer to each question.

1. Unemployment causes a loss for society because:
   a. businesses raise their prices to make up for lower sales.
   b. some goods that could have satisfied society's wants go unproduced.
   c. individuals consume more because they spend fewer hours at work.
   d. all of the above.

2. The economy is at full employment when only the:
   a. cyclically unemployed are out of work.
   b. structurally unemployed are out of work.
   c. cyclically and structurally unemployed are out of work.
   d. frictionally unemployed are out of work.

3. When a person is out of work because the economy is in a recession and spending on the product he or she produces has fallen, the person is:
   a. cyclically unemployed.
   b. frictionally unemployed.
   c. structurally unemployed.
   d. voluntarily unemployed.

4. Which of the following statements is FALSE?
   a. A person must be out of work and actively seeking work to be considered unemployed.
   b. The labor force includes all persons 16 years of age and older who are working or actively seeking work.
   c. The participation rate is the percentage of workers in the labor force currently holding a job.
   d. Discouraged workers are persons who have dropped out of the labor force after an unsuccessful search for a job.

5. Which of the following statements is true?
   a. The economy is at full employment when only the cyclically unemployed are out of work.
   b. The full employment rate of unemployment has been at about 4 percent since the 1960s.
   c. The natural rate of unemployment is typically lower then the full employment rate of unemployment.
   d. The natural rate of unemployment is the rate that includes only the frictionally and structurally unemployed.

6. When the inflation rate goes up, the purchasing power of money:
   a. remains unchanged.
   b. increases.
   c. remains unchanged at first and then increases.
   d. decreases.

7. Which of the following statements is true?
   a. Real income is the amount of goods and services that can be purchased with a particular amount of money income.
   b. The real rate of interest is the nominal, or stated, rate of interest divided by the inflation rate.
   c. Inflation improves the standard of living of persons earning fixed incomes.
   d. Prolonged and severe inflation has no effect on a country's social and political institutions.

8. Inflation coming from the buyers' side of the market is:
   a. demand-pull inflation.
   b. caused by too few buyers in the market.
   c. caused by output increasing faster than spending.
   d. none of the above.

9.   The base year in a price index is:
      a.   always the first year listed in the index.
      b.   always given a value of 0.0.
      c.   the year against which prices in all other years are compared.
      d.   all of the above.

10.   If this year's price index number for good X is 125, then good X is:
      a.   currently priced at $125.
      b.   priced 125 percent higher in the base year than this year.
      c.   priced 25 percent higher this year than in the base year.
      d.   priced 125 percent higher this year than in the base year.

11.   If a product cost $600 in the base year and the price index number for this year is 125.0, the price of the product this year is:
      a. $475.
      b. $480.
      c. $475.
      d. $750.

12.   A product that cost $250 in the base year costs $300 this year. The price index number for this year is:
      a.   50.0.
      b.   83.0
      c.   120.0.
      d.   150.0.

13.   Deflation refers to:
      a.   a decrease in output per worker.
      b.   a decrease in the rate of inflation.
      c.   a sustained decrease in the general level of prices.
      d.   a sustained decrease in the level of an economy's output.

14.   For economic growth to occur, an economy must:
      a.   operate on its production possibilities curve.
      b.   have its production possibilities curve shift outward, or to the right, over time.
      c.   maintain a level of demand sufficient to absorb the economy's expanded output.
      d.   all of the above.

15. Probably the most important factor leading to improved resource efficiency over the long run is:
    a. technological change.
    b. the discovery of new natural resources.
    c. changes in the amount of capital in the economy.
    d. changes in tax laws and government expenditures.

16. Which of the following statements about GDP is FALSE?
    a. Money GDP will increase if there is an increase in the output of the economy.
    b. Real GDP will increase if there is an increase in the output of the economy.
    c. Money GDP will increase if there is an increase in the economy's level of prices.
    d. Real GDP will increase if there is an increase in the economy's level of prices.

17. Real GDP for 1998 is equal to:

    a. $\dfrac{\text{1998 money GDP}}{\text{1998 GDP price index number}} \times 100.$

    b. $\dfrac{\text{1998 money GDP}}{\text{1998 output per worker}} \times 100.$

    c. (1998 money GDP) - (1997 money GDP).

    d. (1998 money GDP) - (1998 GDP deflator) x 100.

18. Real GDP for a particular year would be less than money GDP in that year if:
    a. the GDP price index number was less than 100.0 in that year.
    b. money GDP in that year was less than money GDP in the previous year.
    c. the GDP price index number was greater than 100.0 in that year.
    d. money GDP in that year was greater than money GDP in the previous year.

19. A decrease in productivity means that:
    a. nominal GDP has fallen.
    b. output per worker has fallen.
    c. the production possibilities curve has shifted to the right.
    d. the economy has experienced disinflation.

20. If an economy were to pursue a policy of maintaining full employment, it would likely have to forgo:
   a. price stability.
   b. full production.
   c. economic growth.
   d. maximum current output.

NOTE: Correct answers to the Exercises and the Sample Examination Questions can be found at the end of the Study Guide.

Chapter 5
Foundations of the Macroeconomy

■ CHAPTER OBJECTIVES

- To define and explain business cycles.
- To understand the relationship between total spending and the levels of aggregate employment, production, and prices.
- To examine the spending behavior of households, businesses, government units, and the foreign sector.
- To establish how the relationship between leakages from the spending stream and injections into the spending stream affects the level of economic activity.
- To introduce the multiplier effect.
- To introduce the effect of expectations on output and price levels.
- To identify the role of total spending in the formation of macroeconomic policies.

■ KEY TERMS AND CONCEPTS

Business cycles

Recovery, peak, recession, trough

Total, or aggregate, spending

Personal consumption expenditures

Income-determined spending

Transfer payment

Nonincome-determined spending

Injections into the spending stream

Financial institutions

Leakages from the spending stream

Investment spending

Retained earnings

Saving-investment relationship

Government purchases of goods and services

Exports

Imports

Net exports

Multiplier effect

Expectations

Fiscal policy

Monetary policy

■ STUDY ORGANIZER

1. Understand the relationship between changes in real GDP and in the rate of unemployment.

2. Identify the four phases of a business cycle and explain the change in real GDP that occurs in each phase.

3. Understand the relationship between changes in total spending and changes in the levels of aggregate output, employment, and income in an economy.

4. Compare the size and stability of spending by households, businesses, government units, and foreign buyers.

5. Identify the factors that influence the levels of spending by households and businesses.

6. Explain the effect of household borrowing, transfer payments, saving, and taxes on household spending.

7. Identify the major causes of fluctuations in investment spending.

8. Understand the role of financial institutions in channeling funds from savers to borrowers.

9. Explain how the saving-investment relationship can cause the economy to expand or contract.

10. Understand the influence of government purchases of goods and services, transfer payments, and taxes on the spending stream.

11. Explain how the tax-government expenditures relationship can cause the economy to expand or contract.

12. Distinguish among exports, imports, and net exports, and understand the influence of U.S. exports and imports on the spending stream.

13. Identify the major injections into and leakages from the spending stream.

14. Explain how the relationship between injections and leakages causes economic activity to expand, contract, or stay the same.

15. Differentiate between income-determined and nonincome-determined spending and illustrate the difference by means of a circular flow model.

16. Understand how changes in nonincome-determined spending cause larger changes in output, employment, and income.

17. Be able to calculate the multiplier effect, or the total change in output and income that results from an initial change in nonincome-determined spending.

18. Explain the relationship between total spending and demand-pull inflation when the economy is at or near full employment.

19. Understand how expectations can lead to recessions and inflation.

20. Explain how fiscal policy and monetary policy are designed to affect total spending.

GDP
  business
cycles

rises

1. Recurring periods of expansion and contraction in an economy's real output, or real _____, are referred to as _____ _____. Changes in real GDP influence the level of unemployment: as real GDP falls, the level of unemployment _____.

recovery

peak, recession

trough

a. There are four phases to every business cycle: real GDP grows in the _____ phase, reaches a maximum at the _____, falls in the _____ phase, and is at its lowest point in the _____.

recovery

recession

length
  intensity

b. Since World War II, the U.S. economy has spent more time in _____ phases of business cycles than in _____ phases. The phases of individual business cycles differ in _____ and _____.

theories

spending

c. There are several _____ that explain changes in the level of economic activity. To understand these theories, an overview of the _____ patterns of the major participants in the economy is important.

total
  aggregate

2. Basically, changes in the level of economic activity, or in real GDP, are caused by changes in _____, or _____,

spending. Aggregate spending is equal to the combined spending for new goods and services by all _____, _____, _____ units, and _____ buyers.

households
businesses
government
foreign

a. When total spending decreases, _____ goods and services are sold, and production _____. This leads to a _____ in the employment of resources, which in turn leads to a _____ in the total income going to resource owners.

fewer

decreases

decrease

decrease

b. When total spending goes up and sales increase, producers _____ their output and hire _____ resources, which in turn _____ the total income going to resource owners.

increase
more
increases

3. Households spend _____ on new goods and services than do businesses, government units, and foreign buyers combined. The growth of real household spending over the years has been relatively _____. Economists label the total spending by households on new goods and services as _____ _____ expenditures.

more

stable

personal

consumption

a. The major source of household spending is _____ earned from producing goods and services. Spending from

income

income-determined	this source is labeled _____ - _____ spending. Other sources of funds for household spending include
transfer government	_____ payments, or money from the _____ for which no direct work is performed in return, and
borrowing	_____ from a lender. Spending from sources other
nonincome- determined	than earned income is called _____ - _____ spending.
	b. Spending from sources other than household earned
injection	income causes an _____ into the spending stream,
expansion	which leads to an _____ in output, employment,
income	and _____ in the economy.
spending	c. A household can dispose of its income by _____ it
saving	on goods and services, _____ it for future use, or
taxes	paying _____ to the government. Saving and tax
leakages	payments are _____ from the spending stream,
decreases	which cause _____ in current, output, employment,
	and income in the economy.
financial	d. Savings are channeled to borrowers through _____
institutions	_____, such as banks, savings associations, and
	insurance companies.

investment	4. The purchase of new goods, such as machinery and equipment, by business firms is called _____ spending. Business
fluctuates	investment spending _____ over time and is less stable than personal consumption expenditures or government expenditures. Because of this, changes in investment spending are
primary	a _____ cause of changes in the level of economic activity.
profit	a. Investment spending fluctuates because it is based on businesses' _____ expectations. An investment expenditure may be delayed or dropped from consideration
profitable	if it is not thought to be _____.
expectations	b. The expected profit from an investment is influenced by such factors as _____ of future economic conditions
interest	and the _____ rate. The higher the interest rate, the
more	_____ a business must pay to borrow funds. This in turn
lowers	raises the cost of the investment and _____ the expected profit.
	c. When a business invests, it can borrow from outside sources, or use its own savings, which are called
retained	_____ earnings.

leakage	d. Business saving is a _____ from the spending stream. Investment spending is an _____ into the spending stream because it is a form of _____-_____ spending. Business saving and spending are channeled through _____ _____, such as banks and brokerage houses.
injection	
nonincome-determined	
financial institutions	
saving-investment	e. The relationship between business and household saving, and business investment spending and household spending from borrowing, is called the _____-_____ relationship.
no change	f. If all household and business saving is put back into the spending stream through business investment spending and household spending from borrowing, this relationship will cause _____ _____ in the economy's levels of output, employment, and income. If spending from investment and borrowing is greater than saving, the level of economic activity will _____; and if saving is greater than spending from investment and borrowing, the level of economic activity will _____.
increase	
decrease	
	5. Government purchases of new goods and services is a type of

noninicome-
determined
injection

increase

injection

leakage

no change

contract

expand

foreign

export

injections

_____-_____ spending, which means it is an

_____ into the spending stream. Increases in government

purchases _____ output, employment, and income in the

economy. Spending from government transfer payments is an

_____, and taxes paid to the government by households

and businesses are a _____ from the spending stream.

a. The level of economic activity is influenced by the
relationship between government expenditures and taxes.
If spending from government purchases and transfers
equals spending removed by taxes, this relationship will
cause _____ _____ in the level of economic activity;
if spending from government sources is less than spending
removed by taxes, economic activity will _____; and
if spending from government sources is greater than
spending removed by taxes, economic activity will _____.

6. Transactions between buyers and sellers in the United States
and other countries occur in the _____ sector.

a. A good or service produced in the United States and sold
abroad is an _____. U.S.-produced goods and
services sold abroad create _____ into the spending

94

increase

stream and _____ output, employment, and income in the United States.

b.   A foreign-produced good or service sold in the United States is an _____. Foreign-produced goods and services sold in the United States create _____ from the spending stream and _____ output, employment, and income in the United States.

import

leakages

decrease

net exports

c.   Exports minus imports is termed _____ _____. When net exports is a positive number, leakages are _____ than injections, causing economic activity to _____; when net exports is a negative number, leakages are _____ than injections, causing economic activity to _____; and when net exports is zero, economic activity will _____ _____.

less

expand

greater

contract

not change

7.   Leakages from the spending stream include household _____, business _____, _____ paid to the government by households and businesses, and expenditures on _____ goods and services. These leakages cause the economy's levels of output, employment, and income to _____. Injections into the spending stream include household spending from _____ payments and

saving, saving
taxes

imported

decrease

transfer

95

borrowing investment purchases exported	_____, business _____ spending, government _____ of goods and services, and foreign expenditures on _____ goods and services. These injections cause the economy's levels of output, employment, and income to
increase	_____.
contract	a. If all leakages from the spending stream are greater than all injections, the level of economic activity will _____.
expand	If all leakages from the spending stream are less than all injections, the level of economic activity will _____.
not change	If all leakages from the spending stream are equal to all injections, the level of economic activity will _____ _____.
income	8. Much of the spending in the economy comes from the earned _____ of households. Spending that does not come from
nonincome- determined investment	household earned income is termed _____-_____ spending. This includes business _____ spending,
purchases	government _____ of goods and services, household
transfer borrowing exports	spending from _____ payments and _____, and spending for _____.
larger	a. An increase or decrease in nonincome-determined spending leads to a _____ increase or decrease in

multiplier

nonincome-
determined

income

spend

income

spend

nonincome-
determined
not spent

the level of economic activity. This is referred to as the

_____ effect.

b. The multiplier effect occurs because _____-

_____ spending injected into the economy is spent

over and over again. An initial injection of nonincome-

determined spending provides _____ to those who

own the resources used to produce the goods and services

purchased. These people in turn _____ part of that

income on new goods and services, which provides

_____ to the owners of resources used to produce

those goods and services. These people in turn _____

part of their newly received income to purchase goods and

services, and so on.

c. The total change in output and income that results from

the multiplier effect is found by dividing the initial change

in _____-_____ spending by the percentage

of additional income _____ _____. For example, if

investment spending increases by $8 million and people

spend 75 percent of the additional income they receive, the

effect of this initial change in investment spending on

output and income is found by dividing

97

$8 million
  25% (0.25)
$32 million

_____ by _____, for a total change of

_____.

inflation

full

greater

9. Demand-pull _____ may result if the economy is operating at or near _____ employment when injections into the spending stream are _____ than leakages through saving, taxes, and expenditures on imports.

expectations

10. Economic activity can be affected when households and businesses act on the basis of their _____ of future economic conditions.

inflation

a. Expectations of inflation can cause surges of spending which can in turn cause _____.

recession

b. Fear of a recession can cause reductions in spending and increases in saving which can in turn cause a _____.

fiscal·

11. Changing federal government taxes and/or expenditures to increase or decrease the spending stream in order to change the level of economic activity is referred to as _____ policy. Increasing or decreasing the supply of money to change the level of borrowing and spending, and, through that, the level of

monetary

economic activity, is referred to as _____ policy.

Total Spending and the Level of Economic Activity

1. Label the circular flow diagram in Figure 5.1 with the items listed in a through d below.

    a. The flows of goods and services and factors of production between households and businesses.
    b. The flows of income and personal consumption expenditures.
    c. Business saving and investment spending.
    d. Household saving and household borrowing.

Figure 5.1

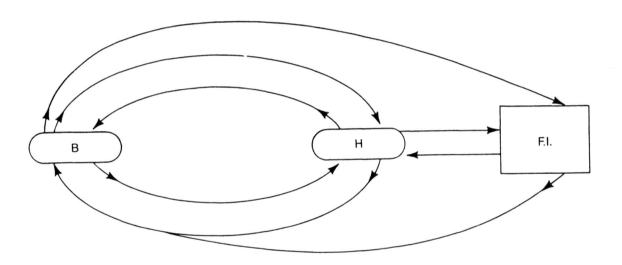

2. Label items a through d below on the circular flow diagram in Figure 5.2.

    a. The flows of goods and services and factors of production between households and businesses.
    b. The flows of income and personal consumption expenditures.
    c. Business and household taxes.
    d. Government purchases of goods and services, and transfer payments.

Figure 5.2

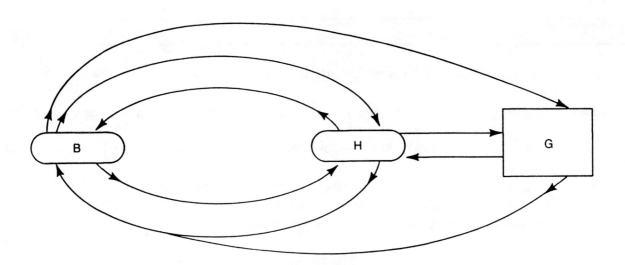

3.   In the column below labeled "Leakages", list the five types of leakages from the spending stream, and in the column labeled "Injections", list the five types of injections into the spending stream.

Leakages   *Injections*

1. _____   1. _____

2. _____   2. _____

3. _____   3. _____

4. _____   4. _____

5. _____   5. _____

4.   Determine whether each of the following, taken alone, would increase or decrease output, income, and employment, or whether demand-pull inflation would result.

a.   Businesses fear that a serious recession will begin in the next three to six months.

b.   The federal government begins a major program to upgrade the interstate highway system with no increase in taxes to pay for the program.

c.   Several American medical equipment manufacturers produce sophisticated testing devices that foreign hospitals begin to buy.

d.   Since the economy is at full employment, spending for automobiles and furniture increases at a rapid rate.

e.   In order to try to balance the federal government budget, taxes are raised and transfer payments are cut.

The Multiplier

1.   Determine the multiplier effect on total output and income in each of the following examples.

a.   There is an initial injection of $6 billion in nonincome-determined spending into the economy, and households spend 75 percent of additional income they receive and do not spend 25 percent.

Change in total output and income = _____

b. $350 million in investment spending is removed from the economy and household spending changes by 80 percent of any change in income.

Change in total output and income = _____

c.   Government increases its purchases of goods and services by $9 billion, investment spending drops by $3 billion, and households spend 60 percent of any increase in their incomes.

Change in total output and income = _____

d.   Nonincome-determined spending falls by $20 billion, and household spending changes by 85 percent of any change in income.

Change in total output and income = _____

Indicate the best answer to each question.

1. When the real output of an economy rises during a business cycle, the economy is:
   a.   at the peak of the business cycle.
   b.   at the trough of the business cycle.
   c.   in the recovery phase of the business cycle.
   d.   in the recession phase of the business cycle.

2. Which of the following statements is FALSE?
   a.   Business cycles are recurring periods of growth and decline in an economy's real GDP.
   b.   All business cycles go through the same sequence of phases.
   c.   The length of time in each phase differs from business cycle to business cycle.
   d.   After World War II the recession phases of business cycles became deeper and longer than previously.

3. The primary cause of changes in the level of economic activity is changes in:
   a.   government tax and expenditure policies.
   b.   total spending.
   c.   imports and exports.
   d.   none of the above.

4. Households spend:
   a.   less on new goods and services than either businesses or government units.
   b.   more on new goods and services than government units, but less than businesses.
   c.   more on new goods and services than businesses, but less than government units.
   d.   more on new goods and services than businesses and government units combined.

5. The level of economic activity and the size of the circular flow would never change if:
   a.   the only spending in the economy were nonincome-determined spending.
   b.   the only spending in the economy were income-determined spending by households, and households spent all that they earned.
   c.   there were no imports or exports.
   d.   government taxes equaled transfer payments to households.

6. Household spending from transfer payments, and payments for personal income taxes are:
   a.   both injections into the spending stream.
   b.   injections into, and leakages from, the spending stream, respectively.

c. both income-determined spending.

d. income-determined spending and nonincome-determined spending, respectively.

7. The least stable component of total spending is:
   a. government purchases of goods and services.
   b. household purchases of food and medical services.
   c. investment spending.
   d. personal consumption expenditures.

8. All other things equal, you would expect business investment spending to increase as a result of:
   a. improved profit expectations.
   b. a decrease in the interest rate for borrowed funds.
   c. expectations of strengthening consumer demand.
   d. all of the above.

9. Financial institutions:
   a. play a role in channeling savings to borrowers.
   b. facilitate investment spending by businesses.
   c. include commercial banks, savings associations, and other similar organizations.
   d. all of the above.

10. Government purchases of goods and services, and spending from transfer payments:
    a. are both nonincome-determined spending.
    b. are nonincome-determined spending and income-determined spending, respectively.
    c. are nonincome-determined spending and a leakage from the spending stream, respectively.
    d. usually exactly offset what the government collects from taxpayers.

11. The payment of taxes by households and businesses is:
    a. income-determined spending.
    b. nonincome-determined spending.
    c. a leakage from the spending stream.
    d. none of the above.

12. Exports minus imports:
    a. is termed net exports.
    b. has created more of an injection into, than a leakage from, the U.S. economy throughout the 1980s and 1990s.

c. has been a small but positive number for the U.S. economy throughout the 1980s and 1990s.

d. has little effect on the economy because it involves dealings with other countries.

13. Which of the following is an injection into the spending stream?

a. Spending from earned income by households.

b. Payments by the government for defense-related goods.

c. Purchases by U.S. buyers of foreign-produced goods and services.

d. Increases in retained earnings by businesses.

14. When injections into the spending stream are greater than leakages, the level of economic activity will:

a. increase.

b. decrease.

c. increase and then decrease.

d. remain unchanged.

15. The multiplier effect:

a. is larger the greater the portion of total spending going toward the purchase of imports.

b. allows for an increase, but not a decrease, in total output and income since wages and other incomes tend not to fall.

c. refers to the fact that a change in nonincome-determined spending leads to a larger change in total output and employment.

d. equals the change in total spending divided by the change in total output.

16. The multiplier effect is equal to:

a. $\dfrac{\text{change in income-determined spending}}{\text{change in nonincome-determined spending}}$.

b. $\dfrac{\text{change in nonincome-determined spending}}{\text{percentage of additional income not spent}}$.

c. $\dfrac{\text{change in total spending}}{\text{change in total output}}$.

d. $\dfrac{\text{percentage of additional income that is spent}}{\text{change in income-determined spending}}$.

17. How much would total output change if 25 percent of additional income were not spent and exports went up by $50 billion?
    a. $12.5 billion.
    b. $62.5 billion.
    c. $75 billion.
    d. $200 billion.

18. If government purchases increased by $30 billion, investment spending decreased by $20 billion, and 80 percent of additional income was spent on new goods and services, total output would:
    a. increase by $8.0 billion.
    b. increase by $10 billion.
    c. increase by $20 billion.
    d. increase by $50 billion.

19. If the economy is at full employment, inflation will result if:
    a. net exports go from a positive to a negative number.
    b. injections into the spending stream exceed leakages from the spending stream.
    c. government purchases and transfers are less than taxes.
    d. expectations of future conditions cause households to delay current purchases.

20. The use of government taxes and expenditures to control the level of economic activity is:
    a. fiscal policy.
    b. monetary policy.
    c. nonincome-management policy.
    d. demand-correction policy.

NOTE: Correct answers to the Exercises and the Sample Examination Questions can be found at the end of the Study Guide.

Chapter 6
The Role of Government in the Macroeconomy

▣ CHAPTER OBJECTIVES

- To identify the major types of expenditures and the major sources of revenue of the federal, state, and local governments.
- To distinguish among progressive, proportional, and regressive taxes.
- To discuss recent tax issues and reforms.
- To introduce fiscal policy, explain its mechanics, and differentiate between discretionary and automatic fiscal policy.
- To define a surplus, balanced, and deficit budget, and identify the economic impact of each.
- To explain the relationship between the federal budget and fiscal policy.
- To discuss some realities of fiscal policy and the budgetary process that can hamper the attainment of fiscal policy objectives.
- To define the national debt, explain its financing, size, and burden on taxpayers, and introduce crowding out.

▣ KEY TERMS AND CONCEPTS

Government purchases of goods and services

Public good

Quasi-public good

Transfer payments

Social insurance program

Progressive tax

Proportional tax (flat tax)

Regressive tax

Tax reform

Tax bracket indexation

Tax Reform Act of 1986

Tax base

Tax abatement

Fiscal policy

Discretionary fiscal policy

Automatic stabilization

Balanced budget

Surplus budget

Deficit budget

Unified budget

Trust fund

Entitlement

On-budget

Off-budget

Full employment budget

Public choice

National debt

U.S. Treasury security (U.S. Treasury bill, note, or bond)

Debt service

Crowding out

1. Describe changes in the size of government spending, and identify the major types of expenditures by the federal government and by state and local governments.

2. Identify significant changes in the allocation of federal government expenditures since 1970.

3. Name the major sources of revenue for the federal government and for state and local governments, and identify some changes in the relative importance of different sources of federal revenue since 1970.

4. Distinguish among progressive, proportional, and regressive taxes.

5. Indicate some of the important tax reforms and issues of the 1980s and 1990s.

6. Explain the appropriate fiscal policy response for controlling unemployment and for controlling demand-pull inflation.

7. Differentiate between discretionary fiscal policy and automatic stabilization.

8. Explain how automatic stabilization works, and how it is affected by recent tax reform.

9. Distinguish among surplus, deficit, and balanced budgets and determine the effect on economic activity of each type of budget.

10. Know the pattern of federal budget deficits in recent years, the relationship between the budget and the Social Security trust fund, the distinction between on-budget and off-budget balances, and budget control problems created by entitlement programs.

11. Explain the budget prescription appropriate for fighting unemployment and for fighting demand-pull inflation, and how automatic stabilization affects the budget.

12. Identify some problems with using fiscal policy and the federal budget to control economic activity.

13. Explain what is meant by the national debt, how it has changed over the last few decades, and how it is financed.

14. Evaluate the national debt's size, the burdens it creates, and the ability to pay it off.

15. Explain the crowding out effect that results from government borrowing.

1. Outlays by government units are referred to as government

    expenditures _____ .

    a. Each year federal government expenditures are

        larger _____ than all state and local government

        expenditures combined, and total government spending

        increased as a percentage of GDP has generally _____ since

        the 1960s.

    b. Government units spend money to _____ goods

        purchase

        transfer and services, provide _____ payments to

        interest households, pay _____ on money they borrow,

        and in other ways.

    c. A good that is provided for everyone in society and not

        public withheld from anyone is called a _____ _____ .
        good
        A government provided good, such as education, that

        could also be obtained in a private market is called a

        quasi-public _____-_____ good.

    d. In recent years, the largest category of federal govern-

        transfer ment expenditures has been _____ payments.

employees

taxes

Social Security

individual

increased

decreased

proportional

progressive

regressive

progressive

regressive

e. The primary expenditure made by state and local governments is for goods and services, particularly the salaries of police, teachers, and other public _____.

2. Government revenue comes mainly from _____ and contributions to social insurance programs, such as the federal government's _____ _____ program.

a. The largest source of federal revenue is _____ income taxes. In recent years, the portion of federal government revenues accounted for by contributions to social insurance has _____ and by other taxes and receipts has _____.

b. When the percentage of income taxed remains the same as income increases, the tax is _____; when the percentage of income taxed increases as income increases, the tax is _____; and when the percentage of income taxed decreases as income increases, the tax is _____. The federal personal income tax is a _____ tax, a 5 percent sales tax on food is a _____ tax, and

110

proportional

a flat 1 percent wage tax on all earned income is a

_____ tax.

c.   The federal income tax structure was significantly altered

Tax Reform

by the _____ _____ Act of 1986 which reduced

brackets
  maximum
increased

the number of tax _____ and the _____ tax

rate.   Further tax reform in 1993 _____ the

number of tax brackets and the maximum tax rate.

d.   Many local governments are concerned about a declining

tax base

_____ _____, which is the particular thing on

which a tax is levied; and state and local governments

abatements

sometimes offer tax _____ that reduce or

eliminate taxes as incentives to attract businesses and

create jobs.

3.   Changing federal taxes and/or expenditures to control un-

demand-pull

employment or _____-_____ inflation is referred to

fiscal

as _____ policy.

a.   Fiscal policy is based on the theory that changes in taxes

and/or government expenditures change the level of

spending

aggregate, or total, _____, which in turn causes

employment

an increase or decrease in the economy's levels of output, income, and _____.

b. To reduce unemployment, fiscal policymakers would want to _____ the level of aggregate spending by _____ taxes, and/or _____ government purchases of goods and services, and/or _____ transfer payments.

increase

decreasing
 increasing
increasing

c. To alleviate demand-pull inflation, fiscal policymakers would want to _____ the level of aggregate spending by _____ taxes, and/or _____ government purchases of goods and services, and/or _____ transfer payments.

decrease

increasing
 decreasing

decreasing

d. The expansionary or contractionary effect of a change in government purchases of goods and services is _____ than the expansionary or contractionary effect of a change in transfer payments or taxes by the same amount. This is because all of the change in government purchases affects total _____, whereas changes in transfer payments and taxes partly affect spending and partly affect _____.

greater

spending

saving

multiplier

nonincome-
   determined

e.   The economy's levels of output and income change by more than an initial change in government expenditures or taxes. That is, increases or decreases in government expenditures or taxes are subject to a _____ effect because they affect _____-_____ spending.

discretionary

4.   Deliberately changing government expenditures and/or taxes to control the level of economic activity is _____ fiscal policy. Changes in government expenditures and/or taxes that occur automatically to control economic activity are referred to

stabilization

transfer

taxes

as automatic _____. The two main automatic stabilizers are _____ payments and personal income _____.

increasing

a.   If the economy were in a recession and the rate of unemployment were _____ and causing a reduction in aggregate income, transfer payments, primarily unemployment compensation, would

increase

automatically _____ and personal income tax payments to the federal government would automatically

decrease

_____ to put more spending into the economy.

b. If the economy were approaching full employment, unemployment compensation would automatically _____ and personal income tax payments to the federal government would automatically _____ to remove some spending that may be causing _____ pressure.

decrease

increase

inflationary

c. Because of changes in the structure of the personal income tax, _____ _____ may become the most important automatic stabilizer.

transfer payments

5. When a government's expenditures equal its revenues, the government is operating with a _____ budget. When a government's expenditures are less than its revenues, the government is operating with a _____ budget. When a government's expenditures are greater than its revenues, the government is operating with a _____ budget. With a deficit budget, the government must _____ money or use its _____ fund to make up the difference between what it spends and what it takes in as revenue.

balanced

surplus

deficit

borrow

reserve

a. Every year since 1969, the federal government has operated with a _____ budget. Concerns over increasing federal deficits include whether the surplus in

deficit

114

Social Security	the _____ _____ trust fund, which is reported
unified	in the _____ budget, reduces the apparent
	magnitude of the deficits, and how easily spending from
entitlement	_____ programs, such as Medicare, can be
	controlled.

b. With a surplus budget, injections of government expenditures into the spending stream are generally

less

_____ than tax leakages from the spending stream. This causes the level of total spending and economic

decrease

activity to _____, and would, therefore, be an appropriate type of budget to counteract a problem with

demand-pull

_____-_____ inflation.

c. With a deficit budget, injections of government expenditures into the spending stream are

greater

_____ than leakages due to taxes. This causes the level of total

increase

spending and economic activity to _____, and would, therefore, be an appropriate policy to counteract

unemployment

a problem with _____.

d. With a balanced budget, despite the fact that the government taxes as much as it spends, the size of the

greater

injections into the spending stream is _____ than

115

the tax leakages, making this type of budget slightly

expansionary

_____.

e. In a recession, with increasing unemployment and falling incomes, automatic stabilization tends to push the

deficit

federal budget toward a _____ . As the economy approaches full employment, automatic stabilization

surplus

tends to push the federal budget toward a _____ .

f. The budget that would result if the economy were to

full

achieve full employment is called the _____

employment

_____ budget.

6. There are several problems that may arise when using fiscal policy and the federal budget to control economic activity.

a. National defense and other objectives may be more important than overcoming inflation or unemployment

spending

in forming taxing and _____ policies.

b. The simultaneous appearance of high rates of both

unemployment
inflation

_____ and _____ , or stagflation, makes it difficult to determine an appropriate fiscal policy.

time	c. Another difficulty with fiscal policy is the _____ lag between the onset of a problem and the implementation of a policy response.
political	d. Problems may arise because the process through which the budget is formed may allow _____ objectives to take precedence over economic objectives.
spend	e. Finally, since the government can operate with a deficit, policymakers may become careless in controlling the amounts of money they _____. Also, large deficits might make it difficult for Congress to implement fiscal
unemployment	policy to counteract high _____.
deficit	7. Over the last few decades, the federal government has tended to run _____ budgets. The total accumulated amount the federal government owes from borrowing to cover its deficit
national debt	spending is referred to as the _____ _____.
Treasury	a. The U.S. government borrows money by issuing U.S. _____ securities. Securities that mature in one
bills	year or less are U.S. Treasury _____; those that
notes	mature in two to ten years are U.S. Treasury _____;

bonds	and those that come due in ten or more years are U.S. Treasury _____.
	b. When the U.S. government borrows money, it does so through a public auction so that it can borrow at the
interest	lowest rate of _____ available.
	c. Over the years, the size of the national debt has
increased	_____ considerably, and is now over $5.1
trillion	_____. In addition, the debt as a percentage of
increasing	GDP has been _____ since the early 1980s and was about 70% of the size of GDP in 1996.
	d. One of the main burdens of the national debt is the
interest	_____ that must be paid to lenders, which has
increased	_____ over the years as a percentage of federal
80s	outlays, especially during the 19_____. Since the debt is not being paid off, this rising interest cost of maintaining
debt service	the debt, or _____ _____, will be passed to future generations.
	e. If the national debt were to be fully paid off, there
redistribution	would be a major _____ of income from taxpayers, who would bear the burden of the repayment,

securities	to holders of government _____, who loaned money to the government. Also, since part of the debt is foreign-held, paying off the debt would result in
out	dollars flowing _____ of the United States. Furthermore, to pay off the debt, the government would
surplus	have to run _____ budgets which would tend to
decrease	_____ the level of economic activity.
	f. If interest rates rise due to an increase in the demand for funds from government borrowing, private borrowers,
businesses households less	such as _____ and _____, who are interest-rate sensitive, will borrow _____. This is
crowding out	referred to as _____ _____.

■ *EXERCISES*

Types of Taxes

1. In each of the following examples, identify the tax as progressive, regressive, or proportional.

   a. A tax of $30 per year on each vehicle owned by the residents of a city.

   b. A tax of 2.8 percent on all income earned within a state.

   c. A state income tax of 2 percent on income less than $20,000, 3 percent on income between $20,000 and $40,000, 4 percent on income between $40,000 and $60,000, and a continuous 1 percent increase for each additional $20,000 of income.

d.   A sales tax of 5.2 percent on food, clothing, and utilities.

e.   An occupancy tax of $12 per room per evening on all hotel rooms within a city.

f.   An earnings tax of 2.5 percent that does not apply to income less than $10,000, doubles for income between $50,000 and $200,000, and triples for income over $200,000.

Government's Impact on the Macroeconomy

1.   Indicate how each of the following actions, taken alone, would affect the economy's levels of output and employment or prices.

a.   Due to political changes in Eastern Europe, the former Soviet Union, and other nations, the federal government cuts back substantially on defense spending.

b.   The federal government runs a large budget deficit while the economy is at full employment.

c.   Many transfer payment programs for poverty-level families are cut from federal and state government budgets.

d.   Politicians elected to office make good on their promise to lower taxes and increase spending on education and health.

e.   Several serious natural disasters increase outlays by the federal government's disaster relief program.

Federal Government Receipts, Outlays, Balances, and the National Debt

1.   Table 6.1 gives data from your text on federal government receipts, outlays, budget deficits, and the national debt for fiscal years 1990 through 1996. Complete the table by filling in this data for the years since 1996. (Hint: The *Economic Report of the President*, an annual government publication, is a good source for this information.)

Table 6.1

Fiscal Year	Receipts (Billions)	Outlays (Billions)	Surplus or Deficit (Billions)	National Debt (Trillions)
1990	$1,032.0	$1,253.2	$ - 221.2	$ 3.21
1991	1,055.0	1,324.4	- 269.4	3.60
1992	1,091.3	1,381.7	- 290.4	4.00
1993	1,154.4	1,409.4	- 255.0	4.35
1994	1,258.6	1,461.7	- 203.1	4.64
1995	1,351.8	1,515.7	- 163.9	4.92
1996	1,453.1	1,560.3	- 107.3	5.18
1997				
1998				
1999				

2. Since 1996, has the national debt increased or decreased as a percentage of GDP? What is the percentage for each year since 1996?

▣ SAMPLE EXAMINATION QUESTIONS

Indicate the best answer to each question.

1. Which of the following statements about public goods is FALSE?
    a. A person must pay to use a public good.
    b. A lighthouse is an example of a public good.
    c. No one can be excluded from using a public good.
    d. Public goods are provided for all members of society.

2. On which of the following does the federal government spend the largest amount?
    a. Defense.
    b. Grants-in-aid to state and local governments.

c.   Interest on the national debt.
d.   Transfer payments.

3.   The primary source of revenue for the federal government is:
a.   excise taxes.
b.   individual income taxes.
c.   corporate income taxes.
d.   tax receipts from state and local governments.

4.   The federal personal income tax is generally regarded as a:
a.   flat tax.
b.   progressive tax.
c.   proportional tax.
d.   regressive tax.

5.   Which of the following taxes is regressive?
a.   A 3 percent sales tax on grocery products.
b.   A 3 percent tax on all earned income.
c.   A 3 percent tax on stock dividend income.
d.   An income tax that increases by 3 percent with each additional $15,000 in income.

6.   One of the most significant changes brought about by the Tax Reform Act of 1986 was to:
a.   increase bracket creep.
b.   abolish the corporate income tax.
c.   reduce the number of federal individual income tax brackets and the maximum tax rate.
d.   require that the federal budget be balanced by 1997.

7.   Which of the following statements is FALSE?
a.   Government expenditures generate nonincome-determined spending and are subject to a multiplier effect.
b.   Fiscal policy affects the level of economic activity by influencing the flows of injections into and leakages from the spending stream.
c.   The appropriate fiscal policy to reduce unemployment is to increase government expenditures and taxes.
d.   The deliberate changing of government expenditures and taxes to control demand-pull inflation or unemployment is discretionary fiscal policy.

8.   If the economy were experiencing a high rate of unemployment, an appropriate corrective measure by the federal government would be to reduce:
a.   transfer payments.
b.   personal income taxes.
c.   purchases of military equipment.
d.   none of the above.

9.   Which of the following would have the greatest contractionary effect on the economy?
a   An increase in income taxes by $100 million.
b.   A decrease in transfer payments by $100 million.
c.   A decrease in government purchases of goods and services by $100 million.
d.   The contractionary effect from each of the above would be the same.

10.   Which of the following would reduce the effectiveness of automatic stabilizers in combating a recession?
a.   A reduction in the number of brackets in the federal personal income tax.
b.   A reduction in the eligibility requirements for receiving unemployment compensation.
c.   An increase in the number of weeks a person can receive unemployment compensation.
d.   All of the above.

11.   Which of the following statements is true?
a.   A balanced budget is slightly expansionary.
b.   The federal government has operated with deficit budgets in roughly 25 of the last 50 years.
c.   Annual federal government budget deficits were in excess of $2 trillion a year during the 1980s and 1990s.
d.   In 1996 a constitutional amendment was passed requiring the federal government to run a balanced budget every year.

12.   If government expenditures were less than tax revenues, the government would be operating with a:
a.   balanced budget.
b.   deficit budget.
c.   surplus budget.
d.   budget that would tend to led to inflation.

13. If the economy were experiencing high rates of inflation, the LEAST appropriate federal government policy would be to operate with a:
    a. balanced budget.
    b. deficit budget.
    c. full employment budget.
    d. surplus budget.

14. Efforts to cut the size of the federal deficit would:
    a. have a contractionary effect on the economy.
    b. be made more difficult due to the behavior of automatic stabilizers.
    c. require cutbacks in government expenditures and/or increases in taxes.
    d. all of the above.

15. The appropriate corrective policy for an economy experiencing stagflation is:
    a. a balanced budget.
    b. a deficit budget.
    c. a surplus budget.
    d. not clear.

16. The national debt is the total accumulated debt of:
    a. the federal government.
    b. the federal government plus all state and local governments.
    c. all private borrowers in the United States.
    d. all government and private borrowers in the United States.

17. The U.S. government security that matures in two to ten years from its date of issue is a Treasury:
    a. bill.
    b. bond.
    c. note.
    d. coupon.

18. During the 1980s and 1990s, the national debt:
    a. decreased in dollar amount and as a percentage of GDP.
    b. increased in dollar amount and as a percentage of GDP.
    c. remained constant in dollar amount and as a percentage of GDP.
    d. increased in dollar amount but decreased as a percentage of GDP.

19. Paying off the entire national debt at one time would:
   a. force interest rates up as the government borrowed funds to pay off the debt.
   b. require that the government run large deficit budgets.
   c. have no effect on the economy since the entire debt is held by U.S. citizens.
   d. have a contractionary effect on the economy.

20. Forcing private borrowers out of the market because government borrowing has raised the rate of interest is:
   a. government foreclosure.
   b. the demand shift effect.
   c. crowding out.
   d. interest rate shock.

Note: Correct answers to the Exercises and the Sample Examination Questions can be found at the end of the Study Guide.

Chapter 7
Money, Financial Institutions, and the Federal Reserve

- To define money and explain the functions of money.
- To identify the various measures and components of the U.S. money supply and different monetary standards.
- To introduce the financial institutions that are important for the maintenance and control of the U.S. money supply, and to highlight commercial banks and commercial bank regulation.
- To explain the role of the Federal Reserve System, its organization, and the functions that Federal Reserve Banks perform.
- To discuss recent legislative and structural changes in the financial institutions system.

◼ KEY TERMS AND CONCEPTS

Money

Medium of exchange

Value of money

Barter system

Functions of money

Definitions of the money supply

M1 and M2

Token money

Federal Reserve Notes

Currency

Demand deposits

Other checkable deposits

Velocity of money

Liquidity

Commodity monetary standard

Paper monetary standard

Financial depository institution

Commercial bank

Dual banking system

National bank

State member bank

Federal Deposit Insurance Corporation (FDIC)

Nonmember state insured bank

Asset

Liability

Net worth

Federal Reserve System

Board of Governors

Open Market Committee

Federal Reserve Banks

Organization of the Federal Reserve System

Reserve account

Correspondent banking

Monetary Control Act of 1980

Garn-St. Germain Act (1982)

Interstate banking

Riegle-Neal Interstate Banking and Branching Efficiency Act (1994)

Branch banking

Unit banking

Bank holding company

Mutual fund

Money market

Federal Savings and Loan Insurance Corporation (FSLIC)

Resolution Trust Corporation (RTC)

■ STUDY ORGANIZER

1. Identify the basic functions of money.

2. Explain how the value of money is determined, and the cause of changes in its value.

3. List the basic components of M1 and indicate the relative importance of each component.

4. Explain the relationship between the size and turnover of the money supply and GDP.

5. Differentiate among M1, M2, M3, and L.

6. Understand the difference between a commodity monetary standard and a paper monetary standard, and the advantages and disadvantages of each.

7. Know what currently backs the U.S. money supply.

8. Identify the basic functions of financial depository institutions and understand why these institutions are important in changing the money supply.

9.   Explain the functions of a commercial bank and why commercial banks are important to the economy.

10.   Name some of the agencies that regulate commercial banks.

11.   Identify the financial depository institutions other than commercial banks, and understand the recent changes in their roles.

12.   Know the purpose, functional structure, and geographic organization of the Federal Reserve System.

13.   Explain the roles of the Board of Governors and the Open Market Committee.

14.   Know the functions of the Federal Reserve Banks.

15.   Explain the effect of check clearing and currency orders and returns on an institution's reserve account.

16.   Evaluate the major changes in the financial depository institutions system that resulted from the Monetary Control Act of 1980, the Garn-St. Germain Act, and the Riegle-Neal Act.

17.   Identify and describe some of the structural changes that have occurred in banking in recent years.

18.   Understand how branch banking, interstate banking, and bank holding companies contribute to the formation of large banking organizations.

19.   Explain how the growth in mutual funds is affecting banks.

20.   Indicate some of the major factors leading to the savings and loan crisis, and explain the government's response to the crisis.

exchange

payment

value

inflation

barter

measure

value

storing
  delaying

1. Money is anything that is generally acceptable as a _____ of _____, which means that people are willing to accept it as _____ for goods, services, and resources.

   a. The _____ of money is measured by the goods, services, and resources the money can purchase. A serious bout of _____ weakens the value of money.

   b. Without money, people would exchange goods and services directly. This is referred to as a _____ system.

   c. Since the values of all goods, services, and resources can be expressed as a fraction or multiple of the basic unit of a nation's money, money functions as a _____ of _____.

   d. Since money is acceptable in the future for the purchase of goods, services, and resources, it provides a method for _____ wealth and _____ payments.

2. There are several definitions of the U.S. money supply. The narrowest definition, known as _____, includes _____ and _____ money in circulation, nonbank issued _____ _____, almost all _____ deposits at commercial banks, and _____ _____ deposits. Other checkable deposits include NOW and ATS accounts, credit union share drafts, and _____ deposits at savings and other thrift institutions.

M1, coins

paper
  traveler's
checks
  demand
other checkable

demand

a. In the United States, coins, which are issued by the U.S. _____, are token money since the value of the metal in the coin is _____ than the face value of the coin. Most paper money in circulation is _____ _____ Notes, which are issued by the _____ _____ Banks. Coins and paper money are _____.

Treasury

less

Federal

Reserve
  Federal
Reserve

currency

b. Demand deposits are better known as balances in _____ accounts, and are held primarily in _____ banks. Other checkable deposits are similar to demand deposits in commercial banks, except that they earn _____ on the balances in the accounts.

checking

commercial

interest

c. The largest part of M1 is made up of _____ deposits and other _____ deposits. This is because it is

demand

checkable

convenient	_____ to use this type of money for large payments, checks and similar instruments serve as _____ of payment, and the safety feature of being able to stop _____ can be used if a check is lost or stolen.
records	
payment	

d. Every year the total expenditure on new goods and services (GDP) is _____ than the money supply. The average annual turnover of the money supply in relation to GDP is termed the _____ of money.

larger

velocity

e. In addition to M1, other definitions of the money supply include _____, _____, and _____. In recent years, M2 has grown in importance as a measure of the money supply since it includes _____ _____ deposit accounts which allow a limited number of checkable type payments. The components of M3 and L are not very _____, which means that they are not easily converted to cash or spendable funds.

M2, M3, L

money market

liquid

3. When an economy's money is backed by something of tangible value, such as gold or silver, the economy is on a _____ monetary standard. For example, if an economy's money is backed by gold, the economy is on a _____ standard. When an economy's money is backed by the strength of the economy or faith

commodity

gold

paper

commodity

gold

frozen

paper

needs

controlled

financial
depository
money

deposits
loans

commercial

banks

demand

money supply

in the money supply, and not by something of tangible value, the economy is on a _____ monetary standard.

    a.   For most of this century, the United States was on a _____ monetary standard since its money was backed by _____. However, in 1971 the gold supply was _____ and the United States is now on a _____ monetary standard.

    b.   A paper monetary standard allows the amount of money in the economy to be adjusted to meet economic _____; however, a money supply based on a paper standard must be properly _____.

4. Commercial banks, savings associations, credit unions, and such are _____ _____ institutions, and are important to the economy since they can create and destroy _____. The two basic functions of a financial depository institution are to accept and maintain _____, and to make various types of _____.

    a.   Of all the financial depository institutions, _____ _____ are the most important because they provide _____ deposits and other accounts that make up a large portion of the _____ _____. Since commercial regulated

banks are so important to the monetary system, they are
_____ by the government.

b. A commercial bank can be chartered either by the
_____ government or by a _____ government,
causing the United States to have a _____ banking
system. Banks incorporated under federal charters are
called _____ banks, and banks incorporated under
state charters are called _____ banks.

federal
  state
dual

national

state

c. Commercial banks can have their deposits up to a certain
amount insured by the Federal _____ _____
Corporation. Most banks are _____.

Deposit Insurance

insured

worth

loan
  deposit

assets
  liabilities

d. A bank fails when its net _____ becomes negative,
which is usually caused by _____ losses and _____
withdrawals. In accounting terms, a bank's loans are
_____ and its deposits are _____.

e. While there are fewer commercial banks than other
financial depository institutions, the total size of
commercial banks is _____. The differences
between commercial banks and other financial depository

larger

lessened

money

regulates

coordinates

Board
  Governors

policies

money

Open Market

12

Bank

same

board

directors

institutions have _____ as a result of recent banking legislation.

5. The Federal Reserve System oversees the U.S. _____ supply, _____ some aspects of all depository institutions, and _____ the operations of commercial banks.

    a.   The Federal Reserve System is headed by the seven-member _____ of _____, which develops objectives pertaining to the money supply and banking practices, and decides on the appropriate _____ to meet those objectives.

    b.   The buying and selling of government securities by the Federal Reserve in the open market, an important method for controlling the _____ supply, is overseen by the _____ _____ Committee.

    c.   The United States is divide into _____ Federal Reserve districts, each headed by a Federal Reserve _____. Although all Federal Reserve Banks carry out the _____ functions, each is independent with its own _____ of _____.

12	6. The _____ Federal Reserve Banks deal primarily with _____ banks and other financial depository institutions.
commercial	
examine	a. Federal Reserve Banks supervise and _____ member banks within their districts.
reserve	b. Federal Reserve Banks maintain _____ accounts for member commercial banks and other financial depository institutions that wish to hold their reserves at the Fed. These accounts earn no _____ for their depositors.
interest	
coins, paper	c. Federal Reserve Banks provide the means for putting _____ and _____ money into, or taking them out of, circulation. When the Fed delivers currency to a financial depository institution, the institution pays for that cash out of its _____ account, and when a financial depository institution returns cash to the Fed, its _____ account is credited with that amount.
reserve	
reserve	
checks	d. Federal Reserve Banks clear _____ for financial depository institutions. When a check that has been deposited at an institution is cleared, the amount of the check is _____ to that institution's _____
added, reserve	

account. When a check is written by someone who has a checking account at a financial depository institution, the amount of the check is _____ from that

subtracted

reserve

institution's _____ account. In addition to the Federal Reserve Banks, other arrangements exist for

clearing

_____ checks. Regardless of the clearing arrangement, the effect on a financial depository institution's reserve account is always the same: checks

increase

deposited _____ reserves, and checks written by

decrease

an institution's customers _____ reserves.

e. The Federal Reserve Banks perform many functions for

government

the U.S. _____, such as maintaining its checking accounts and handling the details concerning U.S. government securities. In this regard, the Federal

fiscal

Reserve Banks are said to be _____ agents for the government.

f. Sometimes a bank will depend upon another bank for Fed-type functions. This relationship is called

correspondent

_____ banking.

deregulation

7. During the 1980s, the _____ of financial depository institutions resulted in a large number and variety of institutions

savings

loan

Monetary

Control
  increased

increased

Garn-St. Germain

branch

state

unit

interstate

holding

stock

performing functions traditionally carried out by commercial banks, larger banking organizations, and problems in the _____ and _____ industry.

a.   The Depository Institutions Deregulation and _____ _____ Act of 1980 _____ the similarity between commercial banks and other financial depository institutions, and _____ the role of the Federal Reserve in monetary matters. This trend was reinforced by the _____-_____ Act in 1982.

b.   The size of a financial depository institution is influenced by its abilities to operate more than one banking facility, which is called _____ banking, and to operate in more than one _____. A banking operation with one facility and no branches is called a _____ bank. The Riegle-Neal Act of 1994 greatly facilitated the growth of _____ banking and branching.

c.   One method for increasing the size of a banking organization is through the formation of a bank _____ company, which is a corporation that owns the controlling shares of _____ in banks. There has

138

increase | been an _____ in the number of bank holding companies in recent years.

d. Because of legislative and other changes, banking activity in the United States is being consolidated into _____

fewer

larger | and _____ banking organizations.

e. In recent years the banking system has faced increased competition for depositors' dollars from _____

mutual

funds | _____, which are pools of depositors' money that are

investments | used to make _____. Some of these funds may

money market | include _____ _____ securities which are short-term corporate and government borrowing instruments. Unlike many deposits in banks, deposits in

insured | mutual funds are not _____.

savings | 8. Deregulation has caused major problems in the _____ and

loan | _____ industry where a large number of institutions have

failed | _____, requiring massive financial assistance from the

government | federal _____.

a. One factor contributing to this crisis was the removal of

interest
deposits | the cap on _____ rates on _____, which prompted

139

loans

reduced

insured

FSLIC

Resolution
Trust

many institutions to offer depositors unprofitably _____ rates.

b. Another factor contributing to this crisis was the heavy losses that resulted from bad _____.

c. The risk of high interest rates and bad loans for savings and loan owners was _____ since most deposits were _____ by the FSLIC.

d. To deal with the savings and loan crisis, Congress terminated the _____, created a new fund which is under the jurisdiction of the FDIC, and created the _____ _____ Corporation to manage failed institutions and their affairs.

Money Supply Data

1. Locate and fill in the figures for the various money supply measures listed in Table 7.1 for 1997 and the following years. The appendix of financial statistics in each issue of the *Federal Reserve Bulletin*, published monthly by the Board of Governors, provides a good source for this information.

Table 7.1

Money Supply Measure	Year		
	1997	1998	1999
M1			
currency			
nonbank-issued traveler's checks			
demand deposits			
other checkable deposits			
M2			
M3			
L			

Banking and the Federal Reserve

1. Answer the following questions for the commercial bank at which you have an account or for a commercial bank familiar to you.

    a.   In which Federal Reserve district is this bank located?

    b.   Does this bank deal directly with a Federal Reserve Bank or one of the Federal Reserve Bank branches?

c.   Is this bank a national or state bank? By whom is this bank insured?

d.   What are the various regulatory agencies with which this bank must deal?

e.   Is this bank owned by a bank holding company?

Changes in a Reserve Account

1.   The OBL Bank starts the day with $7,525,000 in its reserve account. During the day $2,300,000 in deposited checks is cleared, as is $3,450,000 in checks written by the bank's customers. How much does OBL have in its reserve account at the end of the day?

2.   The Mt. Pleasant Bank had $15,560,000 in its reserve account this morning. Its customers wrote $4,580,000 of checks which were cleared, and deposited $3,350,000 of checks which were also cleared. Mt. Pleasant also sent $1,000,000 of currency to the Federal Reserve from its cash on hand. How much does Mt. Pleasant have in its reserve account this evening?

3.   The First National Bank of Ferdon has $9,735,000 in its reserve account **at the end of the day**. During the day it received $600,000 in currency from the Fed and had $1,480,000 in deposits and $1,190,000 in checks written by its checking account holders cleared. How much did Ferdon have in its reserve account **at the beginning of this day**?

Indicate the best answer to each question.

1.   When something is generally acceptable as a means of payment for goods, services, and resources, it is said to be a:
     a.   commodity.
     b.   measure of value.
     c.   medium of exchange.
     d.   store of wealth

2.   Which of the following is NOT a function of money?
     a.   Produce goods and services.
     b.   Provide a method for storing wealth and delaying payments.
     c.   Provide a measure of value for every good, service, and resource.
     d.   Serve as a medium of exchange.

3.   The value of money in the United States is determined by:
     a.   calculations by the Comptroller of the Currency.
     b.   the goods, services, and resources that the money can purchase.
     c.   the amount of gold backing the money.
     d.   none of the above.

4.   The definition of the money supply that includes only coins and paper money in circulation, nonbank-issued traveler's checks, demand deposits primarily at commercial banks, and other checkable deposits is:
     a.   M1.
     b.   M2.
     c.   M3.
     d.   L.

5.   Which of the following statements about the M1 money supply is true?
     a.   The largest component of the money supply is paper money, but demand deposits are growing in importance.
     b.   Coins and paper money are issued by the U.S. Treasury, while demand deposit accounts are held in Federal Reserve Banks.
     c.   Other checkable deposits were the largest component of the money supply until demand deposits were introduced in the 1980s.
     d.   The largest component of the money supply is demand deposits, but other checkable deposits are also important.

6. The velocity of money measures:
   a. the speed with which loan applications are approved by commercial banks and other financial depository institutions.
   b. the speed with which coins and paper money are removed from circulation.
   c. the ratio of coins and paper money to demand deposits and other checkable deposits.
   d. the average number of times the money supply is turned over in a year in relation to GDP.

7. The United States:
   a. is currently on a commodity monetary standard but was previously on a paper monetary standard.
   b. is currently on a paper monetary standard but was previously on a commodity monetary standard.
   c. has always been on a commodity monetary standard.
   d. has always been on a paper monetary standard.

8. When an economy is on a paper monetary standard, its money is backed by:
   a. government securities.
   b. laws assuring that the money will retain its value.
   c. the strength of the economy and faith in the purchasing power of the money.
   d. corporate stocks and bonds.

9. The financial institution that is most important in affecting the money supply is the:
   a. commercial bank.
   b. credit union.
   c. savings and loan association.
   d. stock brokerage house.

10. Which of the following statements is FALSE?
    a. The dual banking system refers to the fact that both the federal and state governments charter commercial banks.
    b. National banks must belong to the Federal Reserve System.
    c. The Federal Deposit Insurance Corporation insures only banks that belong to the Federal Reserve System.
    d. The Federal Reserve imposes some uniform regulations on all commercial banks, whether or not they are members of the system.

11. The Federal Reserve System is headed by the:
    a. Board of Governors.
    b. Open Market Committee
    c. U.S. Secretary of the Treasury.
    d. presidents of the 12 Federal Reserve Banks.

12. The purchase and sale of government securities by the Federal Reserve is authorized by the:
    a. Secretary of the Treasury.
    b. Open Market Committee.
    c. New York Stock Exchange.
    d. U.S. Securities and Exchange Commission.

13. Which of the following functions is NOT performed by the Federal Reserve Banks?
    a. Supervising and examining member banks.
    b. Clearing checks for financial institutions.
    c. Keeping deposits for the general public.
    d. Acting as fiscal agents for the federal government.

14. A reserve account is an account in the name of a:
    a. business that is held at a commercial bank to receive payments on bills.
    b. demand deposit holder at a commercial bank.
    c. financial depository institution that is held at a Federal Reserve Bank or other designated place.
    d. Federal Reserve Bank that is held at the U.S. Treasury.

15. Which of the following would lead to an increase in a bank's reserve account?
    a. An increase in the number of bad checks written by the bank's customers.
    b. An increase in the number of demand deposit accounts at the bank as a result of a promotional program.
    c. An increase in cash on hand in the bank to meet seasonal demands by its customers.
    d. All of the above.

16. Coins and paper money are put into circulation through the:
    a. Board of Governors.
    b. Federal Reserve Banks.
    c. U.S. Treasury.
    d. Open Market Committee.

17. A local bank had $10,000,000 in its reserve account at the opening of business today. Over the course of the day $1,400,000 in checks written by the bank's customers and $2,175,000 in checks deposited by the bank's customers cleared through the Fed, and the bank returned $150,000 in coins and paper money to the Fed. At the close of business today the bank's reserve account was:
    a. $8,925,000.
    b. $9,525,000.
    c. $10,475,000.
    d. $10,925,000.

18. The Depository Institutions Deregulation and Monetary Control Act of 1980:
    a. extended some Federal Reserve Bank services to all financial depository institutions.
    b. increased the similarity of functions between commercial banks and other financial depository institutions.
    c. permitted all depository institutions to offer interest-bearing accounts.
    d. all of the above.

19. Which of the following statements is FALSE?
    a. Interstate banking is not allowed in the United States.
    b. Unit banks operate one facility and have no branches.
    c. A bank holding company is a corporation that owns controlling shares of stock in one or more banks.
    d. Mutual funds compete with commercial banks and other financial depository institutions for households' deposits.

20. The primary problem associated with the deregulation of financial depository institutions in the 1980s has been the:
    a. disappearance of gold from the U.S. after the economy went off its commodity monetary standard.
    b. failure and insolvency of a large number of savings and loans.
    c. reduction of Federal Reserve control over commercial bank lending policies.
    d. uncertainty about what constitutes the U.S. money supply.

Note: Correct answers to the Exercises and the Sample Examination Questions can be found at the end of the Study Guide.

Chapter 8
Money Creation, Monetary Theory, and Monetary Policy

▣ CHAPTER OBJECTIVES

- To explain the relationship between the economy's money supply and output, employment, and prices.
- To explain how money is created and destroyed through the loan-making activities of financial depository institutions.
- To introduce the multiple expansion of money.
- To explain the role of the interest rate in encouraging or discouraging borrowing from financial depository institutions.
- To show how interest rates are affected by changes in financial depository institutions' excess reserves.
- To define monetary policy and explain the major tools for carrying out monetary policy by the Federal Reserve.
- To show the relationship between government borrowing to cover deficit spending and monetary policy.
- To critically evaluate monetary policy.

▣ KEY TERMS AND CONCEPTS

Equation of exchange

Velocity of money

Actual reserves

Reserve requirement

Required reserves

Excess reserves

Creation and destruction of money

Multiplier effect (money)

Money multiplier

Interest rate

Prime rate

Monetary policy

Easy money policy

Tight money policy

Discount rate

Federal Funds market

Open market operations

Open Market Committee

Crowding out

Monetizing the debt

■ STUDY ORGANIZER

1. Understand the relationship between the money supply and the level of total spending and economic activity.

2. Identify the terms in the equation of exchange and explain the effect on output and/or prices of both an increase and a decrease in the money supply.

3. Explain how a financial depository institution's actual reserves, required reserves, and excess reserves are determined.

4. Be able to calculate a financial depository institution's required reserves and excess reserves, and understand the relationship between excess reserves and loan making.

5. Explain how money is created and destroyed.

6. Understand the money multiplier process, and the relationship between the money multiplier and the reserve requirement.

7. Be able to calculate the money multiplier and the change in the money supply that can result from an initial change in excess reserves in the banking system.

8. Explain the role of the interest rate in influencing the level of borrowing by businesses and households.

9. Show graphically how the supply of loans, the interest rate, and the amount of actual lending are affected by changes in excess reserves.

10. Work through the sequence of changes in excess reserves, the interest rate, loan making, the money supply, total spending, and economic activity for an increase and a decrease in excess reserves.

11. Differentiate between easy and tight monetary policy.

12. Explain how changes in the reserve requirement, the discount rate, and open market operations work to increase or decrease excess reserves.

13. Understand the difference between reserve borrowing by a financial depository institution from a Federal Reserve Bank and in the Federal Funds market.

14. Show how each of the basic tools of monetary policy could be used to fight unemployment or demand-pull inflation.

15. Understand how federal government borrowing can cause a crowding out problem.

16. Explain the relationship between federal government borrowing, the interest rate, and monetizing the debt.

17. List the advantages and weaknesses of monetary policy.

money

increase

inflation

decrease

1. The amount that businesses and households spend on goods and services is related to the quantity of _____ in the economy. An increase in the supply of money causes an increase in total spending, which leads to an _____ in output, employment, and income, or if the economy is at or near full employment, to _____. A decrease in the supply of money causes a _____ in total spending and economic activity.

increases

loans

decrease

commercial

   a.   Money is created and the level of spending _____ when commercial banks and other financial depository institutions make _____. The supply of money and the level of spending fall when there is a _____ in loan making by _____ banks and other financial depository institutions.

equation
  exchange
money
  velocity

spending

prices

output

GDP

2. MV = PQ is the _____ of _____. In this equation, M stands for the supply of _____ and V is _____, or the number of times a dollar is spent for new goods and services per year. MV represents total _____ on new goods and services in the economy. P stands for the level of _____ and Q is the _____ of goods and services. PQ represents the dollar value of output, or current _____. According to the

output	equation of exchange, total spending in the economy equals the value of the economy's _____.
	a. If there were an increase in the supply of money, and if velocity remained unchanged, MV, or total spending, would
increase increase	_____. This, in turn, would cause PQ to _____. If the economy were experiencing unemployment, an increase in the money supply would primarily cause an
increase Q	_____ in output and employment, or in the _____ term in the equation. If the economy were at or near full employment and the money supply were increased, the
P	increase in spending would cause the _____ term in the
inflation	equation to increase, or would cause _____.
	b. If the supply of money were to decrease and the velocity of
decrease	money remained unchanged, MV would _____, which
decrease	would cause PQ to _____ as well. A decrease in the
decrease	supply of money would primarily cause a _____ in output, income, and employment, but it could also reduce
prices	spending pressure on _____.
	3. A financial depository institution's reserve account plus its vault
actual	cash make up the institution's _____ reserves.

deposits	a.	The percentage of _____ that a financial depository institution must keep as actual reserves is called the _____ requirement, and the reserves needed to back deposits are called _____ reserves.
reserve		
required		
	b.	The amount remaining after a depository institution subtracts its required reserves from its actual reserves is the institution's _____ reserves.
excess		
	c.	If a commercial bank has demand deposits of $100 million and a reserve requirement of 10 percent on those deposits, its required reserves are _____. If this bank has actual reserves of $25 million, its excess reserves are _____.
$10 million		
$15 million		
	d.	Depository institutions can make new loans up to an amount equal to their _____ reserves. This is because when the money that is loaned is spent and cleared against the lending institution, that institution _____ reserves. If a bank or other depository institution lends more than its excess reserves, that institution will not be able to meet its _____ requirement when the loans are spent and cleared.
excess		
loses		
reserve		

e. If a commercial bank has $340 million in deposits, a 5 percent reserve requirement on those deposits, and $50 million in actual reserves, then its required reserves are _____, its excess reserves are _____, and it can make new loans of up to _____.

$17 million
$33 million
$33 million

f. Commercial banks and other financial depository institutions do not take money away from depositors when they make loans. Instead, they _____ new money for their borrowers. Money is destroyed when loans are _____.

create

repaid

4. An initial change in excess reserves in the banking and depository institutions system will cause a change in the _____ _____ that is a multiple of the initial change in _____ _____.

money supply

excess reserves

a. The multiple by which the money supply can increase or decrease following an initial change in excess reserves in the banking and depository institutions system is the _____ multiplier.

money

b. The size of the money multiplier depends upon the _____ requirement. If the reserve requirement is 1/10, or 10 percent, the money multiplier is _____; if the money multiplier is five, the reserve requirement is _____, or _____

reserve

10

1/5, 20

153

reciprocal

money
multiplier

$100 million

$50 million

interest

$75,000

demand
  supply
downward

inverse

decreases

upward

direct

percent. Technically, the money multiplier is the _____ of the reserve requirement.

c. The initial change in excess reserves times the _____ _____ equals the maximum total change in the money supply. If the reserve requirement were 10 percent and excess reserves in the system increased by $10 million, the money supply could increase by a maximum of _____. If the reserve requirement were 20 percent and excess reserves in the system fell by $10 million, the money supply could shrink by as much as _____.

5. The price to borrow money is the _____ rate. If this rate were 15 percent, the cost of borrowing $500,000 for one year would be _____.

a. The equilibrium interest rate is determined by the _____ for and _____ of loans. The demand curve for loans is _____ sloping because of the _____ relationship between the interest rate and the quantity of loans demanded: as the interest rate increases, the quantity of loans demanded _____. The supply curve for loans is _____ sloping, indicating a _____ relationship between the interest rate and the

increases	quantity of loans supplied: as the interest rate increases, the quantity of loans supplied _____.
equilibrium	b. The intersection of the supply and demand curves for loans indicates the _____ interest rate.
increase right fall increase left interest rate, decrease	c. An increase in excess reserves would _____ the supply of loans, or shift the supply curve of loans to the _____. As a result, the equilibrium interest rate would _____, and the equilibrium quantity of loans made would _____. A decrease in excess reserves would shift the supply curve of loans to the _____, causing an increase in the equilibrium _____ _____ and a _____ in lending and borrowing.

interest rate
 	
decrease
 	
increase
  money
supply
  increases
 	
increase
 	
inflation
	d. In summary, the link between changes in excess reserves in the system and changes in loan making or the money supply is the _____ _____. An increase in excess reserves causes a _____ in the interest rate which causes an _____ in loan making, or the _____ _____. This increased loan making _____ the level of total spending in the economy, which will _____ total output, income, and employment, or will cause _____ if the economy is at full employment.

increase	A decrease in excess reserves causes an _____ in the interest rate which causes a _____ in loan making, or the _____ _____. This decrease in loan making _____ total spending, which _____ the economy's levels of output, income, and employment.
decrease	
money supply	
decreases decreases	

6. Deliberate changes in the money supply by the Federal Reserve to reduce unemployment or inflation are known as _____ policy.

a. When the Federal Reserve attacks unemployment by taking steps to _____ excess reserves in order to _____ the money supply and total spending, it is said to be following an _____ money policy. When the Fed attacks demand-pull inflation by _____ excess reserves to _____ loan making and total spending, it is said to be following a _____ money policy.

b. The main tools of Federal Reserve monetary policy are the _____ requirement, the _____ rate, and _____ _____ operations.

c. An increase in the reserve requirement _____ excess reserves, which reduces the ability of financial

Left margin word bank:

monetary

increase
increase
easy
decreasing
decrease
tight

reserve
discount
open market

decreases

loans

increases

same

deposit

interest

Federal Reserve

discourages

encourages

Federal Funds

created

existing

buying

selling

Federal

Reserve

buy

increase

d. depository institutions to make _____. A decrease in the reserve requirement _____ excess reserves, which increases the ability to make loans. Reserve requirements are the _____ for all financial depository institutions, but differ according to type of _____.

d. The discount rate is the _____ rate that a financial depository institution must pay to borrow reserves from a _____ _____ Bank. An increase in the discount rate _____ reserve borrowing, and a decrease in the discount rate _____ reserve borrowing. Banks can also borrow reserves from each other in the _____ _____ market. When institutions borrow from the Federal Reserve, new reserves are _____ in the system, and when banks borrow from each other, _____ reserves are exchanged.

e. Open market operations refers to the _____ and _____ of securities, primarily those of the U.S. government, on the open market by the _____ _____. If the Fed wanted to increase the level of economic activity, it would _____ securities from banks and dealers. This would _____ excess reserves and the loan-making abilities of depository institutions. If the

Fed wanted to fight demand-pull inflation, it would

sell

_____ securities to banks and dealers, which would

decrease

_____ depository institutions' excess reserves and their

loan-making abilities. Of the three major tools of monetary

open market
  operations

policy, _____ _____ _____ is the most

important and most often used.

f. In summary, if the Fed wanted to increase the money supply

unemployment
  decrease
decrease

in order to fight _____ it could _____

the reserve requirement, _____ the discount rate,

buy

and/or _____ securities on the open market. If the Fed

wanted to decrease the money supply in order to fight

inflation
  increase
increase

_____ it could _____ the reserve

requirement, _____ the discount rate, and/or

sell

_____ securities on the open market.

7. When government borrowing is added to that of businesses and

households, the demand curve for loanable funds shifts to the

right
  increases

_____, and the equilibrium rate of interest _____.

As an increase in government borrowing raises the interest rate,

decreases

borrowing by households and businesses _____, causing a

crowding out

_____ _____ problem.

increase

monetize

speed

size

political

loan
recession

inflation

independent

a. An increase in the rate of interest resulting from government borrowing could be prevented if the Federal Reserve would _____ excess reserves to compensate for government borrowing, or if the Fed would _____ the debt.

8. Some advantages of monetary policy are: the _____ with which it can be implemented; flexibility in the _____ of excess reserve changes; and less _____ pressure on the Fed than on Congress. Some disadvantages of monetary policy are: indirect control over the money supply since no one can be forced to make a _____; decreased effectiveness during a _____ since people may not borrow even at a low interest rate in such a period; the possible worsening of a problem with _____ if businesses pass on higher interest costs in higher prices; and the possibility that the Fed may be too _____.

Reserves and Loans

1. Assume that Hometown Bank has demand deposits of $350 million, a reserve requirement of 15 percent on demand deposits, and actual reserves of $85 million. Determine the bank's required reserves and excess reserves.

    Required reserves = _____.

    Excess reserves = _____.

2. If Downtown Bank has $750 million in deposits, a reserve requirement of 10 percent, and $95 million in actual reserves, how much in new loans can it make?

    New loans = _____.

3. First Bank of Youngwood, which has a reserve requirement of 4 percent on its demand deposits, determines that it has $32.5 million in its reserve account at the Fed, $10.5 million in vault cash, and $220 million in its demand deposit accounts at the close of business today. Based on this information for the First Bank of Youngwood, determine the following.

    Actual reserves = _____.

    Required reserves = _____.

    Excess reserves = _____.

    Maximum new loans = _____.

Reserves and Monetary Policy Tools

1.   How much in new excess reserves is created for a bank with deposits of $90 million and actual reserves of $35 million when its reserve requirement is lowered from 15 percent to 13 percent?

       New excess reserves = _____ .

2.   El Paso Community Bank, which is meeting its reserve requirement of 5 percent, sells $1.75 million in Treasury notes to the Federal Reserve through open market operations. By how much have El Paso's excess reserves increased?

       Increase in excess reserves = _____ .

3.   Midtown Bank sells the Fed a $2 million Treasury security. Midtown had $112 million in deposits, a 10 percent reserve requirement, and $10 million in actual reserves before the security sale. What is the bank's excess reserve position after it sells the security?

       Excess reserves after sale = _____ .

4.   How much would Prescott Bank need to borrow from the Fed or in the Federal Funds market if its deposits were $250 million, its reserve requirement were 18 percent, and its actual reserves were $35 million?

       Amount borrowed = _____ .

Money Multiplier

1. What is the money multiplier and the maximum amount of new money that could be created in the banking and depository institutions system with an injection of $70 million in new excess reserves and a reserve requirement of 12.5 percent?

    Money multiplier = _____.

    Maximum increase in money = _____.

2. If all banks are meeting their reserve requirement of 20 percent and the Fed buys $350 million of securities from these banks, what is the maximum amount of money that can be created in the banking system as a result of this purchase?

    Maximum increase in money = _____.

Summary

1. The Deer Grove Bank had $45.75 million in its reserve account at the Fed and $5.6 million in vault cash at the close of business on Thursday. On Friday, Deer Grove Bank officials sold $10 million in securities to the Fed, cashed $1.78 million in checks written by its customers, and received $900,000 in cash for deposits. At the Fed, $1.79 million in checks deposited at the Deer Grove Bank were cleared, as were $2.55 million in checks written by Deer Grove's holders of checking accounts. In addition, a $150,000 check written by a customer who just received a loan from the bank for farm equipment was cleared. What are the actual reserves of the Deer Grove Bank at the close of business on Friday?

    Actual reserves = _____.

Indicate the best answer to each question.

1. The equation of exchange is:
   a. M = PQ+V.
   b. P = MQ/V.
   c. MP = QV.
   d. MV = PQ.

2. If the money supply increased when the economy was at full employment, which of the following terms would you NOT expect to increase in the equation of exchange?
   a. M.
   b. P.
   c. Q.
   d. PQ.

3. A financial depository institution's reserve requirement is a specified percentage of:
   a. actual reserves that must be kept at a Federal Reserve bank.
   b. deposits that must be kept as actual reserves.
   c. excess reserves that must be backed by required reserves.
   d. required reserves that must be kept as actual reserves.

4. If a commercial bank has demand deposits of $200 million, actual reserves of $40 million, and a reserve requirement of 15 percent, its required reserves are:
   a. $6 million.
   b. $15 million.
   c. $30 million.
   d. $40 million.

5. If a commercial bank has demand deposits of $150 million, actual reserves of $20 million, and a reserve requirement of 10 percent, the bank has excess reserves of:
   a. $5 million.
   b. $15 million.
   c. $18 million.
   d. $135 million.

6. A financial depository institution can make new loans up to an amount equal to its:
   a. actual reserves.
   b. excess reserves.
   c. required reserves.
   d. deposits.

7. If ABC Bank has $80 million in deposits, $22 million in actual reserves, and a 20 percent reserve requirement, it can make new loans totaling:
   a. $6 million.
   b. $14 million.
   c. $16 million.
   d. $22 million.

8. The money multiplier:
   a. is directly - not inversely - related to the size of the reserve requirement.
   a. can cause the money supply to increase but not decrease.
   c. can be weakened by actions such as converting some portion of deposits to cash.
   d. all of the above.

9. If the reserve requirement were 5 percent, an initial $25 million increase in excess reserves in the depository institutions system could lead to an increase in the money supply of:
   a. $1.25 million.
   b. $20 million.
   c. $125 million.
   d. $500 million.

10. A decrease in excess reserves would cause:
    a. a decrease in the interest rate and the quantity of loans made.
    b. a decrease in the interest rate and an increase in the quantity of loans made.
    c. an increase in the interest rate and the quantity of loans made.
    d. an increase in the interest rate and a decrease in the quantity of loans made.

Answer questions 11 and 12 on the basis of the following figure.

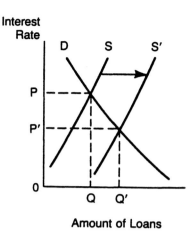

11. The movement from S to S' in the figure is most likely due to:
     a. a decrease in the interest rate.
     b. an increase in excess reserves.
     c. an increase in required reserves.
     d. an increase in the reserve requirement.

12. Which of the following statements concerning the movement from S to S' in this figure is FALSE?
     a. Both excess reserves and the interest rate have fallen.
     b. The Federal Reserve is following an easy money policy.
     c. This situation could be the result of a decrease in the reserve requirement.
     d. This situation could be the result of the Fed's purchase of government securities.

13. If the Federal Reserve is trying to reduce inflationary pressure, it should:
     a. increase the discount rate.
     b. increase the reserve requirement.
     c. sell securities to banks and dealers.
     d. all of the above.

14. In addition to borrowing reserves from the Federal Reserve, banks can borrow them from one another in the:
     a. Federal Funds market.
     b. Inter-bank Market.
     c. market for mutual funds.
     d. stock market.

15. The difference between a commercial bank's borrowing reserves from the Fed and borrowing them from another commercial bank is that:
    a. borrowing from other banks is illegal.
    b. new reserves are created in the system when borrowing from the Fed, but not when borrowing from other banks.
    c. the Fed can not refuse loan requests, but other banks can.
    d. the Fed charges no interest, while other banks do charge interest.

16. The Fed's sale of government securities in the open market would:
    a. increase depository institutions' excess reserves, interest rates, and borrowing by households and businesses.
    b. decrease depository institutions' excess reserves, interest rates, and borrowing by households and businesses.
    c. decrease depository institutions' excess reserves, increase interest rates, and decrease borrowing by households and businesses.
    d. increase depository institutions' excess reserves, lower interest rates, and increase borrowing by households and businesses.

Answer questions 17 and 18 on the basis of the following figure.

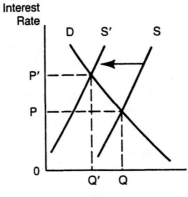

17. Which of the following would cause the change from S to S' shown in this figure?
    a. lowering the discount rate.
    b. monetizing the debt.
    c. reducing excess reserves.
    d. the Fed's purchase of government securities.

18. The change from S to S' in this figure is consistent with:
    a. a tight money policy.
    b. an easy money policy.
    c. a policy to monetize the debt.
    d. a policy to reduce unemployment.

19. Crowding out:
    a. occurs when the discount rate is lowered.
    b. occurs when the Fed monetizes the debt.
    c. results from an increase in interest rates due to federal government borrowing.
    d. becomes more of a problem for households and businesses when the Fed follows an easy money policy.

20. Which of the following is an advantage of monetary policy?
    a. The first steps toward changing the money supply can be taken the day the decision to do so is made.
    b. It is largely removed from politics.
    c. It is flexible with regard to the size of the change to be implemented.
    d. All of the above.

Note: Correct answers to the Exercises and the Sample Examination Questions can be found at the end of the Study Guide.

Chapter 9
Macroeconomic Viewpoints and Models

- To understand that there are several major macroeconomic models with different assumptions that focus on different relationships.
- To recognize the historical dimension of macroeconomic theory.
- To discuss the fundamental relationships of the classical, new classical, Keynesian, new Keynesian, and monetarist schools of thought.
- To describe the classical aggregate demand-aggregate supply model and its conclusions.
- To understand the basic relationships in the Keynesian model, the concept of macro-equilibrium and the factors that influence it, and the policy implications of the model.
- To explain the aggregate demand curve, the difference between the short-run and the long-run aggregate supply views, and the policy implications of the new classical model.
- To identify the basic focus of new Keynesian economics and of monetarism.
- To introduce the Phillips curve, examine U.S. rates of inflation and unemployment, and identify reasons for shifts in the Phillips curve.

◪ KEY TERMS AND CONCEPTS

Classical economics

Keynesian economics

Macroeconomic equilibrium

Inventories

Stagflation

New classical economics

Interest rate effect

Wealth effect

Foreign trade effect

Natural rate hypothesis

Adaptive expectations

Rational expectations

New Keynesian economics

Monetarism

Monetarists

Supply-side economics

Phillips curve

Closed economy

Open economy

▣ STUDY ORGANIZER

1. Understand the role of model building in explaining macroeconomic relationships, and give some reasons why different models focus on different economic variables.

2. Illustrate the aggregate demand-aggregate supply model of classical economics.

3. Identify the classical economic position concerning the output level at which the macroeconomy is expected to operate, and the assumptions supporting that position.

4. Explain the process in the classical model by which an economy that is not at full employment would move to full employment.

5. Explain what is meant by equilibrium in the Keynesian model, the conditions necessary to achieve equilibrium, and be able to illustrate equilibrium in a table and graph.

6. Identify the difference between Keynesian economics and classical economics in terms of their views about the economy automatically operating at full employment.

7. Understand how the relationship between total planned spending and total output is affected by the relationship between leakages from and injections into the spending stream, and explain the role of inventories in the Keynesian model.

8. Compare the assumptions and policy positions of classical economics and new classical economics.

9. Explain the role of household and business' expectations in new classical economics.

10. Give the reasons new classical economists offer for the downward-sloping aggregate demand curve.

11. Illustrate the short-run and long-run aggregate supply curves in new classical economics and explain the difference between them.

12. List the main points of new Keynesian economics, monetarism, and supply-side economics.

13. Understand the tradeoff between demand-pull inflation and unemployment.

14. Construct a Phillips curve and discuss the behavior of the Phillips curve for the United States from the 1960s through the 1990s.

15. Identify several factors that could contribute to shifts in the Phillips curve for the U.S. economy, and explain how each factor could cause the curve to shift to the right or left.

16. Indicate some warnings that must be remembered when evaluating economic theories and policies, and how living in an open economy complicates the task of evaluating economic theories and policies.

model

variables

1. Much of the work of economists is _____ building, which allows them to explain the relationships between economic _____.

output

output

output

a. Different macroeconomic models focus on the relationships between different variables in the economy. For example, one major model focuses on the relationship between prices and _____, another on the relationship between spending and _____, and a third on the relationship between the supply of money and _____.

problem

historical

values

data

b. Different models may highlight different macroeconomic variables because they were designed to address a major economic _____ at the time the model was developed, or they have an _____ dimension. Sometimes the assumptions in a model reflect the _____ of the model builder. It is useful to know the components that go into a model, including the variables, assumptions, and _____ collection.

schools

c. Different economic theories can be better understood by placing them in different _____ of economic thought.

classical Keynesian, new new monetarism	The major macroeconomic schools, or viewpoints, include _____ economics, _____ economics, _____ classical economics, _____ Keynesian economics, and _____.

2. The classical school of economics, popular before the 1930s, theorized that a free market economy always automatically adjusts

full employment government	to _____ _____, and, therefore, needs no _____ intervention.

	a. The classical position that a free market economy always adjusts to full employment is based on three assumptions:
demand	supply creates its own _____ in the macroeconomy;
increase, decrease	prices and wages will _____ or _____ to ensure the economy always operates at full employment;
equals	and savings always _____ investment to ensure that
spending	every dollar leaked from the _____ stream is returned.

	b. The line marked AS in Figure 9.1 shows how classical
aggregate supply	economists viewed _____ _____. The AS curve is vertical and at the full employment level of output because the classical economists thought the economy would operate at full employment regardless of the level of
prices, wages	_____ and _____. The lines AD and AD1

aggregate demand

falls

represent _____ _____, and indicate that the classical economists thought that more would be demanded as the level of prices _____.

Figure 9.1

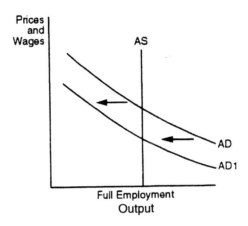

c. If the economy in Figure 9.1 were at full employment where AD intersects AS, and aggregate demand fell to AD1, prices

fall

AD1

and wages would _____ to ensure that the economy continued to operate at full employment, or where _____ intersects AS.

3. Keynesian economics, named after John Maynard Keynes, came to the forefront of economic thinking in the 1930s, when classical

depression

economics could not satisfactorily explain the _____ which took place in most industrialized countries. Keynes focused on

spending

aggregate, or total, _____, and rejected the classical

full employment

equilibrium

equals

full employment

change

less

greater

inflation

increases

inventories

decrease

increase

economic position that the economy automatically adjusts to

_____ _____.

a.   Keynes proposed that an economy seeks an _____ level of output where total planned spending by households, businesses, government units, and foreign buyers _____ the economy's current total output. According to Keynesian economics, this equilibrium output need not occur at _____ _____.

b.   When the economy is in equilibrium, there is no tendency for _____ in its level of activity. Output, employment, and income will decrease when total planned spending is _____ than production. Output, employment, and income will increase when total planned spending is _____ than production, unless the economy is at full employment, which causes _____ to occur.

c.   An important element in adjusting current output to changes in total planned spending is business _____. When total planned spending is greater than current output, business inventories _____, causing businesses to _____ their production. When total planned spending is less than output, unintentional business

174

increase

decrease

leakages

injections

equilibrium

greater

less

contract

less

greater

inventories _____, causing businesses to _____ their production.

4. An important factor, highlighted in Keynesian economics, which determines whether the economy is expanding, contracting, or in equilibrium is the relationship between _____ from and _____ into the spending stream.

a. If leakages equal injections, the amount leaving the spending stream is equal to the amount entering, so that spending equals current output and the economy is in _____.

b. If leakages are greater than injections, the amount leaving the spending stream is _____ than the amount entering, and the size of the spending stream is _____ than current output, causing the level of economic activity to _____.

c. If leakages are less than injections, the amount leaving the spending stream is _____ than the amount entering, and the size of the spending stream is _____ than current output, causing the level of economic activity to

expand, full

_____, provided _____ employment has not been reached.

d. If the economy produces $2 trillion of current output and total planned spending is $1.5 trillion, then injections are _____ than leakages by _____, business inventories will _____, and the economy will _____. If the economy produces $2 trillion of output and total planned spending is $2.5 trillion, then injections _____ leakages by _____, business inventories will _____, and the economy will _____. If the economy produces $2 trillion of output, equilibrium will occur where total planned spending is _____, or where leakages _____ injections.

less
  $0.5 trillion
increase
  contract

exceed

$0.5 trillion

fall
  expand

$2 trillion

equal

expenditures

taxes

5. Keynes pioneered the idea of using government _____ and _____ to influence the level of macroeconomic activity. If the economy were in equilibrium at less than full employment, government expenditures and transfer payments could be _____ and/or taxes _____ to increase total _____ and move the economy toward _____ _____ equilibrium.

increased
  decreased
spending
  full
employment

stagflation

new

classical

free
  prices
downward

full

natural

cyclical

inverse

interest rate

wealth
  foreign

6. Simultaneous increases in unemployment and prices, or _____, in the 1970s and early 1980s led to renewed interest in the relationship between price levels and output explored in classical economics, and to the birth of _____ _____ economics.

a. Like classical economics, new classical economics assumes a _____ market economy, flexible _____, and a _____-sloping aggregate demand curve. While classical economics holds that the economy will operate at _____ employment, new classical economics holds that, over the long run, the economy operates at the _____ rate of unemployment, which is the rate at which there is no _____ unemployment.

b. New classical economists attribute the downward-sloping aggregate demand curve with its _____ relationship between price and output levels for the economy as a whole to three effects: the _____ _____ effect, the _____ effect, and the _____ trade effect.

c. In the short run, according to the new classical economics view of aggregate supply, total output can be increased when the economy is at low levels of output without having any

prices	effect on the level of _________; at higher levels of output,
increases	increases in output will be accompanied by __________ in
	prices; and when the economy is at very high levels of
	output, efforts to increase output will lead only to higher
prices	_________. In the long run, the aggregate supply curve is
vertical natural	seen as perfectly __________ at the __________ rate of
	unemployment. The economy moves toward this output
prices	level and _________ are flexible.
	d. The new classical economists argue that because of the long-
no	run view there should be _______ government intervention
	in the economy. The ineffectiveness of government policy
	to reduce unemployment below its natural rate is called the
hypothesis	natural rate _________. Arguments supporting this
expectations	position are based on household and business __________.
adaptive	Past and current experiences contribute to __________
	expectations, and thoughts about the effect of those policies
rational	lead to __________ expectations.
	7. New Keynesian economists continue the Keynesian view that the
full	economy can persistently operate at less than _______
	employment, and attribute this problem largely to the downward
wages, prices	inflexibility of _________ and _________. According to the new
	Keynesian position, decisions by individual firms in the

microeconomy	_____ affect the movements of wages and prices in the macroeconomy.
monetarists	8. Those who favor altering the supply of money to stabilize the level of economic activity are known as _____, and the school of thought that emphasizes the role of money in the macroeconomy
monetarism free	is _____. Monetarists tend to favor _____ markets and proper control over the money supply as the ideal strategies for
full employment	reaching _____ _____.
supply-side	9. An alternative to demand-oriented macroeconomic policies popular in the 1980s was _____-_____ economics. Supply-side
lowering investment saving	include _____ taxes to stimulate _____ by businesses and _____ by individuals, and government
deregulation	_____ to increase productivity.
inverse	10. Economies seldom simultaneously achieve full employment and stable prices: Instead, there is typically an _____ relationship, or tradeoff, between unemployment and demand-pull inflation. This
downward	relationship can be illustrated with a _____- sloping
Phillips	_____ curve, indicating that higher rates of unemployment are
lower	associated with _____ rates of inflation.

higher	a. In the United States during the 1970s and early 1980s, annual rates of unemployment were generally associated with _____ rates of inflation than in the 1960s, and late 1980s and 1990s. These changes can be illustrated by shifts of the 1960s downward-sloping Phillips curve to the
right	_____ for the 1970s and early 1980s, and then to the
left	_____ for the late 1980s and 1990s.
	b. Several factors that may contribute to shifts in the Phillips
labor	curve include: structural changes in the _____
force women teenagers, part	_____, particularly the participation of _____ and _____, and involuntary _____-time employment; changes in the rate of price increases coming
cost	from the sellers' side of the market, or _____-
push	_____ inflation; and changes in the availability of unemployment compensation and other government
transfer payments	_____ _____.
	11. In evaluating macroeconomic theories and policies, it must be remembered that knowledge of the way the economy works must be
updated	continually _____, and that the solutions to economic
simple	problems are not always _____.

a. The task of evaluating economic theories and policies would be easier if we lived in a _____ economy where events outside the country's borders would have _____ effect on output, employment and prices. However, we live in an _____ economy, where outside influences can have a major effect on the domestic economy.

closed

no

open

Aggregate Demand and Aggregate Supply

1. Figure 9.2 gives the aggregate demand-aggregate supply model of the classical school. Answer questions a through c based on this graph.

Figure 9.2

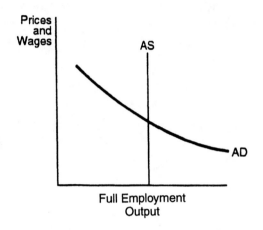

a. Explain why the classical economists would draw a perfectly vertical line to represent aggregate supply. How does this line differ from long-run aggregate supply in the new classical model?

b. Why does the aggregate demand curve slope downward? What explanations for this relationship were contributed by the new classical school?

c. Illustrate in Figure 9.3 an increase in aggregate demand and a decrease in aggregate demand, and explain the effect of each of these changes on prices and wages and full employment GDP. Would the effect be the same in the new classical model?

Equilibrium in the Macroeconomy

1. Answer questions a through e on the basis of Table 9.1, which lists levels of output and total spending (in trillions of dollars) for a hypothetical economy.

Table 9.1

Total Output	Total Spending	Injections Minus Leakages	Economic Condition
$0.00	$0.75	$	
0.50		0.50	
1.00	1.25		
1.50	1.50		
2.00	1.75		
2.50		-0.50	
3.00	2.25		

a. Calculate and fill in the "Total Spending" and "Injections Minus Leakages" columns of Table 9.1.

b. Equilibrium occurs at an output level of $_____ trillion.

c. Indicate in the "Economic Condition" column of Table 9.1 whether the economy is expanding, contracting, or at equilibrium for each total output level.

d. If the economy operated at a level of output of $1.00 trillion, business inventories would (increase or decrease) _____, and if the economy operated at a level of output of $2.00 trillion, business inventories would (increase or decrease) _____.

e. How is economic expansion or contraction explained by the relationship between injections and leakages?

2. Table 9.2 lists levels of total output and total spending (in trillions of dollars) for a hypothetical economy. Answer questions a through c based on this table.

Table 9.2

Total Output	Total Spending
$0.00	$1.00
1.00	1.50
2.50	2.25
3.50	2.75

Figure 9.3

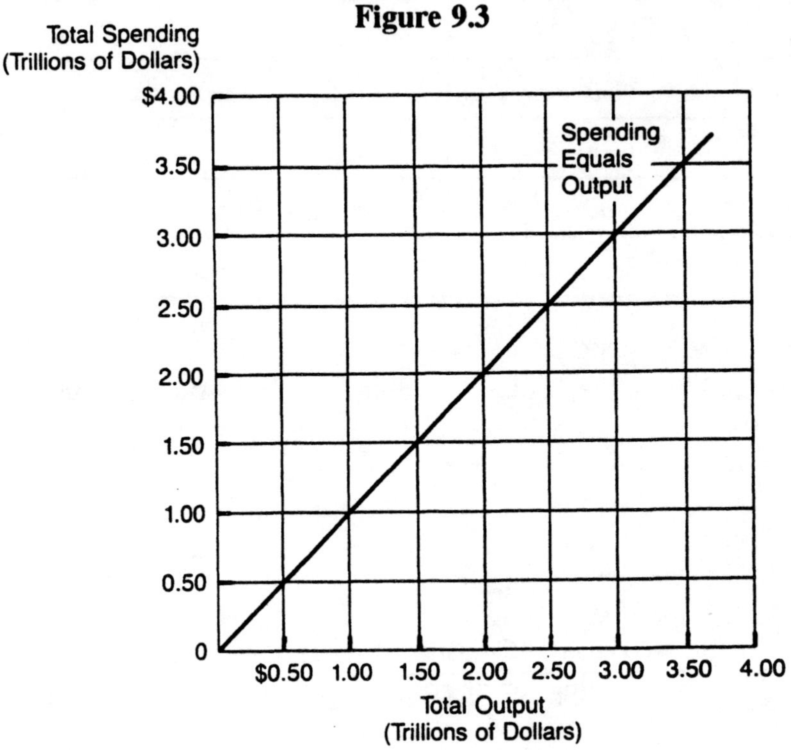

a. Plot, in Figure 9.3, total spending at each level of output shown in Table 9.2, and connect the points with a line labeled Total Spending.

b. According to Figure 9.3, equilibrium occurs at an output level of $_____ trillion, because at this point _____.

c. At an output level of $1.00 trillion, injections minus leakages is $_____ trillion; at an output level of $2.00 trillion, injections minus leakages is $_____ trillion; and at an output level of $3.00 trillion, injections minus leakages is $_____ trillion.

The Phillips Curve

1. Plot in Figure 9.4, which illustrates Phillips curves for the U.S. economy, the annual inflation rate and unemployment rate for each year since 1996. The inflation rate is the annual percentage change in the GDP implicit price deflator, and the unemployment rate is the percentage of the civilian labor force that is unemployed. Both figures can be located in the annual *Economic Report of the President*, a government publication, as well as in other sources.

    Does it appear that the Phillips curve is shifting or staying in the range of PC3?

Figure 9.4

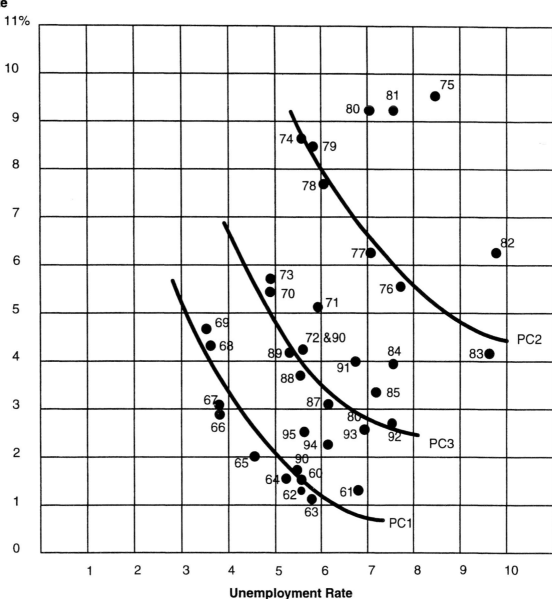

Indicate the best answer to each question.

1. Which of the following statements most accurately describes the current state of thinking about the macroeconomy?
    a. Over time, economists have been unable to develop any theory that helps us understand the behavior of the macroeconomy.
    b. There are several theories focusing on different variables that help us understand the behavior of the macroeconomy.
    c. There is almost complete agreement among economists that the classical model fully and accurately portrays the macroeconomy.
    d. No theory of the macroeconomy is necessary because there are good theories that explain the behavior of businesses and households, whose actions drive the macroeconomy.

2. Which of the following schools of economic thought would favor active intervention into the macroeconomy through fiscal policy?
    a. The classical school.
    b. The Keynesian school.
    c. The monetarist school.
    d. The new classical school.

3. Classical economics holds that a market economy will tend to operate at full employment when:
    a. it is free of government intervention.
    b. exports are greater than imports.
    c. the government runs deficit budgets.
    d. the money supply grows at an increasing rate.

4. Which of the following statements is NOT consistent with classical economic theory?
    a. Saving always equals investment.
    b. Supply creates its own demand.
    c. Prices and wages can be expected to rise but not fall.
    d. None of the statements are consistent with classical economic theory.

Answer questions 5 through 8 on the basis of the following figure.

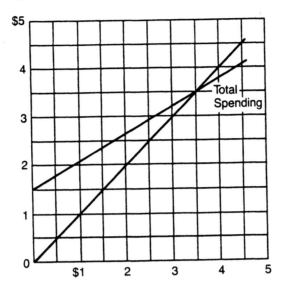

Total Spending
(Trillions of Dollars)

Total Output
(Trillions of Dollars)

5.   The economy is in equilibrium at an output of:
      a. $1.5 trillion.
      b. $2.0 trillion.
      c. $3.5 trillion.
      d. $4.0 or more trillion.

6.   At an output level of $4.0 trillion, injections into the spending stream:
      a.   equal leakages, and the economy is in equilibrium.
      b.   exceed leakages, and total output will increase.
      c.   are less than leakages, and equilibrium output will increase.
      d.   are less than leakages, and total output will decrease.

7.   Injections into, and leakages from, the spending stream are:
      a.   both zero at an output of zero.
      b.   equal at an output of $1.5 trillion.
      c. $1.5 trillion and zero, respectively, at an output of zero.
      d.   none of the above.

8. At an output level of $2.0 trillion:
   a. businesses will experience reductions in inventories
   b. the economy will go into equilibrium if spending decreases.
   c. there are no leakages from the spending stream.
   d. injections into the spending stream are less than leakages from the spending stream.

9. In which of the following economic theories is the short-run aggregate supply curve thought to be upward sloping, and the long-run aggregate supply curve thought to be perfectly vertical at the natural rate of unemployment?
   a. The new classical theory.
   b. The new Keynesian theory.
   c. Supply-side economics.
   d. All of the above.

10. According to the rational expectations concept:
    a. monetary policy adjustments should be announced in advance so that businesses and households have time to react.
    b. businesses and households may distort the effects of economic policies through their reactions to those policies.
    c. we should expect the economy to always face high rates of inflation.
    d. we should expect most government economic policies to be successful.

11. A Keynesian economist would favor stabilizing the economy through:
    a. only private efforts with no government involvement.
    b. military force.
    c. changes in the level of prices.
    d. changes in taxes and government expenditures.

12. According to new classical economics, aggregate demand in the economy increases as the level of prices decreases because of the:
    a. interest rate effect.
    b. wealth effect.
    c. foreign trade effect.
    d. all of the above.

13. Which of the following approaches to the macroeconomy would be least likely to advocate limiting government intervention to bring the economy to full employment?
    a. Classical economics.
    b. New Classical economics.
    c. New Keynesian economics.
    d. Monetarism.

14. Milton Friedman and the "Chicago School" are most closely associated with:
    a. classical economics.
    b. new classical economics.
    c. supply-side economics.
    d. monetarism.

15. Which of the following schools of thought would argue that an economy could persistently operate well below full employment?
    a. The classical school.
    b. The new classical school.
    c. The new Keynesian school.
    d. All of the above.

16. The Phillips curve that shows a tradeoff between the rate of unemployment and the rate of inflation is:
    a. downward sloping.
    b. upward sloping.
    c. downward sloping at low rates of unemployment and upward sloping at high rates of unemployment.
    d. upward sloping at low rates of unemployment and downward sloping at high rates of unemployment.

17. From the mid 1970s and early 1980s to the late 1980s and 1990s, the Phillips curve for the U.S. has:
    a. shifted to the left.
    b. remained stationary.
    c. shifted to the right.
    d. become horizontal.

18. An increase in the amount of time a person can receive unemployment compensation, and an increase in the labor force participation rate of teenagers would:
    a. both cause the Phillips curve to shift to the left.
    b. cause the Phillips curve to shift to the left, and shift to the right, respectively.
    c. both cause the Phillips curve to shift to the right.
    d. cause the Phillips curve to shift to the right, and shift to the left, respectively.

19. You would expect stagflation to cause the Phillips curve to shift to:
    a. the left.
    b. the right.
    c. a perfectly vertical position.
    d. a perfectly horizontal position.

20.	An economy that has its levels of output, employment, and prices affected by developments in other countries is:
a.	a closed economy
b.	an open economy.
c.	not a capitalist economy.
d.	a pass-through economy.

*Note:	Correct answers to the Exercises and the Sample Examination Questions can be found at the end of the* Study Guide.

Chapter 10
Households and Businesses: An Overview

◼ CHAPTER OBJECTIVES

- To provide an overview of households and businesses.
- To introduce the sources and sizes of household income and types of household expenditures.
- To define the basic objective of economic decision making by individuals.
- To introduce the balancing process involved in an individual's spending and earning decisions.
- To identify the legal forms of business, and to discuss business ownership of other businesses.
- To discuss the goal of profit maximization or loss minimization in business decision making, and to explore some questions about this goal.
- To identify sources of information on households and businesses.

◼ KEY TERMS AND CONCEPTS

Microeconomics

Household

Personal income

Transfer payment

Durable good

Nondurable good

Maximizing economic well-being

Utility

Total utility

Utility maximization

Business

Proprietorship

Unlimited liability

Partnership

General partner

Corporation

Preferred stock

Common stock

Corporate board of directors

Bond

Merger (acquisition)

Conglomerate merger

Vertical integration

Horizontal integration

Holding company

Revenue

Profit and loss

Profit maximization

◼ STUDY ORGANIZER

1. Identify some basic characteristics of U.S. households.

2. Indicate the relative importance of wages, rent, interest, profits, and transfer payments as sources of household income.

3. Identify the major government transfer programs.

4. Know how factors such as a household head's age, gender, and education affect average household income.

5. Indicate the major uses of household income and the major categories of household expenditures.

6. Identify the basic objectives of household and business economic decision making.

7. Recognize how the basic economic problem applies to individuals.

8. Understand the balancing process involved in individual spending and earning decisions and in business decisions.

9. Understand the relationship between utility and price in maximizing satisfaction from an expenditure decision.

10. Identify the basic characteristics of the three legal forms of business organization and know the advantages and disadvantages of each form.

11. Explain the structure of a corporation in terms of ownership and management.

12. Distinguish among preferred stock, common stock, and bonds.

13. Recognize the relative importance of each form of business organization in terms of number of firms and share of business receipts.

14. Distinguish among conglomerate, vertical, and horizontal integration, and recognize the purpose of a holding company.

15. Describe the trend in merger activity in the United States in recent years.

16. Know how profit or loss is calculated.

17. Recognize the various points of controversy over the definition and goal of profit maximization.

18. Identify some basic sources of information on households and businesses in general, and on specific products, firms, and industries.

household

increasing

decreasing

personal

resources
   transfer

labor

increased

Social Security

more

less
   direct

1. A person living alone or a group of persons occupying a housing

    unit constitute a _____.

    a. Over the years, the number of households in the United States

        has been _____, but the average number of persons

        per household has been _____.

2. Household income before taxes is termed _____ income

    and comes from the sale of _____ or from _____

    payments.

    a. The main source of income for households is from the sale of

        _____ resources. Over the years, transfer payments have

        _____ in importance as a source of income. The

        largest amount of transfer funds goes to recipients of

        _____ _____.

    b. In 1995 average household income was approximately $32,300.

        Households headed by a college graduate averaged _____

        than this amount, and households headed by a high school

        graduate averaged _____. This illustrates a _____

relationship between household income and the level of education of the household head.

purchase

taxes

saved

services

nondurable

durable

c. Most household income is used to _____ goods and services, but household income is also used to pay _____ to the government and can be _____ for future use. Most household purchases are for _____, followed by spending for goods with a short useful lifetime, or _____ goods, and for goods with a useful lifetime of more than one year, or _____ goods.

benefits
costs
greatest

3. To maximize economic well-being, an individual must balance the _____ and _____ of possible alternative actions and choose the one that adds the _____ amount to total economic satisfaction.

utility

income

a. In making spending decisions, an individual tries to find the combination of goods and services that provides the greatest amount of satisfaction, or _____, from a given limited _____.

utility

b. To maximize the total utility from consuming goods and services, an individual must weigh the added _____ received from each additional unit of an item that can be

price	purchased against the _____ of the item. If a person with $20 to spend would receive twice as much utility from a $14 steak dinner as he would from an $8 pasta dinner, then this
steak	person would maximize utility by purchasing the _____ dinner.
satisfaction	c. In making earning decisions, the additional _____ from income gained by working more hours must be balanced
dissatisfaction	against the additional _____ from having to forgo other activities in order to work those extra hours.
three	4. There are _____ legal forms of business organization.
proprietorship unlimited	a. A one-owner business is a _____. In this form of business, the owner has _____ liability for the debts
money	of the firm, and may find it difficult to raise large sums of _____ to finance expansion, improvements, and other activities.
partnership general	b. An unincorporated business owned by two or more persons is a _____. The partner(s) with unlimited liability for the debts of the firm are _____ partners.

corporation

charter

c. A business that has a "life of its own" and can continue to operate while owners come and go is a _____. In order to form a corporation, a _____ stating details about the nature and purpose of the firm must be obtained.

stockholders

preferred

common

limited

bonds

d. The owners of a corporation are its _____. If a stock pays a specified dividend to its holder and the holder is paid before holders of other types of stock, it is _____ stock. If there is no specified dividend, it is _____ stock. Owners of corporations have _____ liability. A corporation can borrow money on a long-term basis for expansion or other purposes through _____.

own

elected
    governs
appointed

runs

e. Stockholders _____ a corporation; the board of directors, which is _____ by the stockholders, _____ a corporation; and top management, which is _____ by the board of directors, _____ a corporation.

proprietorships

corporations

f. In the United States, most business firms are organized as _____. However, the majority of business receipts goes to _____.

owned

merger

acquisition

conglomerate

horizontally

vertically

holding

increased

maximize
  minimize

revenue
  revenue
costs

5. Many businesses are _____ by other businesses. When one firm obtains control of another firm, a _____ or _____ has occurred.

    a. When a corporation acquires another corporation that produces an unrelated product, it is called a _____ merger. When a firm acquires another firm that competes with it, it has _____ integrated; and when a firm acquires a firm that is a supplier or distributor, it has _____ integrated.

    b. A corporation that is organized to own the stock of other corporations is a _____ company.

    c. Through the 1980s and 1990s, the number of mergers in the United States has generally _____.

6. In economics, it is generally assumed that the basic objective of a business firm is to _____ its profit or to _____ its loss.

    a. The money that a firm receives from selling its product is called _____. Profit or loss is equal to _____ minus _____. If revenue is greater than costs, the firm is

profit	earning a _____; if revenue is less than costs, the firm is sustaining a _____.
loss	
stockholders	b. Profit goes to proprietors, partners, or _____ in corporations.
maximization	c. There is some controversy surrounding the goal of profit maximization or loss minimization. Two controversial points are exactly what is meant by profit _____, and whether a firm may seek alternative _____ in the short run.
objectives	
stockholders	d. The management of a corporation may be motivated to maximize profit in order to satisfy the corporation's _____, or because its failure to maintain satisfactory profits may lead to a hostile _____.
takeover	
Statistical Abstract	7. A good source of general information on households and businesses that is published annually by the U.S. government is the _____ _____ of the United States.
annual report	a. Information on an individual corporation can be found in the firm's _____ _____, or, for many large corporations, in _____ *Industrial Manual.*
Moody's	

b. For firms listed on major stock exchanges, much financial
information can be found in _____ _____ _____
S&P Reports, and articles on specific firms, products, and such
are listed in *F & S* _____. Also, CD-ROM reference
services for both government and private documents are
increasing in availability.

■ EXERCISES

Household Income

1. Given in Table 10.1 are average incomes for all households and various subgroups of households in 1995, as shown in your text. Complete the table by locating and filling in the average income for each group in each year since 1995. (Hint: The annual *Statistical Abstract of the United States* is a good source for this information.)

Table 10.1

Household/Family Group	Average Income[a]			
	1995	**1996**	**1997**	**1998**
All Households	$32,264			
Family headed by a married couple	$45,041			
Household head aged 25 - 34 years	$33,151			
Household head graduated high school	$30,071			
Household head with a bachelor's degree	$52,370			
[a] The average income used is the median.				

Maximizing Satisfaction

1. Assume that your friend is trying to decide whether to spend $60 for a shirt and wallet or $60 for a pair of pants. The amount of additional utility anticipated from each item, as well as the item's price, are given in the following table.

Item	Price of Item	Additional Utility
Pants	$60	125 units
Shirt	$40	100 units
Wallet	$20	50 units

How should your friend spend the $60 to maximize satisfaction? Why?

2. Assume that you have $6 to spend on lunch and have narrowed your choices to the items in the following table. This table, which lists the price of each item and the anticipated additional utility from each, also indicates that you receive 6 units of additional utility from not spending a dollar. In other words, if you saved all of your $6 and did not buy lunch you would receive a total of 36 units of utility (6 x $6).

Item	Price of Item	Additional Utility
Salad	$4	36 units
Sandwich	$3	36 units
Desert	$2	22 units
Soup	$2	16 units
Cola	$1	15 units
Nothing	$1	6 units

How will you spend your $6 at lunch if you will not buy more than one of each food item? Will you spend all of it or save some of it? What items will you buy to maximize your total satisfaction?

Data Sources

1. Your textbook gives several sources of information about households and businesses. Where could you locate the information listed in a through g below?

   a. The goods and services produced by General Electric Corporation.

   b. Articles on mergers between firms in a particular industry.

   c. The average annual salaries of men and women.

   d. The annual profit of Pacific Bell.

   e. The federal income tax bill of the average U.S. household.

   f. The number of partnerships in the United States.

   g. The board of directors of General Motors.

■ SAMPLE EXAMINATION QUESTIONS

Indicate the best answer to each question.

1. Over recent years in the United States the number of households:
   a. and the average number of persons per household have been increasing.
   b. and the average number of persons per household have been decreasing.
   c. has been increasing and the average number of persons per household has been decreasing.
   d. has been decreasing and the average number of persons per household has been increasing.

2. The majority of earned income in the United States is:
   a. interest
   b. profits.
   c. transfer payments.
   d. wages.

3. From 1970 through the mid-1990s:
   a. labor income remained the largest component of total income.
   b. transfer payments increased as a percentage of total income.
   c. labor income decreased as a percentage of total income.
   d. all of the above.

4. You would expect the highest average money income to go to households headed by a:
    a.   person 65 years of age or older.
    b.   person with a bachelor's degree.
    c.   person between 25 and 34 years of age.
    d.   married couple.

5. A good with a useful lifetime of more than one year is a:
    a.   consumer good.
    b.   normal good.
    c.   durable good.
    d.   nondurable good.

6. Individuals in households maximize their economic well-being by:
    a.   acquiring as many goods and services as possible.
    b.   buying the lowest priced items they can find.
    c.   working as few hours as possible.
    d.   none of the above.

7. To maximize satisfaction from consuming goods and services, a person should purchase the:
    a.   trendiest goods available.
    b.   least expensive goods available.
    c.   goods they have wanted for the longest time.
    d.   goods that add the most utility per dollar spent.

8. If you receive the same amount of satisfaction from a grocery store's house brand soda as you do from a popular name brand soda that costs twice as much, to maximize satisfaction you should drink:
    a.   the house brand soda.
    b.   equal amounts of each.
    c.   one-half as much as you normally do, but drink the name brand soda.
    d.   neither one since you cannot arrive at a perfect relationship between them.

9. Suppose Good X costs twice as much as Good Y. To maximize satisfaction, you should buy Good X only if it adds at least:
    a.   half as much satisfaction as is added by Good Y.
    b.   as much satisfaction as is added by Good Y.
    c.   twice as much satisfaction as is added by Good Y.
    d.   none of the above.

10. To maximize satisfaction from earning income you should:
    a. determine which goods and services you want, and then work only as much as is needed to afford those products.
    b. balance the additional satisfaction from the income against what is given up to earn that income.
    c. work as many hours as possible in order to purchase more want-satisfying goods and services.
    d. always choose the higher paying of two jobs.

11. Which of the following statements about a partnership is FALSE?
    a. A partnership is a business organization owned by two or more persons.
    b. It is possible to form a partnership where none of the partners have unlimited liability for the debts of the business.
    c. It is not necessary to obtain a charter to form a partnership.
    d. Total partnership receipts are less than total corporate receipts.

12. Who of the following is NOT personally responsible for all the debts of a business?
    a. A stockholder in a corporation.
    b. A general partner in a partnership.
    c. A sole proprietor.
    d. None of the above are personally responsible for all the debts of the business.

13. The ownership share in a corporation that does not return a specified dividend to its holder is:
    a. common stock.
    b. preferred stock.
    c. a letter of credit.
    d. a bond.

14. Which of the following is NOT an owner of a company?
    a. A sole proprietor.
    b. A general partner.
    c. A bondholder.
    d. A preferred stockholder.

15. The majority of business firms in the United States are organized as:
    a. sole proprietorships.
    b. partnerships.
    c. corporations.
    d. trusts.

16. The majority of business receipts in the United States goes to:
    a.   sole proprietorships.
    b.   partnerships.
    c.   corporations.
    d.   trusts.

17. A communications company acquiring a clothing manufacturer is an example of:
    a.   conglomerate integration.
    b.   horizontal integration.
    c.   vertical integration.
    d.   none of the above.

18. A holding company is a corporation:
    a.   that has been acquired in an unfriendly takeover.
    b.   owned by another corporation for the purpose of issuing bonds.
    c.   whose purpose is to own stock in other corporations.
    d.   whose charter is under review by a state government.

19. In economics, it is generally assumed that the basic goal of a firm is to:
    a.   drive its rivals out of business.
    b.   maximize profit or minimize loss.
    c.   maximize sales revenue.
    d.   maximize the recognition of the company among its buyers.

20. Information on the financial condition of a specific corporation can always be found in:
    a.   the corporation's annual report.
    b.   *F & S Index.*
    c.   the *Statistical Abstract.*
    d.   all of the above.

Note: Correct answers to the Exercises and the Sample Examination Questions can be found at the end of the Study Guide.

Chapter 11
Benefits, Costs, and Maximization

◘ CHAPTER OBJECTIVES

- To explain the basic process of balancing costs and benefits in economic decision making.
- To introduce marginal analysis, and to define marginal benefit and marginal cost and explain their relationship to total benefit and total cost.
- To explain the manner in which individuals measure the costs and benefits of actions, and to introduce the Law of Diminishing Marginal Utility.
- To explain the measurement of business costs, revenues, and profit, and to differentiate between normal and economic profit.
- To identify the rules for maximizing satisfaction by individuals and maximizing profit by businesses.
- To introduce the concepts of externalities and social costs and benefits.
- To examine how individual costs and benefits form the basis of collective, or public, choices.

◘ KEY TERMS AND CONCEPTS

Cost-benefit analysis

Opportunity cost

Marginal benefit (marginal utility)

Total benefit (total utility)

Law of Diminishing Marginal Utility

Total cost

Marginal cost

Net benefit

Net benefit (profit) maximizing rules

Explicit costs

Implicit costs

Normal profit

Economic cost of production

Excess profit (economic profit)

Total revenue

Marginal revenue

Profit or loss

Externality

Positive externality

Negative externality

Social benefits and costs

Public choice

Rational ignorance

Special interest group

■ STUDY ORGANIZER

1. Recognize how an individual's benefits and costs of an action can be measured in terms of utility.

2. Be able to calculate marginal cost and marginal benefit or revenue, total cost and total benefit or revenue, and net benefit or profit.

3. Understand the relationship between marginal and total costs, and between marginal and total benefits or revenues.

4. Explain how the Law of Diminishing Marginal Utility affects marginal and total utility.

5. Know the two net benefit maximization rules and understand the relationship between the two rules.

6. Determine the net benefit maximizing level of activity when total benefit and total cost and when marginal benefit and marginal cost are given tabularly and graphically.

7. Differentiate between a business's explicit and implicit costs, and between normal profit and excess profit.

8. Identify the two profit maximization rules.

9. Given total cost and total revenue, tabularly and graphically determine the profit-maximizing level of output.

10. Given marginal cost and marginal revenue, tabularly and graphically determine the profit-maximizing level of output.

11. Explain the effect on net benefit or profit when marginal benefit or revenue is greater than, equal to, and less than marginal cost.

12. Distinguish between positive and negative externalities and give examples of each.

13. Explain the difference between private costs and benefits and social costs and benefits.

14. Understand how the net benefit maximizing level of an activity for society is affected by external costs and external benefits.

15. Know the basic idea behind public choice and explain the effects of rational ignorance and special interest groups on collective decision making.

costs, benefits

1. All rational decision making involves a balancing of the _____ and _____ of the decision.

utility

opportunity

utility

2. When an individual makes a purchase or takes an action, he or she receives satisfaction, or _____. The cost of a purchase or an action can be measured by the value of the alternative forgone to make the purchase or take the action, or by its _____ cost. Opportunity cost for an individual can be measured in terms of forgone _____, or satisfaction.

total

marginal

a. The satisfaction from consuming a particular number of units of a good, service, or activity is _____ benefit or utility. The change in total satisfaction from consuming an additional unit of a good, service, or activity is _____ benefit or utility.

20

10

b. If the total utility from consuming five units of an item is 300 points, the total utility from consuming six units is 320 points, and the total utility from consuming seven units is 330 points, then the marginal utility of the sixth unit consumed is _____ points and the marginal utility of the seventh unit consumed is _____ points.

less

lower

total

marginal

10

40

100

net benefit

cost

c. The Law of Diminishing Marginal Utility states that, as additional units of a good, service, or activity are consumed, a point is eventually reached where each additional unit consumed adds _____ to total utility, or has a _____ marginal utility, than the unit consumed just before it.

d. The cost of consuming a specified number of units of a good, service, or activity is _____ cost. The change in total cost from consuming one more unit of a good, service, or activity is _____ cost.

e. If the marginal cost of the first unit of an activity is 10 utility points, the marginal cost of the second unit is 30 utility points, the marginal cost of the third unit is 60 utility points, and the total cost of no units of the activity is zero, then the total cost of the first unit of the activity is _____ utility points, the total cost of two units of the activity is _____ utility points, and the total cost of three units is _____ utility points.

3. The objective of making a purchase or taking an action is to maximize _____ _____, which is total benefit minus total _____.

a. There are two net benefit maximization rules. Net benefit is maximized where total _____ exceeds total _____ by the greatest amount. Net benefit is also maximized where marginal benefit _____ marginal cost.

benefit
cost

equals

b. When marginal benefit is greater than marginal cost, net benefit _____; when marginal benefit is less than marginal cost, net benefit _____.

increases

decreases

c. Graphically, net benefit is positive as long as the total _____ curve is above the total _____ curve. Also, the vertical distance by which the total benefit curve exceeds the total cost curve is greatest at the point where the marginal benefit curve _____ the marginal cost curve.

benefit, cost

equals (crosses)

4. To maximize its profit, a business evaluates the _____ from the sale of its product and the _____ of producing and selling the product at various levels of output.

revenue

cost

a. The dollar payments made by a business to outsiders who provide land, labor, and capital are _____ costs. The opportunity costs to a business owner from using his or her own resources in the business rather than in some other way are _____ costs, which must be recovered by

explicit

implicit

211

operate | the owner(s) for the business to continue to _____.

The return necessary to cover these implicit costs is called

normal | _____ profit.

b.   In economics, the total cost of operating a business is equal

explicit
  implicit
normal | to both _____ and _____ costs, or includes

_____ profit.

excess | c.   Profit greater than normal profit is called _____, or

economic | _____, profit. If total profit earned is $50,000 and

$20,000 | normal profit is $30,000, economic profit is _____.

5.   The total amount received from selling a particular number of units

revenue | of a firm's product is total _____. The change in total

revenue when one more unit of a firm's product is demanded is

marginal revenue
  price | _____ _____. Total revenue equals _____

times the quantity demanded.

a.   If the total revenue from selling four units of a product were

$1,000, and the total revenue from five units were $1,150,

the marginal revenue from the fifth unit would be

$150 | _____.

b.   If the total revenue from selling ten units of a product were $2,000, and the marginal revenue from the eleventh unit were $25, the total revenue from eleven units would be

$2,025

_____ .

c.   The cost of producing a particular number of units of a

total cost

product is _____ _____ ; the change in total cost

marginal

from producing one more unit of a product is _____

cost

_____ .

6.   The primary economic objective of a business is to maximize

profit
   cost

_____ , which is equal to total revenue minus total _____ .

a.   There are two profit-maximizing rules. A firm will maximize its profit by operating where total revenue

exceeds

_____ total cost by the greatest amount. Profit is also maximized by operating where marginal revenue

equals

_____ marginal cost.

b.   If marginal revenue is greater than marginal cost, profit

increases

_____ ; if marginal revenue is less than marginal

decreases

cost, profit _____ .

	c.	Graphically, a firm is maximizing its profit by operating

total revenue

total cost

equals (crosses)

c. Graphically, a firm is maximizing its profit by operating where the _____ _____ curve exceeds the _____ _____ curve by the greatest amount, or where the marginal revenue curve _____ the marginal cost curve.

7. The effect of an action on another person or thing that is not a

externality

primary party to the action is called an _____. As a

result of this effect, the level of activity that maximizes private net

society's

benefit might not maximize _____ net benefit.

negative

cost

a. Air pollution is an example of a _____ externality, which is a _____ to a nonprimary party to an action. The reduction in robberies in an area because of a small but active neighborhood watch group is an example of a

positive
   benefit

_____ externality, which is a _____ to a nonprimary party to an action.

social

b. The private benefits from an action plus any positive externalities from the action equal the _____ benefits of the action. The private costs of an action plus any negative externalities resulting from the action equal the

social

_____ costs of the action. The social benefits minus

the social costs of an action equal society's _____

_____ from the action.

net

benefit

c. If there are negative externalities associated with an activity, the amount of the activity that maximizes society's net benefit is _____ than the amount that maximizes private net benefit. If an activity creates positive externalities, the amount of the activity that maximizes society's net benefit is _____ than the amount that maximizes private net benefit.

less

greater

d. If the activity given in Figure 11.1 had negative externalities, the _____ social cost curve would be to the _____ of the private marginal cost curve, and the best activity level for society would be _____ than activity level N in the figure. If the activity given in Figure 11.1 had positive externalities, the _____ social benefit curve would be to the _____ of the _____ marginal benefit curve, and the best activity level for society would be _____ than activity level N in the figure.

marginal

left

less

marginal

right
private

greater

Figure 11.1

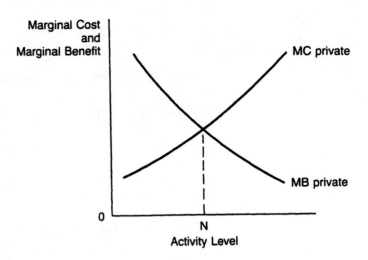

e.   Society's net benefit from an action is maximized at the

social benefit   activity level where total _____ _____ exceeds

social cost   total _____ _____ by the greatest amount, or where

marginal, benefit   _____ social _____ equals _____ social
  marginal
cost   _____.

8.   Many decisions in the U.S. economy are made collectively, or as a

group   _____. Collective decision making occurs mainly at the

                 government level, and individuals participate in these decisions

voting   through the _____ mechanism.

                 a.   The study of the economic motives and attitudes of voters

                       and public officials in making collective decisions is called

public choice   _____ _____. The basic idea behind public

maximize

collective

choice is that individuals try to _____ their own well-being when making _____ decisions.

b.   In making collective decisions, as in making individual

costs, benefits

decisions, people weigh the _____ and _____ of their choices. For example, some people do not seek information about a candidate or an issue before an election

cost

because the perceived _____ of acquiring the

benefit

information is greater than the perceived _____.

rationally ignorant

These people choose to be _____ _____.

c.   Persons who share and promote a common position on an

special interest

issue are a _____ _____ group.

Maximizing by an Individual

1. Assume that the costs and benefits given in Table 11.1, which are measured in utility points, apply to a student planning to spend an evening studying. Answer questions a through e below Table 11.1 based on this information.

Table 11.1

Number of Hours Studying	Marginal Cost	Total Cost	Marginal Benefit	Total Benefit	Net Benefit
0		0		0	0
	75		500		
1					
	150		400		
2					
	225		300		
3					
	300		200		
4					
	375		100		
5					
	450		50		
6					

a. In Table 11.1, calculate and fill in the total cost and total benefit for each number of hours spent studying.

b. Calculate and fill in the net benefit column.

c. This individual would maximize net benefit by studying for _____ hours. At this maximizing level, the net benefit will be _____ points. Prior to the maximizing level, marginal cost is _____ (greater or less) than marginal benefit, causing net benefit to _____ (rise or fall). Beyond the maximizing level, marginal cost is _____ (greater or less) than marginal benefit, causing net benefit to _____ (rise or fall).

d. Graph total cost and total benefit in Figure 11.2.

Figure 11.2

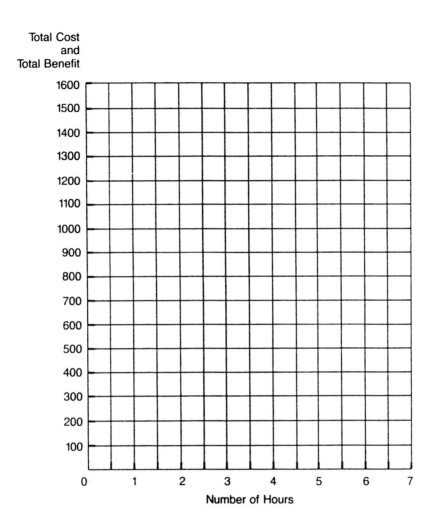

e. According to Figure 11.2, net benefit is maximized where _____ _____ , or at an activity level of _____ hours.

Maximizing by a Business

1. Assume that the costs and benefits in Table 11.2 apply to the manufacture and sale of an item. Answer questions a through e below based on Table 11.2.

Table 11.2

Number of Units of Output	Total Cost	Marginal Cost	Price per Unit	Total Revenue	Marginal Revenue	Profit
0	$ 50		$440	$		$
		$ ___			$___	
1	150		420			
2	300	___	400		___	
3	500	___	380		___	
4	750	___	360		___	
5	1050	___	340		___	
6	1400	___	320		___	
7	1800	___	300		___	
8	2250	___	280		___	

a. Calculate and fill in total revenue.

b. Calculate and fill in marginal cost and marginal revenue.

c. Determine profit.

d. This company would maximize its profit by producing and selling _____ units of output at a price of $_____ each. At this level of sales, it would earn $_____ in total profit.

e. Graph total cost and total revenue in the upper graph of Figure 11.3, marginal cost and marginal revenue in the middle graph, and profit in the lower graph. (Remember: Marginal cost and marginal revenue are plotted at the midpoints.)

Figure 11.3

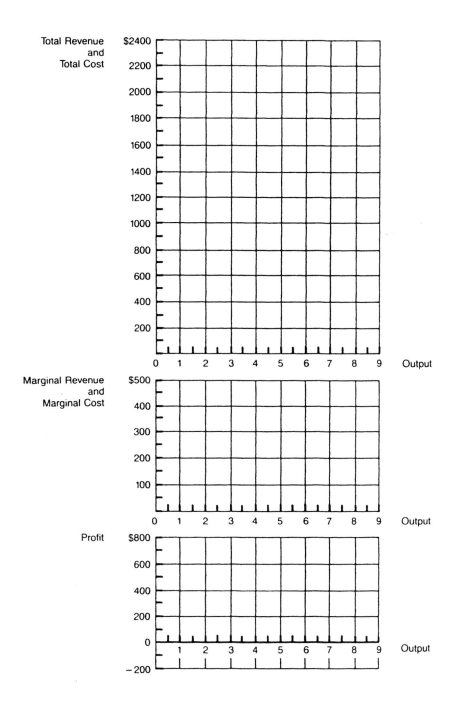

Indicate the best answer to each question.

1. The cost of a purchase or action measured in terms of its forgone alternative is its:
   a. forgone cost.
   b. opportunity cost.
   c. money cost.
   d. sunk cost.

2. Marginal utility and total utility are, respectively:
   a. the change in total satisfaction from consuming one more unit of a good, and the total satisfaction from consuming a particular amount of a good.
   b. the satisfaction one person gets, and the satisfaction all people get from consuming a particular amount of a good.
   c. the satisfaction from consuming one type of good, and the satisfaction from consuming several different types of goods.
   d. the satisfaction from the least-liked good consumed, and the satisfaction from all the goods consumed.

3. The total utility from consuming four units of an item is 200 utility points and the marginal utility of the fifth unit of the item consumed is 50 utility points. The total utility from consuming five units of the item is:
   a. 125 utility points.
   b. 150 utility points.
   c. 250 utility points.
   d. 450 utility points.

4. A person receives 25 marginal utility points from the first piece of pizza she consumes, 40 total utility points from two pieces of pizza, and 10 marginal utility points from the third piece. How many total utility points does she receive from three pieces of pizza?
   a. 15 points.
   b. 25 points.
   c. 50 points.
   d. 75 points.

5.   According to the Law of Diminishing Marginal Utility:
     a.   the second unit of a good consumed adds less to total satisfaction than was added by the first unit consumed.
     b.   beyond some point, the next unit of a good consumed adds less to total satisfaction than was added by the unit consumed just before it.
     c.   there is less satisfaction from consuming when there is a wide range of goods to choose from than when there is a narrow range.
     d.   marginal utility is increasing when total utility is decreasing.

The following table applies to questions 6 and 7. Total Cost is given in utility points.

Quantity of Good X	Total Utility	Total Cost
0	0	0
1	60	30
2	110	70
3	150	120
4	180	190

6.   According to the information in this table, diminishing marginal utility:
     a.   sets in when the second unit is consumed.
     b.   sets in when the third unit is consumed.
     c.   sets in when the fourth unit is consumed.
     d.   does not set in.

7.   To maximize net benefit, this individual should consume:
     a.   1 unit of Good X.
     b.   2 units of Good X.
     c.   3 units of Good X.
     d.   4 units of Good X.

8.   Net benefit is equal to:
     a.   total benefit.
     b.   total benefit plus marginal benefit.
     c.   total benefit minus total cost.
     d.   marginal benefit minus marginal cost.

Answers questions 9 and 10 on the basis of the following figure.

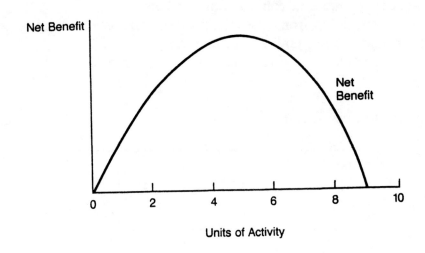

9. According to this figure, an individual's:
   a. total benefit from this activity increases up to five units and then decreases.
   b. total benefit from this activity exceeds total cost by the greatest amount at five units.
   c. total cost from this activity decreases up to five units and then increases.
   d. all of the above.

10. According to this figure, at six units of activity this individual's marginal cost would:
    a. equal marginal benefit from the activity.
    b. be less than marginal benefit from the activity.
    c. be greater than marginal benefit from the activity.
    d. be less or greater than marginal benefit, depending on whether the activity was decreasing or increasing at the time.

11. The amount of profit that must be earned to keep a business in operation is:
    a. economic profit.
    b. normal profit.
    c. considered to be an explicit cost of production by economists.
    d. none of the above.

12. Profit is at a maximum where:
   a. marginal revenue equals marginal cost.
   b. total revenue equals total cost.
   c. marginal revenue is at a maximum.
   d. total revenue is at a maximum.

The following table applies to questions 13 and 14.

Units of Output	Marginal Revenue	Marginal Cost
0		
	$160	$ 60
1		
	120	80
2		
	80	100
3		
	40	120
4		

13. According to this table, to maximize profit this firm should produce and sell:
   a. 1 unit of output.
   b. 2 units of output.
   c. 3 units of output.
   d. 4 units of output.

14. The firm's profit at its profit-maximizing output is:
   a. $40.
   b. $80.
   c. $140.
   d. $280.

Answer questions 15 and 16 on the basis of the following figure.

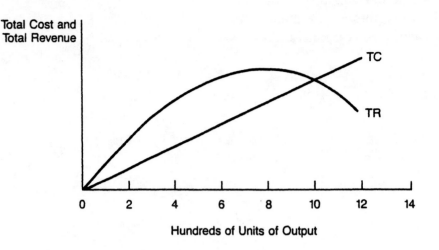

15.   According to this figure, profit is maximized at:
       a.   zero or 1,000 units of output.
       b.   500 units of output.
       c.   800 units of output.
       d.   1,000 units of output.

16. ′   According to this figure, at 800 units of output, marginal revenue:
       a.   is at its maximum level.
       b.   equals marginal cost.
       c.   exceeds marginal cost.
       d.   is less than marginal cost.

17.   Which of the following statements is true?
       a.   Society maximizes its net benefit by operating where total social benefit exceeds
             total social cost by the greatest amount.
       b.   Society maximizes its net benefit as long as marginal social benefit is greater than
             marginal social cost.
       c.   The social benefit of an action is equal to the private benefit minus any negative
             externalities.
       d.   All of the above.

18.   If an activity creates negative externalities:
   a.   less of the activity is performed than is in the best interest of society.
   b.   the level of the activity that maximizes society's net benefit is greater than the level that maximizes the net benefit of the individuals performing the activity.
   c.   the marginal social cost of the activity is less than its private marginal cost.
   d.   imposing taxes and other restraints on the activity's producers could be an appropriate policy to induce them to reduce the externalities.

19.   Suppose the private marginal cost of an activity exceeds its private marginal benefit at the level of the activity where society's net benefit is maximized. Based on this, society should want the amount of the activity to:
   a.   remain at the private-maximizing level.
   b.   decrease from the private-maximizing level.
   c.   increase from the private-maximizing level.
   d.   either decrease or increase from the private-maximizing level, depending on how much private marginal cost exceeds private marginal benefit.

20.   According to public choice theory, individuals, in making collective decisions, try to maximize:
   a.   overall voter turnout on major issues.
   b.   the well-being of society.
   c.   their own total benefits, regardless of the total costs they will incur.
   d.   their own well-being.

Correct answers to the Exercises and the Sample Examination Questions can be found at the end of the Study Guide.

Chapter 12
Production and the Costs of Production

■CHAPTER OBJECTIVES

- To identify categories of productive activity in the U.S. economy.
- To explain the nature and importance of production methods.
- To explore the relationship between production methods and technology.
- To differentiate between production in the short run and production in the long run.
- To define the various types of costs associated with production.
- To explain the behavior of costs as the level of production changes in the short run and the long run.
- To provide (in an appendix) a more detailed understanding of short-run average costs.

■ KEY TERMS AND CONCEPTS

Producing sectors

Industry

Production function

Efficient method of production

Technology

Creative destruction

Short run

Variable factors

Variable costs

Fixed factors

Fixed costs

Long run

Total fixed cost

Total variable cost

Total cost

Average total cost

Marginal cost

Law of Diminishing Returns

Long-run total, average total, and marginal costs

Economies of scale

Diseconomies of scale

Constant returns to scale

■ STUDY ORGANIZER

1. Differentiate between producing sectors and industries, and give examples of each.

2. Identify some changes that have occurred in the relative importance of the major producing sectors in the U.S. economy.

3. Explain what is meant by a production function.

4. Explain the relationship between profit and the choice of a method of production.

5. Understand how technology affects the range of production techniques from which a business can choose.

6. Explain what is meant by creative destruction and give some examples.

7. Differentiate between production in a short-run and a long-run time frame.

8. Differentiate between fixed factors and costs, and variable factors and costs.

9. Be able to calculate total cost when total fixed cost and total variable cost are given, and be able to calculate average total cost and marginal cost when total cost is given.

10. Know the pattern of total fixed cost, total variable cost, total cost, average total cost, and marginal cost as output increases in the short run.

11. Explain how the relationship between fixed and variable factors causes total cost, average total cost, and marginal cost to behave as production increases in the short run.

12. Explain the relationship between average and marginal costs as production increases.

13. Know the role of the Law of Diminishing Returns in short-run production.

14. Relate the shape of a long-run average total cost curve to economies of, diseconomies of, and constant returns to scale.

15. Give some reasons for economies and diseconomies of scale.

Appendix

16. Explain the relationship between short-run average total cost and average fixed and average variable costs.

17. Describe how average fixed cost and average variable cost change as the level of output changes in the short run.

production

businesses

1. The process of transforming inputs into outputs is _____. Most production for sale in the United States is carried out by _____.

a. Products and firms that are grouped into the same very broad category, such as agriculture or manufacturing, are in the same producing _____. The dominant producing sector in the U.S. economy is the _____ sector.

sector

services

industry
    narrower

b. Firms producing goods and services that are similar, either because their production processes are similar or because buyers view them as substitutes for one another, are in the same _____. This classification is _____ than the producing sector classification. Many firms that produce several different products operate in several different _____ at the same time.

industries

production function

2. The type and quantity of output that can be produced when certain inputs are combined in a particular way is indicated by a _____ _____.

least-cost

efficient

differs

a. To maximize its profit, a firm will try to produce its output using the _____-_____, or most _____, method of production. This method of production depends upon a producer's particular set of circumstances and _____ from seller to seller.

technology

obsolete

profit

creative

b. The body of knowledge that exists about production and its processes is _____. Over time, as technology changes, many production methods become _____. When older methods and resources become less efficient and more costly than newly developed ones, businesses may replace the old with the new in an effort to maximize _____. The replacement of less efficient old processes and resources with new ones and the ultimate disappearance of the old, is referred to as _____ destruction.

short

3. A firm can vary the amounts of some, but not all, of its factors of production when it is producing in a _____-run time frame.

fixed

fixed

a. Factors of production that can not be changed in amount over the short run are _____ factors, and their costs are _____ costs. Factors that can be changed in

232

variable

variable

amount over the short run are _____ factors, and
their costs are _____ costs.

fixed

zero

change

increases

decreases, zero

b. There is no change in the cost of _____ factors over
the short run, and a firm must pay for these factors even if
its level of production is _____. As a result, total fixed
cost does not _____ as the level of output changes.
Since the quantity of variable factors changes as production
changes in the short run, total variable cost increases and
decreases as the level of output _____ and
_____, and is zero when output is _____.

fixed

variable

c. The total cost of producing a particular amount of output in
the short run is equal to the total _____ cost plus the
total _____ cost at that level of output.

average
total

marginal

d. The cost per unit of output at a particular level of output is
_____ total cost, which is equal to _____ cost
divided by the number of units of output produced. The
change in total cost from producing one more unit of output
is _____ cost.

e. Assume that the total fixed cost of producing Good X is $25 and that the total variable cost of producing 4, 5, 6, and 7 units of Good X is as follows.

Output	TVC
4	$ 23
5	25
6	53
7	101

Based on this information we can conclude that the total

cost of producing 4 units of Good X is _____, the total

cost of producing 6 units is _____, the marginal cost of

the fifth unit is _____, the marginal cost of the seventh

unit is _____, the average total cost when producing 4

units is _____, and the average total cost when

producing 7 units is _____.

4. The various short-run costs exhibit specific patterns of change as the output level changes.

a. As output increases over the short run, total cost increases

_____ at first and then increases more _____ at higher levels of output. This occurs because, at higher levels of output, the ability to produce more is hindered by

234

fixed	the limitations imposed by the _____ factors, and
variable	many more _____ factors are required to compensate
	for these limitations. In other words, the total cost pattern
variable	results from changes in total _____ cost as output
fixed	increases since total _____ cost does not change.
decrease	b. Both marginal cost and average total cost _____ and
increase	then _____ as the level of output goes up in the short
	run. When marginal cost is less than average total cost,
falls	average total cost _____, and when marginal cost is
rises	greater than average total cost, average total cost _____.
	c. The behavior of short-run costs is governed by the Law of
Diminishing Returns	_____ _____. According to this law, as
	additional units of a variable factor are added to a
fixed	_____ factor, beyond some point the additional
	product from each additional unit of the variable factor will
decrease	_____.
	8. In the long-run time frame all factors of production are
variable, variable	_____, and, therefore, all costs are _____.
	a. In the long run, the total cost of producing a particular level
long, total	of output is _____-run _____ cost; the cost per unit

long	when producing a particular level of output is _____-run
average	_____ total cost; and the change in total cost from
marginal	producing one more unit of output is long-run _____
cost	_____. Unlike short-run total cost, which includes
	expenditures that must be made for fixed factors even when
zero	nothing is produced, long-run total cost is _____ when
	output is zero.
	b. Generally, as the level of output increases, long-run average
decreases	total cost _____, reaches a minimum, and then
increases	_____.
	c. The initial decrease in long-run average total cost as output
economies	increases is due to _____ of scale, such as cost
	savings from increased specialization or from quantity
	discounts. Economies of scale allow a business to produce
	each unit of output more cheaply than it could with a
smaller	_____ size operation. Increases in long-run average
	total cost at very large levels of output are due to
diseconomies	_____ of scale resulting, for example, from
	difficulties in maintaining communication and control in an
	organization as it grows larger. If long-run average total
	cost does not change as the level of output increases, the
constant returns	firm is experiencing _____ _____ to scale.

236

Appendix

fixed

variable

total

total

output

1. Short-run average total cost is equal to average _____ cost plus average _____ cost. Average fixed cost and average variable cost are found by dividing _____ fixed cost and _____ variable cost, respectively, by the number of units of _____ produced.

decreases, decreases

minimum, increases

less

equal

greater

a. As the level of output increases, average fixed cost _____, and average variable cost _____ reaches a _____ and then _____. Marginal cost is _____ than average variable cost when average variable cost is decreasing, _____ to average variable cost when average variable cost is at its minimum, and _____ than average variable cost when average variable cost is increasing.

Law, Diminishing Returns

b. The basic economic reality explaining the behavior of short-run marginal cost, average variable cost, and average total cost is the _____ of _____ _____.

Cost Determination

1.   Marcia Deal bakes and decorates large, elaborate, multi-layered, special occasion cakes. She produces these in her own home without any help, unless she has a large number of orders on a particular day.

   a.   Given the following information, complete Table 12.1, which lists the various costs for producing from 0 through 8 cakes per day.

   - The total cost of producing 5 cakes is $135.
   - Deal's total fixed cost for 1 cake is $25.
   - The marginal cost of the 8th cake is $91.
   - The average total cost per cake when 3 cakes or when 4 cakes are made is $25.
   - The total variable cost of producing 7 cakes is $220.
   - The marginal cost of the 6th cake is $45.
   - The total cost of 2 cakes is $60.
   - The total variable cost of 1 cake is $25.

Table 12.1

Number of Cakes	Total Cost	Total Fixed Cost	Total Variable Cost	Average Total Cost	Marginal Cost
0					
1					—
2					—
3					—
4					—
5					—
6					—
7					—
8					—

b.   Notice in Table 12.1 that the marginal costs of the seventh and eighth cakes are fairly high. Why is this so?

c.   If Deal can sell from 0 through 8 cakes at $40 each, how many will she choose to produce and sell per day if she is trying to maximize her profit?

d.   Complete Table 12.2 to check your answer to question c. Do the numbers in the *Total Profit* column and in the *Marginal Revenue* and *Marginal Cost* columns support your answer?

Table 12.2

Number of Cakes	Total Revenue	Total Cost	Total Profit	Marginal Revenue	Marginal Cost
0					
1				—	—
2				—	—
3				—	—
4				—	—
5				—	—
6				—	—
7				—	—
8				—	—

e.   On Figure 12.1, plot the total cost of producing from 0 through 8 cakes, as given in Table 12.1.

Figure 12.1

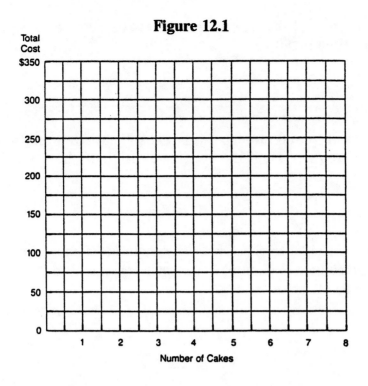

f.   Why does total cost exhibit this pattern in this exercise?

g.   On Figure 12.2, plot the average total cost and marginal cost of producing from 0 through 8 cakes, as given in Table 12.1. (Remember to plot marginal cost at the midpoints.)

Figure 12.2

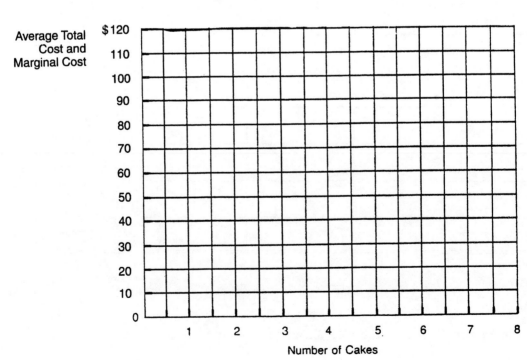

240

2. Marcia Deal is considering giving up her cake baking and decorating business to begin a daycare center in her home. Table 12.3 gives the total cost of providing 8 hours of care per day for from 0 through 5 children.

    a. Complete Table 12.3 by calculating total fixed cost, total variable cost, average total cost, and marginal cost for each number of children.

Table 12.3

Number of Children	Total Cost	Total Fixed Cost	Total Variable Cost	Average Total Cost	Marginal Cost
0	$15				
1	40				——
2	44				——
3	48				——
4	68				——
5	90				——

    b. (appendix) On the basis of the information in Table 12.3, complete Table 12.4 by calculating average fixed cost and average variable cost.

Table 12.4

Number of Children	Average Fixed Cost	Average Variable Cost
0		
1		
2		
3		
4		
5		

c.   On the basis of the calculations in Tables 12.3 and 12.4, graph in Figure 12.3 below Marcia Deal's average total cost, average variable cost, and marginal cost of providing daycare services to 1 through 5 children.

Figure 12.3

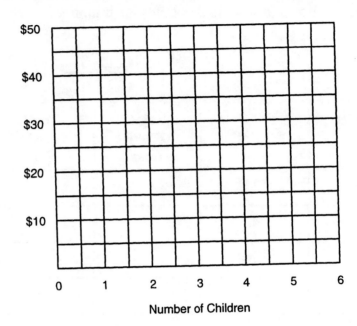

d.   Why does the distance between the average total cost curve and the average variable cost curve narrow as the number of children in daycare increases?

e.   Can Marcia Deal make a decision about whether to go into the daycare business on the basis of the above cost information? What information does she need to know before she can make this decision?

242

Indicate the best answer to each question.

1. Firms producing similar products are in:
   a. the same industry and the same producing sector.
   b. the same industry but different producing sectors.
   c. different industries but the same producing sector.
   d. different industries and different producing sectors.

2. Which of the following statements about production is FALSE?
   a. Production functions exist for virtually every good and service.
   b. A production function shows the output that can be attained when a particular group of inputs is combined in a certain way.
   c. The relative cost and availability of different types of inputs is an important consideration when choosing a production method.
   d. There is usually only one method available to a business for producing its product.

3. A profit-maximizing firm would choose the production method that:
   a. does not require the use of any high-priced inputs.
   b. provides the desired output at the lowest cost.
   c. uses the smallest amount of inputs.
   d. all of the above.

4. Which of the following statements about technology is FALSE?
   a. Technology is the body of knowledge that exists about production and its processes.
   b. What is known about production at a particular time becomes embodied in the equipment and methods used for production at that time.
   c. Technology refers only to our knowledge about the design and use of machines and other capital equipment.
   d. Technology affects the range of production methods from which a business can choose.

5. If a manager chooses not to use the latest available cost-saving technology to produce a business's product:
   a. you must conclude that the manager is not looking out for the best interest of the owners of the business.
   b. the business's profit will be less than it would be if the technology were adopted.
   c. the cost of switching to the new technology may be more than the cost-savings the technology can deliver.
   d. the manager is probably keeping costs high so that the price of the product can be kept at a high level as well.

6. Creative destruction refers to the:
   a. disappearance of less efficient resources and processes as more efficient resources and processes are introduced.
   b. opportunity cost that results when materials that go into one good cannot be used in other goods.
   c. pollution of the environment that results from the production of different types of goods.
   d. loss of trees and countryside due to mining.

7. Over the short run, total cost:
   a. is zero when output is zero.
   b. and average total cost are equal when one unit of output is produced.
   c. increases and then decreases as the business increases the amounts of all the inputs it employs.
   d. all of the above.

8. If a firm incurs a cost of $50,000 when nothing is produced and $50,010 when one unit is produced:
   a. the firm is operating in the short run.
   b. the total variable cost of the first unit produced is $10.
   c. the average total cost of the first unit produced is $50,010.
   d. all of the above.

The following table applies to questions 9 through 11.

Output	Total Cost	Marginal Cost
0	_____	
		$200
1	$600	
		_____
2	$720	

9. Total fixed cost for this firm is:
   a. $0.
   b. $200.
   c. $400.
   d. $600.

10. The marginal cost of the second unit of output is:
    a. $120.
    b. $360.
    c. $660.
    d. $720.

11. The average total cost when two units of output are produced is:
    a. $120.
    b. $320.
    c. $360.
    d. $720.

12. The total cost of producing 299 units of a product is $1,195, and the average total cost when producing 300 units is $4. From this we know:
    a. the marginal cost of the 300th unit is $4.
    b. the marginal cost of the 300th unit is $5.
    c. total fixed cost is $1,000.
    d. the total cost of 300 units is $1,199.

13. The average total cost when four units of output are produced is $12, and the average total cost when five units of output are produced is $11. The marginal cost of the fifth unit of output is:
    a. -$1.
    b. $7.
    c. $11.
    d. $55.

14. A cost that, when graphed, decreases to a minimum and then increases as the level of output increases could be:
    a. short-run average total cost.
    b. short-run marginal cost.
    c. long-run average total cost.
    d. all of the above.

15. The Law of Diminishing Returns applies to production:
    a. where some factors are fixed in amount.
    b. where a firm is facing severe diseconomies of scale.
    c. in the manufacturing sector, but not in the services sector.
    d. in the long run.

16.   If the long-run total cost of producing the first unit of output is $600, then the:
       a.   total cost when nothing is produced must be $600.
       b.   variable cost of producing the first unit must be $600.
       c.   marginal cost of producing the second unit must be $600.
       d.   none of the above.

17.   If long-run average total cost is greater than long-run marginal cost:
       a.   long-run average total cost is falling.
       b.   long-run average total cost is increasing.
       c.   the firm is experiencing diseconomies of scale.
       d.   the firm is experiencing the Law of Diminishing Returns.

18.   Long-run average total cost rises as the level of output increases because of:
       a.   economies of scale.
       b.   the Law of Diminishing Returns.
       c.   the direct relationship between price and quantity supplied.
       d.   the increasing difficulty of maintaining control of an organization as the level of
             output grows.

Appendix
Answer questions 19 and 20 on the basis of the following figure.

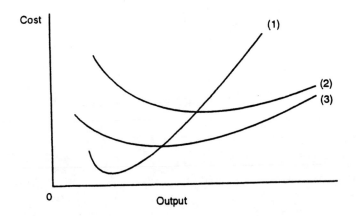

19.   Marginal cost is:
       a.   shown by line (1).
       b.   shown by line (2).
       c.   shown by line (3).
       d.   not shown in this figure.

20. Average fixed cost is shown by:
    a. line (1).
    b. the distance between lines (2) and (3).
    c. the distance between line (2) and the horizontal axis.
    d. the distance between line (3) and the horizontal axis.

Correct answers to the Exercises and the Sample Examination Questions can be found at the end of the Study Guide.

Chapter 13
Competition and Market Structures

■ CHAPTER OBJECTIVES

- To define a market and explain how its boundaries are determined.
- To explain how a firm's pricing and profit behavior are related to the amount of competition it faces in the market.
- To give the basic characteristics of the four market structures: pure competition, monopolistic competition, oligopoly, and monopoly.
- To describe an individual firm's demand curve, pricing behavior, and nonprice competitive behavior in each of the four market structures.
- To explain how a firm's long-run pricing and profit behavior and the degree of efficiency it achieves are affected by the amount of competition it faces in a market.
- To develop (in an appendix) the explanation of how a firm determines its profit-maximizing price and output level.

■ KEY TERMS AND CONCEPTS

Market structures

Industry

Market

Geographic boundary of a market

Product boundary of a market

Pure competition

Barriers to entry

Price taker

Market demand curve

Individual firm's demand curve

Economic profit, loss, or breaking even

Nonprice competition

Efficient production

Monopolistic competition

Identical vs. differentiated outputs

Oligopoly

Mutual interdependence

Leadership pricing

Kinked demand curve

Monopoly

Natural monopoly

Cartel

Price searcher

■ STUDY ORGANIZER

1. Differentiate between a market and an industry, and explain how the boundaries of a market are determined.

2. List the basic characteristics differentiating purely competitive, monopolistically competitive, oligopolistic, and monopolistic markets.

3. Graphically illustrate the demand curve for the product of a firm in pure competition, monopolistic competition, and monopoly.

4. Explain the extent of a firm's control over price in each market structure.

5. Understand the relationship between price and average total cost when a firm in any market structure is earning an economic profit, a loss, or breaking even.

6. Understand how product differentiation and nonprice competition affect firms in each market structure.

7. Explain the ease or difficulty of entering and exiting each of the market structures, and the effect of entry and exit conditions on price and economic profit over the long run in each market structure.

8. Explain the long-run position of a firm in each market structure with respect to price, cost, economic profit, and efficiency.

9. Explain what is meant by mutual interdependence.

10. Differentiate between price leadership and pricing with a kinked demand curve.

11. Identify some barriers to entry that may permit a firm to monopolize a market.

12. Explain the relationship between the market demand curve and the individual seller's demand curve for a product in pure competition and monopoly.

13. Know how each market structure affects consumers.

Appendix

14. Identify how an individual seller's marginal revenue curve is related to its demand curve when the demand curve is horizontal, and when the demand curve slopes downward.

15. Determine, and graphically illustrate, the profit-maximizing or loss-minimizing price and output for a firm in pure competition, monopolistic competition, and monopoly.

16. Understand the marginal cost-marginal revenue relationship in determining the best output level for a firm, and the price-average total cost relationship in measuring profit or loss at that output level.

1. The four market structures into which firms can be classified according to the competitive environment in which they operate are

pure
 monopolistic
oligopoly
 monopoly

_____ competition, _____ competition, _____, and _____.

    a. Firms are in the same market when they produce

similar

_____ products and compete for the same group of

buyers

_____.

    b. The boundaries of a market are established by the size of

geographic

the area in which sellers compete, or by _____

considerations, and by the degree to which buyers view the

substitutes

products of different sellers as _____. The

differ

perceived boundaries of a market may _____ among

the persons evaluating the market, and may be important in

antitrust

court cases involving the _____ laws.

2. A purely competitive market has a very large number of

sellers
 identical

independent _____ whose products are _____.

Entry into and exit from a purely competitive market is

easy, barriers

_____: there are no substantial _____ to

entry

_____ into this type of market.

a. The price of a product sold in a purely competitive market is determined by the interaction of its downward-sloping

market demand

_____ _____ curve and its upward-sloping

market supply

_____ _____ curve. At the market price, an individual purely competitive firm can sell as _____ or

much

little, no

as _____ as it wishes: The individual seller has ____

taker

control over price, or is a price _____. As a result, the demand curve for the individual firm's product is a

horizontal

_____ line at the market price.

b. If there is an increase in the number of sellers in a purely competitive market and no change in demand, the

fall

equilibrium market price will _____. This will, in turn, cause the demand curve for each individual seller's product

downward

to shift _____. If the equilibrium market price increases, the demand curve for each individual seller's

upward

product will shift _____.

c. If the price a purely competitive seller receives for its product is greater than its average total cost, the firm will

economic

earn an _____ profit; if price equals average total

· break even

cost, the firm will _____ _____; and if price is less than average total cost, the firm will sustain a

loss

_____. Graphically, an economic profit results when

below

above

the average total cost curve is _____ the demand curve, and a loss results when the average total cost curve is _____ the demand curve.

nonprice

lower

d. Because purely competitive sellers' products are identical, they do not engage in _____ competition. Without nonprice competition, the firms' costs are _____ than they would otherwise be.

cost

price
  economic

average total

e. In the long run, a purely competitive seller operates efficiently, or at its lowest average total _____, charges the lowest _____ possible, and earns no _____ profit. Under these conditions, the demand curve for each individual seller's product just touches the lowest point on its long-run _____ _____ cost curve.

easy

enter

increase

fall

exit

f. The long-run behavior of purely competitive sellers is due to _____ entry into and exit from the market. If firms are earning economic profits, other firms will _____ the market, causing market supply to _____ and the equilibrium price and demand curve for each seller's product to _____ until it equals minimum long-run average total cost. If firms in the market are losing money, some sellers will _____ the market and market supply decrease

rise

will _____, causing the equilibrium price and each individual seller's demand curve to _____ until it equals minimum long-run average total cost.

g. The purely competitive model helps us understand the behavior of certain markets in the economy and provides an

ideal

_____ against which all markets can be judged.

large

competition

differentiated

easy

3. In a monopolistically competitive market there is a _____ number of sellers, but not as many as in pure _____; each seller's product is _____; and entry into and exit from the market is fairly _____.

a. Because of product differentiation, buyers do not view monopolistically competitive sellers' products as perfect

substitutes

control

_____ for each other. Therefore, each individual seller has some _____ over the price of its product: When it raises its price by a small amount, the seller will not

all

limited

similar

lose _____ of its buyers. However, the individual seller's control over its price is _____ by the presence of many other firms producing _____ products in its market.

b. Since a seller of a product in a monopolistically competitive market will not lose all of its buyers when it raises its price

downward

by a small amount, the demand curve for the individual seller's product is _____ sloping.

c. A monopolistic competitor will earn an economic profit if it operates where its demand curve is _____ its average total cost curve, or where price is _____ than cost per unit. A monopolistic competitor will sustain a loss if it operates where its demand curve is _____ its average total cost curve, indicating that _____ is less than _____ per unit.

above

greater

below

price

cost

d. Competition not directly involving price, such as that stressing quality, guarantees, and the like, is called _____ competition. Nonprice competition can _____ the demand for a firm's product or make the _____ appear unique.

nonprice

increase

product

e. Because of easy entry into and exit from the market, over the long run monopolistic competitors earn only _____ profit, or operate where _____ equals long-run average total cost. However, because each seller's demand curve is downward sloping, over the long run a monopolistic competitor does not operate at the _____ point on its

normal

price

lowest

efficiently

few

differentiated

difficult
  dominant

long-run average total cost curve, or does not operate _____.

4. An oligopolistic market has a _____ large firms selling _____ or identical products. Entry into this type of market is _____. Oligopoly is the _____ market structure in the U.S. economy.

control

rivals

a. With only a few sellers in an oligopolistic market, each firm has some _____ over its price. But with few sellers in a market, each firm's actions will affect its _____. Therefore, in oligopoly, a firm must consider not only the effects of its policies on its buyers, but also the effects of those policies on its rivals, and how its rivals will react. This is referred to as _____ _____.

mutual
  interdependence

leadership

b. When a seller in an oligopoly market sets a price and other sellers follow that price, there is _____ pricing. This type of pricing may occur because firms do not want to challenge the pricing of the _____ rival, or because a firm is seen by others as particularly sensitive to changing _____ conditions.

largest

market

kinked

many

flat

few

steep

differentiated

increases

mutual
    interdependence

prices

economic

inefficiently

c.   If a seller's rivals follow its price decreases but not its price increases, the firm faces a _____ demand curve. With this type of demand curve, a seller that raises its price stands to lose _____ buyers, causing the demand curve above the current price to appear relatively _____, and a seller that lowers its price stands to gain _____ buyers, causing the demand curve below the current price to appear relatively _____.

d.   Nonprice competition may be found in oligopolistic markets where products are _____. It is useful where price cuts would not lead to large _____ in sales. Like price competition in oligopoly, nonprice competition is subject to _____ _____.

e.   Since entry into oligopoly markets is difficult, over the long run sellers can charge higher _____ than would be the case if entry were easy. This, in turn, can lead to _____ profit. Difficult entry may also allow a firm to operate _____, or not at its lowest long-run average total cost.

one, entry

barriers, entry

scale

natural

regulatory

patent

sole

cartel

market

more

less

more

5. A monopoly market has _____ seller, and _____ of additional sellers into the market is blocked by impassable _____ to _____.

a. It may be impossible to enter a monopolized market if economies of _____ make it more efficient to have one firm, rather than several, in that market. In this case, a _____ monopoly exists. A seller may also maintain a monopoly position if a _____ authority controls entry into its market, if it owns a key _____ on a product or process, or if it is the _____ owner of a factor necessary to operate.

b. When several sellers join together and form an organization in which they act like a monopolist, a _____ is created.

c. The demand curve for a monopolist's product is the same as the _____ demand curve for that product. This demand curve is downward sloping, indicating that _____ of the product will be demanded at lower prices and _____ will be demanded at higher prices.

d. The monopolist has _____ control over price than does a firm in any of the other market structures. The

searches

maximize

profit

market

lower

markets

seller

economic

efficiently

pure

monopolistic

oligopoly

monopolist _____ its demand curve to find the one price-output combination that will _____ its _____. Once the monopolist chooses this price and output level, that level is established for the _____: There is no direct competition to force the monopolist to _____ its price. The monopolist, however, does need to be concerned about potential competition from products in closely related _____.

e.   Nonprice competition by a monopolist is designed to make buyers more aware of the product itself than of the _____.

f.   As long as entry of new rivals is impossible, in the long run a monopolist can earn _____ profit, and not operate _____, or at lowest average total cost.

6.   The market for an agricultural crop, such as corn, would be classified as _____ competition; the market for lawn care in the suburbs of a large city would be classified as _____ competition; the market for VCRs or aluminum would be classified as an _____; and the market for electric power provided by one firm in a city would be classified as a

monopoly
purely
competitive

_____. Buyers fare best when facing _____ _____ sellers.

Appendix

cost, revenue

intersects

revenue

demand

below

cost

maximizing
profit

minimizing

loss

1. A firm will maximize its profit or minimize its loss by producing where marginal _____ equals marginal _____, or where the marginal cost curve _____ the marginal revenue curve.

a. In pure competition, a firm's marginal _____ curve is a horizontal line at the prevailing market price, or is identical to the firm's _____ curve. When a seller faces a downward-sloping demand curve, as in monopolistic competition or monopoly, its marginal revenue curve is also downward-sloping and _____ the demand curve. The typical marginal _____ curve for a seller decreases and then increases as output increases, regardless of the slope of the demand curve.

b. If price is greater than average total cost at the output level where marginal cost equals marginal revenue, the firm is _____ its _____; if price is less than average total cost at the output level where marginal cost equals marginal revenue, the firm is _____ its _____.

operating

shutting

down

fixed

c. If, in the short run, price is less than average total cost but greater than average variable cost, the firm will minimize its loss by _____ at the output level where marginal cost equals marginal revenue. If price is less than average variable cost, the firm will minimize its loss by _____ _____. A firm's shut down loss over the short run is equal to its total _____ costs.

Pure Competition

1. Figure 13.1a gives the market supply and demand curves for a product sold under purely competitive conditions.

Figure 13.1

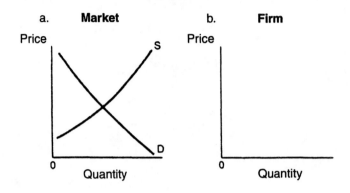

a.   In Figure 13.1b, illustrate the demand curve for an individual firm's product in this market, and label it D.

b.   Graphically show in Figures 13.1a and 13.1b the effect on the market and the individual firm of entry by new sellers into this market.

2. Draw an average total cost curve in each of the following figures to indicate that the firm in Figure 13.2a is operating with an economic profit, the firm in Figure 13.2b is taking a loss, and the firm in Figure 13.2c is breaking even.

Figure 13.2

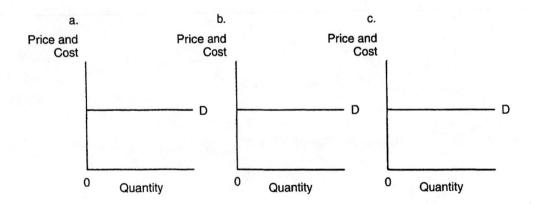

3.   Figure 13.3 applies to an individual purely competitive firm. Draw a long-run average total cost curve in this figure that is representative of the long-run position of a purely competitive firm, and answer question a below.

Figure 13.3

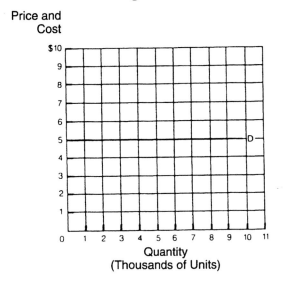

Price and Cost

Quantity
(Thousands of Units)

a.   In the long run, this firm will produce _____ units of output that will be sold for $_____ each.

4.   Figures 13.4a and 13.4b illustrate a short-run purely competitive market situation that permits firms to earn an economic profit. Illustrate in Figure 13.4a the change that would occur in the market, and in Figure 13.4b the change that would occur for the firm, in the long run.

Figure 13.4

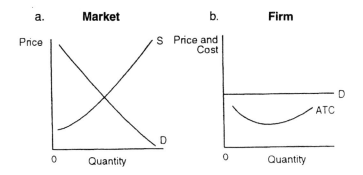

a.   **Market**   b.   **Firm**

Price   S   Price and Cost

Quantity   Quantity

5.   **(Appendix)**   Figure 13.5 applies to a firm operating in a purely competitive market. Answer questions a through d below based on this figure.

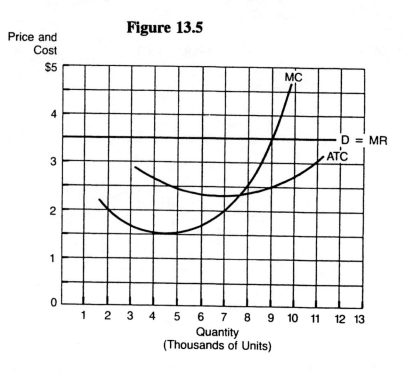

Figure 13.5

a.   This firm will be operating at a _____ (profit or loss) because its average total cost curve lies _____ (below or above) its demand curve.

b.   To maximize profit, this firm should sell _____ units of output.

c.   At the profit-maximizing output, the cost per unit is $_____ and the price per unit is $_____, causing the firm to make an economic profit of $_____ per unit.

d.   Total economic profit at the profit-maximizing output is $_____. (Total economic profit is economic profit per unit times the number of units demanded.)

6.   **(Appendix)**   Figure 13.6 applies to a pure competitor operating at a loss in the short run. Answer questions a through c below the figure.

Figure 13.6

Price and Cost

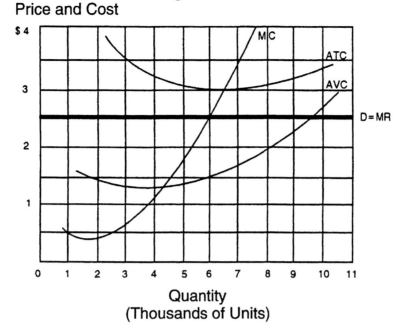

Quantity
(Thousands of Units)

a. If this firm were to operate, its best price-output combination would be $_____
and _____.

b. At this output the firm's average total cost would be $_____ and its average
variable cost would be $_____.

c. Would the firm minimize its loss by operating or by shutting down? Why?

Monopolistic Competition

1. Figure 13.7 applies to a firm in monopolistic competition in the long run. Answer
questions a and b below the figure.

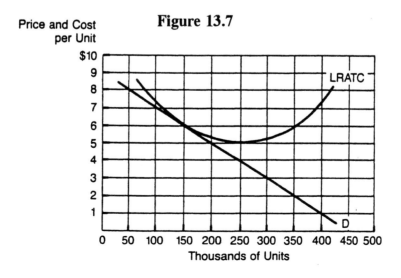

265

a. In the long run, this firm will sell _____ units of output at a price of $_____ each. At this output and price, this firm will make an economic profit of $_____.

b. If the long-run average total cost curve in Figure 13.7 applied to a firm in pure competition, then the purely competitive firm would produce _____ units of output and charge a price of $_____ per unit.

2. *Appendix* Figure 13.8 could apply to a firm in monopolistic competition or to any other firm with a downward-sloping demand curve in any other market structure. Answer questions a and b below the figure.

Figure 13.8

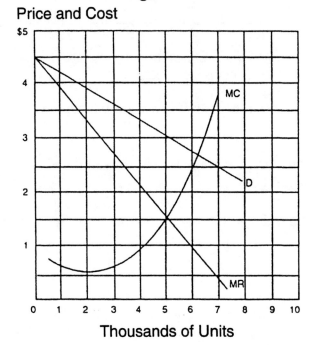

a. The profit-maximizing or loss-minimizing output for this firm is _____ units. At this output, the firm will charge a price of $_____ per unit.

b. Draw a long-run average total cost curve in Figure 13.8 to indicate that this firm is just breaking even.

Oligopoly

1. Draw a kinked demand curve in Figure 13.9, using point P to indicate the current price and output.

Figure 13.9

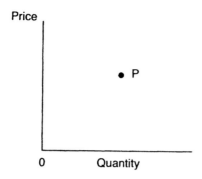

Monopoly

1. *Appendix* Figure 13.10 applies to a pure monopolist. Answer questions a through c based on this figure.

Figure 13.10

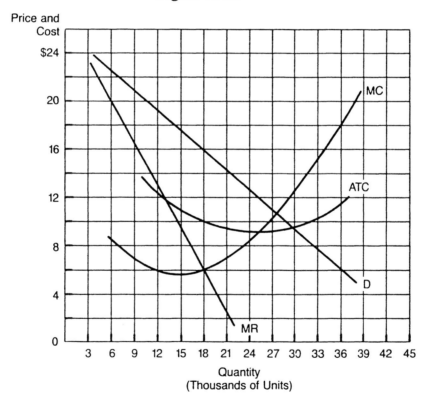

Quantity
(Thousands of Units)

a. The profit-maximizing or loss-minimizing output is _____ .

b. At this output, the monopolist would charge a price of $_____ .

c. At the profit-maximizing output, the cost per unit is $_____ , the price per unit is $_____ , economic profit per unit is $_____ , and total economic profit is $_____ .

Indicate the best answer to each question.

1. Producing similar products and competing for the same group of buyers are the main criteria for classifying firms into:
   a. producing sectors.
   b. industries.
   c. markets.
   d. foreign or domestic producer categories.

2. Which of the following is a primary way firms in the four market structures differ from one another?
   a. Pure competitors' short-run costs are affected by the Law of Diminishing Returns while short-run costs of sellers in the other market structures are not.
   b. Firms in some market structures can earn excess profits over the short run while firms in other market structures can not.
   c. Each firm's control over price differs from one market structure to the next.
   d. The profit-maximizing rule is different from one market structure to the next.

3. Ranking the market structures from that with the smallest number of sellers to that with the largest number of sellers, respectively, we have:
   a. monopoly, monopolistic competition, oligopoly, pure competition.
   b. monopoly, oligopoly, monopolistic competition, pure competition.
   c. monopolistic competition, pure competition, oligopoly, monopoly.
   d. oligopoly, monopoly, pure competition, monopolistic competition.

4. Which of the following statements about pure competition is FALSE?
   a. Sellers can earn excess profits over the long run.
   b. The market demand curve for the product is downward sloping.
   c. There is no nonprice competition.
   d. There is a very large number of sellers in the market.

5. The individual seller's demand curve in pure competition is:
   a. the same as the market demand curve.
   b. downward sloping, but not as steep as the market demand curve.
   c. perfectly horizontal at the going market price.
   d. impossible to determine since the seller has no control over its price.

6. An increase in the price a pure competitor can receive for its product would cause:
    a. the seller to move upward on its downward-sloping demand curve.
    b. the seller's downward-sloping demand curve to shift to the right.
    c. the seller to move to the left on its horizontal demand curve.
    d. the seller's horizontal demand curve to shift upward.

7. If purely competitive sellers were earning excess profits, you would expect:
    a. existing sellers to collect their profits and leave the market over the long run.
    b. new sellers to enter the market, and the market price to fall over the long run.
    c. new sellers to enter the market, and the market price to rise over the long run.
    d. no sellers to enter the market, and the market price to remain where it is over the long run.

8. If, over the long run, an increase in the number of sellers in a purely competitive market causes a decrease in price, you would expect that, before the decrease in price, sellers in the market were:
    a. earning excess profits.
    b. just breaking even.
    c. just earning enough to cover their normal profits.
    d. losing money.

9. The market structure characterized by many small firms, each attempting to differentiate its product through nonprice methods, is:
    a. monopoly.
    b. monopolistic competition.
    c. pure competition.
    d. oligopoly.

10. The market structure where a seller earns no excess profit in the long-run and operates at greater than minimum long-run average total cost is:
    a. pure competition.
    b. monopolistic competition.
    c. both pure competition and monopolistic competition.
    d. none of the above.

11. Mutual interdependence means that:
    a. businesses depend on the government to ensure that there will be no illegal competitive practices.
    b. buyers in households depend on sellers for goods and services, and sellers depend on households for resources to produce them.

c.   sellers in pure competition depend on market supply and demand to determine the price they will receive.

d.   rivals take each others' reactions into account when formulating their pricing and other competitive policies.

12.   The following demand curve for an individual seller's product is associated with:

a.   price leadership in pure competition.
b.   monopolistic competition over the long run.
c.   one theory of oligopoly pricing.
d.   monopoly over both the short and long run.

13.   Excess profits can be earned over the long run by:
a.   oligopolists.
b.   monopolistic competitors.
c.   oligopolists and monopolistic competitors.
d.   monopolistic competitors and pure competitors.

14.   The main factor allowing excess profit over the long run in certain market structures is:
a.   barriers to entry.
b.   no mutual interdependence.
c.   price taking.
d.   product differentiation.

15.   A natural monopoly occurs:
a.   only where there are no strong antitrust laws.
b.   primarily in monopolistic competition.
c.   where one firm has complete control of a raw material.
d.   where it is more efficient to have one seller, rather than several, in a market.

16. The individual seller's demand curve and the market demand curve are the same in:
    a. monopoly.
    b. monopolistic competition.
    c. oligopoly.
    d. all of the above.

17. Firms operate at minimum average total cost in the long run in:
    a. oligopoly.
    b. monopoly.
    c. monopolistic competition.
    d. pure competition.

Appendix

18. A firm in any market structure will maximize its profit or minimize its loss by operating where:
    a. total revenue equals marginal revenue.
    b. total revenue equals total cost.
    c. marginal revenue equals marginal cost.
    d. marginal revenue is greater than marginal cost.

19. As a seller in pure competition offers more of its product for sale:
    a. both the price of its product and its marginal revenue fall.
    b. the price of its product falls, but its marginal revenue remains unchanged.
    c. the price of its product remains unchanged, but its marginal revenue falls.
    d. both the price of its product and its marginal revenue remain unchanged.

20. Suppose a monopolist's price is less than average total cost but greater than average variable cost at the output level where marginal revenue equals marginal cost. The firm will:
    a. maximize its profit by operating at that output level.
    b. minimize its loss by operating at that output level.
    c. increase its profit by increasing its output level.
    d. increase its profit by decreasing its output level.

Correct answers to the Exercises and the Sample Examination Questions can be found at the end of the Study Guide.

Chapter 14
Government and the Markets

■ CHAPTER OBJECTIVES

- To introduce the main forms of government intervention in the operation of markets and some reasons for government intervention.
- To identify the major federal antitrust statutes, the business practices at which they are directed, and the penalties they carry.
- To distinguish among horizontal, vertical, and conglomerate mergers, and to indicate the relative importance of each.
- To identify the forms and organization of government regulation and distinguish between industry regulation and social regulation.
- To explain some justifications for industry regulation and to study price regulation, an important aspect of industry regulation.
- To introduce the controversy over the effectiveness and desirability of regulation and deregulation, and to discuss the implications for antitrust and regulatory policy of the growing internationalization of economic activity.

■ KEY TERMS AND CONCEPTS

Antitrust laws

Monopolization and attempts to monopolize

Combinations and conspiracies in restraint of trade

Sherman Act

Per se violations

Price fixing

Territorial division

Rule of Reason violations

Trade association

Joint venture

Federal Trade Commission Act

Clayton Act

Exclusionary practices

Tying contract

Interlocking directorates

Robinson-Patman Act

Price discrimination

Celler-Kefauver Act

Horizontal, vertical, and conglomerate mergers

Leveraged buyout

Junk bonds

Government regulation

Industry regulation

Natural monopoly

Public interest justification for regulation

Cost-plus pricing

Incentive regulation

Price caps

Social regulation

Deregulation

1. Identify some basic reasons for government intervention in a market system.

2. Differentiate between antitrust enforcement and government regulation of business.

3. Identify the two broad categories of antitrust violations.

4. Explain how the antitrust laws are administered and enforced, and identify the penalties for antitrust offenses.

5. Know the basic provisions of the Sherman, Federal Trade Commission, Clayton, Robinson-Patman, and Celler-Kefauver Acts.

6. Know the difference between Section One and Section Two Sherman Act violations.

7. Differentiate between a per se and a Rule of Reason violation.

8. Understand what is meant by monopolization and the importance of the definition of the relevant market in monopolization cases.

9. Identify the activities prohibited by the Clayton Act and its amendments.

10. Distinguish among horizontal, vertical, and conglomerate mergers, and explain how each type of merger can be anticompetitive.

11. Differentiate between industry and social regulation.

12. Explain how a regulatory agency is created, and how its range of authority is generally defined.

13. Identify some of the types of business decisions overseen by industry regulation.

14. Explain the two basic justifications for industry regulation.

15. Explain the relationship among natural monopoly, economies of scale, and efficiency.

16. Recognize the major advantage and disadvantage of cost-plus pricing, and explain the meaning and purpose of incentive regulation.

17. Give some examples of social regulation.

18. Discuss deregulation, the concern over the costs and benefits of regulation, and the effect of the internationalization of economic activity on firms subject to U.S. antitrust and regulatory enforcement.

1. The two main forms of government intervention in the operation of markets in the United States are _____ enforcement and government _____.

    antitrust
    regulation

    a. Government intervention in the operation of a market might be sought if the amount of _____ in the market is too limited to be effective; if the public interest would be better served by one large, efficient _____ seller rather than by several smaller and _____ efficient competing sellers; or if more _____ for participants in the market is desirable.

    competition

    regulated
    less

    security

2. The antitrust laws are designed to promote competition among sellers by condemning two broad categories of actions: those by individual firms seeking to _____ a market; and those by two or more firms that _____ or _____ with one another to monopolize or reduce competition in a market.

    monopolize

    combine
    conspire

    a. Antitrust issues are settled through the judicial system and are handled for the federal government

Justice

Trade Commission

Sherman

prices
  sales
per se

guilt

Rule, Reason

trade association

joint ventures

restrain

by the Department of _____ and the Federal _____ _____.

3.   The first federal antitrust statute was the _____ Act of 1890.

     a.   Sellers violate Section One of this act if they combine or conspire with one another to fix _____ or divide _____ territories among themselves. Both of these actions are _____ ____ violations, which are anticompetitive agreements where proof of the agreement is sufficient to establish _____.

     b.   Other activities involving several sellers which, depending upon the circumstances, may or may not be in violation of Section One of the Sherman Act are _____ of _____ violations. Activities of a _____ _____ that represents firms in a particular industry or _____ _____ of limited scope by two or more firms may be anti-competitive under Section One of the Sherman Act if they unreasonably _____ trade.

monopolization monopolize	c. Sherman Act Section Two cases, which deal with _____ and attempts to _____, depend in an important way on the specific actions taken by a firm against its rivals and the firm's share
market	of its _____. Generally, the more broadly a market is defined in terms of its geographic boundaries and/or number of substitute products, the
smaller	_____ will be a firm's share of that market.
Trade Commission	4. The Federal _____ _____ Act, which was passed in 1914, grants the commission the power to prohibit
unfair methods	_____ _____ of competition. These include antitrust violations.
Clayton	5. The _____ Act, also passed in 1914, prohibits certain specific practices when they are found to be anticompetitive.
exclusionary	a. When the seller of a product follows a policy that keeps its rivals from competing, it engages in an _____ practice. One example of this occurs when a firm agrees to sell one product to a buyer only if the buyer agrees to purchase another related product exclusively from the seller and not

tying

from its rivals. This arrangement is called a

_____ contract.

b. When the same person sits on the boards of directors

interlocking

directorate

of two or more corporations, an _____

_____ exists.

price discrimination

c. A seller is practicing _____ _____

when it sells different buyers the same product for

different prices. Price discrimination can injure

seller

competition between a _____ and its rivals, or

buyer

between the _____ of a product and its rivals.

The price discrimination provisions of the Clayton

Robinson-Patman

Act were amended by the _____-_____

Act of 1936.

6. The Clayton Act provisions dealing with anticompetitive

mergers and acquisitions were amended in 1950 by the

Celler-Kefauver

_____-_____ Act.

a. A merger between two firms that are competitors in

horizontal

a market is a _____ merger; a merger

between two firms where one is a supplier or

vertical

distributor for the other is a _____ merger;

278

conglomerate

fewer

suppliers
distributors

rivals

waves

large

leveraged

buyouts

junk bonds

imprisonment

fines, structural
triple

and a merger between two unrelated firms is a

_____ merger.

b. A horizontal merger can reduce competition by leaving _____ and larger sellers in a market; a vertical merger can reduce competition by making it difficult for a seller's rivals to find adequate _____ or _____; and a conglomerate merger can reduce competition because of the deep pocket of financial resources that can be made available to an acquired firm to use against its _____.

c. Historically, merger activity in the United States has occurred in _____. During the 1980s and 1990s, _____ numbers of acquisitions were completed. Many of these acquisitions were _____ _____ financed by borrowed funds to be paid off by the newly formed company. One method for acquiring these funds was by issuing _____ _____.

7. The penalties under the antitrust laws include _____, _____, _____ remedies, and _____ damages. With triple damages, a party injured by an

three | antitrust violation can sue for _____ times the damages incurred.

8. Government regulation involves the participation by government in business _____ _____. Regulation is carried out through agencies and _____ that oversee various aspects of the operations of business firms.

decision making

commissions

a. Unlike the antitrust laws, which are aimed at protecting the _____ relationships between sellers in a market, regulation is concerned with protecting specific _____ within society, such as buyers, workers, or the general public.

competitive

groups

b. One type of regulation involves _____ participation by the government in pricing and other decision making by firms. This type of participation is usually associated with _____ regulation. Another type of regulation involves _____ participation through the setting of rules and standards to which firms are expected to conform. This type of participation is usually associated with _____ regulation.

direct

industry

indirect

social

Congress

interstate

intrastate

mandate

agency

industry

economies

costly

natural

regulated

c. Federal regulatory agencies are created by acts of _____ and oversee activities that involve _____ commerce. State agencies oversee activities that involve _____ commerce. In the legislation creating a federal regulatory agency, a general _____ for the agency is given. Detailed rules and regulations to carry out the mandate are then made by the _____.

9. The type of regulation that is concerned with matters such as pricing, entry of new sellers into the market, and quality of service for firms such as natural gas distributors or electric power companies is termed _____ regulation.

   a. One justification for industry regulation is that, in certain markets, significant _____ of scale make it more efficient, or less _____, to have a monopoly producer rather than several competing firms. This is referred to as a _____ monopoly. In order to protect the consumer, the natural monopolist needs to be _____.

   b. A second justification for industry regulation is that certain businesses are important enough to the well-

public	being of society that there is a _____ interest in their operation and, therefore, they may be subject
regulation	to _____. The public interest justification
more	for regulation applies to _____ situations than does the natural monopoly justification.
	c. Pricing by a firm subject to industry regulation has
cost-plus	typically been done on a _____-_____ basis: that is, the regulatory authority approves a price that is designed to allow the firm to cover its costs plus
return (profit)	an adequate _____ to persons investing in the company. One problem with cost-plus pricing is that
efficiency	it does not promote economic _____.
	d. One approach to increasing the efficiency of
incentive	regulated firms is to subject them to _____
caps	regulation, such as price _____ which allow the firm to charge what it wants up to a designated maximum price and retain any additional profit from
efficiently	operating more _____.
	10. Regulation that addresses specific problems, such as pollution or worker safety, found in many industries is
social	_____ regulation. Social regulation does not involve

direct

_____ government participation in pricing and other related decisions of a business.

more

a. At the federal level, much _____ is spent on social regulation than on industry regulation.

11. There have been several important recent developments concerning regulation in the U.S. economy.

deregulation

a. During the late 1970s and 1980s the economy went through a period of _____ that was prompted in part by a concern that the costs of

greater

regulation may be _____ than its benefits.

disadvantage

b. As U.S. business firms face increased rivalry from foreign firms, some believe that the U.S. firms will be at a competitive _____ because U.S. government antitrust enforcement and regulation is national in scope.

Antitrust

1.   Find at least one article in a major newspaper, such as *The Wall Street Journal*, published in the last six months, that pertains to some aspect of antitrust enforcement. Analyze this article in terms of the material in this chapter.

Government Intervention

1.   Listed in Table 14.1 are the long-run total costs for Firm X at several levels of output. Suppose that this firm is currently selling 40,000 units of output a year and that, at most, 50,000 units would be demanded by all buyers in the market. In short, Firm X is well on its way to monopolizing its market.

Table 14.1

Units of Output	Long-Run Total Cost	Long-Run Average Total Cost
0	$ 0	-----
10,000	1,000,000	$
20,000	1,600,000	
30,000	1,950,000	
40,000	2,200,000	
50,000	2,500,000	

a.   Calculate the long-run average total cost at each level of output in Table 14.1 and fill in the appropriate column.

b.   On the basis of your calculations, would you recommend using the antitrust laws to break up this potential monopolist, or would you subject the firm to industry regulation? Explain the reasoning behind your recommendation.

Indicate the best answer to each question.

1. People who favor free markets might seek government intervention into the operation of a market because they:
    a.   think the amount of competition in that market is too limited to be effective.
    b.   think the public interest would be best served by one large efficient regulated seller in that market, rather than several smaller sellers.
    c.   desire to reduce the risks that accompany decision making in free markets.
    d.   all of the above.

2. Suppose the government sues a business in a court of law for anticompetitive practices in a market. Once the suit is settled, no ongoing action is taken against the business regarding this matter. This approach is most closely associated with:
    a.   antitrust enforcement.
    b.   laissez-faire enforcement.
    c.   social regulation.
    d.   industry regulation.

3. Which is the correct order of federal antitrust laws, from the earliest to the most recent?
    a.   Clayton Act, Celler-Kefauver Act, Federal Trade Commission Act.
    b.   Robinson-Patman Act, Clayton Act, Sherman Act.
    c.   Sherman Act, Celler-Kefauver Act, Federal Trade Commission Act.
    d.   Sherman Act, Federal Trade Commission Act, Robinson-Patman Act.

4. Price fixing and division of sales territories among competing sellers are examples of:
    a.   Rule of Reason violations of the Sherman Act.
    b.   per se violations of the Sherman Act.
    c.   practices normally found in purely competitive markets.
    d.   practices firms are allowed to carry out in the United States, but not in foreign markets.

5. Per se violations of the antitrust laws:
    a.   apply primarily to Section Two of the Sherman Act.
    b.   are anticompetitive agreements among sellers where proof of the agreement is sufficient to establish guilt.
    c.   make all activities of trade associations and joint ventures illegal.
    d.   none of the above.

6. To which of the following would the Rule of Reason apply?
   a. An agreement by sellers in a market as to how buyers will be allocated among those sellers.
   b. The setting of minimum prices by competing sellers in a market.
   c. The reporting of general supply and demand conditions to a trade association by competing sellers in a market.
   d. All of the above.

7. Cases charging a single seller with monopolizing its market:
   a. are brought primarily under Section One of the Sherman Act.
   b. depend in an important way on the definition of the relevant market.
   c. typically involve per se violations of the antitrust laws.
   d. all of the above.

8. The federal government agency that plays a major role in antitrust enforcement is the:
   a. Council on Wage and Price Stability.
   b. Equal Employment Opportunity Commission.
   c. Federal Trade Commission.
   d. Renegotiation Board.

9. The Sherman Act differs from the Clayton Act in that the Sherman Act:
   a. applies to interstate commerce, and the Clayton Act applies to intrastate commerce.
   b. disallows combinations and conspiracies in restraint of trade, and the Clayton Act disallows monopolization and attempts to monopolize.
   c. is not as specific as the Clayton Act in terms of the practices that are not allowed.
   d. has no per se violations, but there are per se violations of the Clayton Act.

10. An exclusionary practice, as the term is used in the Clayton Act, occurs when the:
    a. government passes a law to keep foreign sellers out of domestic markets.
    b. government places a private business beyond the reach of the antitrust laws.
    c. seller of a product is prevented by the government from entering into a price fixing agreement.
    d. seller of a product forecloses its rivals from the market by making it impossible for the rivals to compete.

11. The Robinson-Patman Act deals with:
    a. interlocking directorates.
    b. mergers and acquisitions.
    c. price discrimination.
    d. tying contracts.

12. The Clayton Act provisions dealing with anticompetitive mergers and acquisitions were amended by the:
   a. Celler-Kefauver Act.
   b. Federal Trade Commission Act.
   c. Robinson-Patman Act.
   d. Sherman Act.

13. Two rival movie theater chains in the same city coming together to form a single organization would be an example of a:
   a. horizontal merger.
   b. conglomerate merger.
   c. vertical acquisition.
   d. natural monopoly.

14. Historically in the U.S. economy:
   a. leveraged buyouts have been per se violations of the antitrust laws.
   b. junk bonds have been the most commonly used method for financing mergers.
   c. merger activity has occurred in waves.
   d. the majority of mergers has been with foreign firms.

15. Under the antitrust laws, a firm found guilty of injuring another firm may be required to pay the other firm:
   a. all its damages.
   b. one and one-half times its damages.
   c. three times its damages.
   d. ten times its damages.

16. Generally speaking:
   a. individual states are responsible for entering into agreements to regulate interstate commerce.
   b. there is widespread agreement about the costs and benefits to businesses and society from regulation.
   c. there is widespread agreement that internationalization of economic activity benefits regulated firms.
   d. none of the above.

17. The overseeing by a government agency of several aspects of the operations of a group of firms, such as their pricing and quality of service, is a characteristic of:
   a. antitrust enforcement.
   b. industry regulation.
   c. social regulation.
   d. special purpose regulation.

18. Government regulation of a firm could be justified on the grounds that:
    a.   it is more efficient to have one seller, rather than several sellers, in the market.
    b.   the well-being of the public is affected by the product the firm produces.
    c.   the firm experiences significant economies of scale and is a natural monopoly.
    d.   all of the above.

19. A major problem with cost-plus pricing is that it:
    a.   does not promote economic efficiency.
    b.   is not designed to give a fair return to the investors in a business.
    c.   has been struck down as unconstitutional by the Supreme Court.
    d.   forces a firm to operate where marginal cost equals marginal revenue.

20. Regulatory and antitrust enforcement:
    a.   generally put U.S. firms at an advantage in international trade.
    b.   are generally national in scope, but economic activity has become increasingly internationalized.
    c.   are international in scope.
    d.   are carried out in joint programs between the United States and other nations' governments.

Correct answers to the Exercises and the Sample Examination Questions can be found at the end of the Study Guide.

Chapter 15
Labor Markets, Unions, and the Distribution of Income

- To understand the behavior of the demand for labor.
- To explain, using a basic supply and demand model, how wages are determined.
- To introduce some real world considerations that modify the basic labor supply and demand model.
- To describe the types and structure of unions, collective bargaining, and major legislation affecting labor.
- To examine the distribution of income in the United States and some explanations for that distribution.
- To define poverty, and identify the poverty population in the United States.
- To discuss some government programs for alleviating poverty.

Wage

Derived demand

Law of Diminishing Returns

Marginal physical product

Marginal revenue product

Demand curve for labor

Supply curve of labor

Change in labor demand or supply

Change in the quantity of labor demanded or supplied

Minimum wage law

Labor union

Craft union

Industrial union

AFL-CIO

Collective bargaining

Strike

National Labor Relations Act (Wagner Act)

National Labor Relations Board (NLRB)

Taft-Hartley Act

Right to work laws

Distribution of income

Human capital investment

Discrimination

Poverty levels

■ STUDY ORGANIZER

1. Graph a supply curve and a demand curve for labor in a competitive market, and determine the equilibrium wage and level of employment.

2. Understand the meaning of derived demand.

3. Understand how the Law of Diminishing Returns and the Law of Demand cause the labor demand curve to slope downward.

4. Be able to calculate marginal physical product and marginal revenue product.

5. Explain how marginal revenue product determines a firm's labor demand curve.

6.   Understand the impact of nonwage factors on labor supply.

7.   Give some of the major factors that could cause a change in the demand for and the supply of labor.

8.   Distinguish between a change in the demand for (or supply of) labor and a change in the quantity demanded (or supplied) of labor, and illustrate each change graphically.

9.   Explain how wage rigidities, legislation, and unequal bargaining power can modify the competitive labor supply and demand model.

10.   Demonstrate graphically how a minimum wage law affects a labor market.

11.   Differentiate among a craft union, industrial union, and the AFL-CIO.

12.   Illustrate graphically how craft union membership policies can result in increased wages for their members.

13.   Explain what is meant by collective bargaining, and the purpose and risks of a strike.

14.   Identify some basic provisions of the National Labor Relations Act and the Taft-Hartley Act, and describe what is meant by right to work laws.

15.   Describe how the distribution of income is measured and how income is distributed among households in the United States.

16.   Give some explanations for an unequal distribution of income.

17.   Understand what is meant by a human capital investment.

18.   Explain how the U.S. government officially defines poverty.

19.   Identify groups of persons with a high incidence of poverty and some government programs to aid low-income households and individuals.

demand

derived

productivity

downward

falls

fall

decreasing

lower

1. The demand for labor, or any other factor of production, depends upon the _____ for the good or service that factor produces. That is, the demand for any factor of production is a _____ demand.

   a. The amount that a business is willing to pay for labor, or any other factor of production, depends upon the value of the factor's _____ to the business.

   b. An individual firm's demand curve for labor is _____ sloping, indicating that the firm will increase its quantity of workers demanded only if the wage _____.

   c. If a firm will increase the quantity of workers demanded only when the wage is lowered, and if wages are based on the value of labor's productivity, then as more labor is hired, the value of each additional worker's productivity must _____. The declining value of labor's productivity is due to _____ marginal productivity as more workers are utilized and, in most markets, to the need to _____ a product's price in order to sell the increased output.

marginal

Diminishing

Returns

less

decreases

lessens

lower

lessens

marginal revenue

$750

d. The change in total product that results when one more worker is utilized is that worker's _____ physical product. Over the short run, marginal physical product decreases because of the Law of _____ _____, which sets in when the additional output of an additional worker is _____ than the additional output of the preceding worker, or when each additional worker's marginal physical product _____. In other words, declining marginal physical product _____ the value of each additional worker to the firm.

e. Since almost all firms face a downward-sloping demand curve for their products, they must _____ a product's price to sell more units. Since the additional output from hiring more labor can only be sold at lower prices, this also _____ the value of labor's productivity as more workers are hired.

f. The change in total revenue from sales that result from using one more unit of a factor of production is _____ _____ product. If total revenue is $1,000 utilizing one worker and $1,750 utilizing two workers, the marginal revenue product of the second worker is _____.

demand

demand

3
4

upward

higher

nonwage

supply

increase
increase

more

g. A firm's marginal revenue product of labor determines that firm's _____ for labor, or, in other words, the marginal revenue product curve becomes the firm's _____ curve for labor. If a firm finds that the marginal revenue product of the third worker is $90 and the marginal revenue product of the fourth worker is $75, then that firm should be willing to hire _____ workers for $90 each or _____ for $75 each.

2. Typically, the supply curve in a labor market is _____ sloping, indicating that more labor will be supplied at a _____ wage.

   a. In addition to the wages offered for jobs, _____ considerations, such as the prestige of the job and location, influence people's labor _____ decisions.

3. An increase in the demand for labor with no change in supply will _____ the equilibrium wage and _____ the number of workers hired.

   a. The demand for labor may increase if an input for which labor can be substituted becomes _____ expensive to use than labor, if a production technique that requires

294

more, increase

economic

demographic

nonwage

shifts

quantity

movement along

falling

minimum wage

unequal

_____ labor is adopted, or if there is an _____ in the demand for the good or service produced by the labor.

b.   A change in supply in a labor market could result from a change in factors such as _____ conditions and _____ trends.

c.   When there is a change in a _____ factor influencing the demand or supply of labor, there is a change in demand or supply, and the demand or supply curve _____ to the right or left. When there is a change in the wage rate, there is a change in the _____ of labor demanded or supplied, and there is a _____ _____ the demand or supply curve from one wage-quantity combination to another.

4. In the real world, the operation of the simple labor supply and demand model is affected and modified by such factors as wage rigidities that keep money wages from _____; legislation such as the _____ _____ law which specifies the lowest hourly wage an employer may pay an employee; and _____ bargaining power where one side in a wage negotiation has a stronger bargaining position than the other.

5. An organization of workers that bargains with management on its members' behalf is a labor _____. In the United States, labor union membership has _____ over the last few decades.

union

fallen

a. A union that represents persons with a particular skill is a _____ union. This type of union helps to raise the incomes of its members by _____ the supply of labor. A union that represents all workers in a particular industry is an _____ union.

craft

limiting

industrial

b. The best-known organization to which many unions in the United States belong to further their common interests is the _____ _____ of Labor-_____ of _____ _____, better known as the _____.

American
  Federation
Congress, Industrial
  Organizations
AFL-CIO

c. The process through which union and management representatives negotiate the terms of a labor contract is _____ _____. The objectives bargained for by a union and management are primarily _____, but the bargaining process itself is largely _____.

collective bargaining

economic

political

d. If a contract agreement cannot be reached, a union may try to bring economic pressure on an employer with a _____.

strike

riskless	A strike is not _____ for a union, and its outcome depends in large part on whether the workers or the
employer	_____ can better survive the work stoppage.
	e. The legislation passed in 1935 that permits and supports organized labor and the collective bargaining process is the
Labor Relations	National _____ _____ Act, or the Wagner Act.
Labor Relations	This act also created the National _____ _____
Board	_____, which hears and acts on complaints concerning
labor	unfair _____ practices. The legislation that limits some union activities and defines some unfair union
Taft-Hartley	practices is the _____-_____ Act of 1947. State laws prohibiting union membership as a condition of
right, work	work are _____ to _____ laws.
	7. The way in which income is divided among the members of society
distribution	is referred to as the _____ of income.
equally	a. Generally, income is not divided _____ among the members of society. In the United States, the poorest 20
less	percent of all households receives much _____ than 20 percent of the total income and the most affluent 20 percent
more	receives much _____ than 20 percent of the total income.

resources
capital

discrimination

bargaining

inheritance

b. Some explanations for an unequal distribution of income include: differences in the quantity, quality, and uses of the _____ one owns; differences in human _____ investments, such as schooling or on-the-job training; _____ based on a person's age, race, gender, or another characteristic; differences in _____ power that allow some persons to command higher incomes; and _____, or the passing of wealth from generation to generation.

poverty levels

greater

disagreement

7. The minimum annual income that an individual or household must receive to not be included in the official measure of poverty is given by the government designated _____ _____. The poverty-level income for a large household is _____ than the poverty-level income for a small household. There is some _____ over how the official poverty levels are measured.

children

woman
works

a. Many of the poor are _____, live in households headed by a _____, or where the head _____.

public

b. The most likely source of government cash transfers to persons living in poverty is _____ aid. A problem the poor face in obtaining government assistance is that regular

298

employment | _____ is required for benefits under many programs, such as unemployment compensation and Social Security.

time

work

c. Sweeping welfare reform in 1996 limited the maximum _____ some types of aid could be received, and introduced a "_____ activity" requirement certain recipients must meet to qualify for aid.

Demand for Labor

1. Table 15.1 gives a hypothetical producer's total product as more units of labor are used. Calculate the marginal physical product of each additional unit of labor and fill in the appropriate column.

Table 15.1

Units of Labor	Total Product	Marginal Physical Product
0	0	
1	480	_____
2	940	_____
3	1360	_____
4	1720	_____
5	1960	_____
6	2100	_____
7	2120	_____
8	2120	

2. Given in Table 15.2 is the product and price information for a manufacturer of Good Z. Answer the questions following the table.

Table 15.2

Number of Workers	Total Product	Price per Unit	Total Revenue	Marginal Revenue Product
0	0	$7.25		
1	150	7.00		———
2	275	6.75		———
3	375	6.50		———
4	450	6.25		———
5	500	6.00		———
6	525	5.75		———
7	525	5.75		———

a. Calculate and list the firm's total revenue for each total product level.

b. Calculate and list the marginal revenue product of each additional worker.

c. If the wage paid in the market for workers who produce Good Z is $600, how many workers will this firm demand? _____ At a wage of $250, how many will it demand? _____ At $175? _____ At $25? _____

d. Fill in Table 15.3 (on the next page), giving the wage that this firm would be willing to pay for each number of workers demanded.

e. In Figure 15.1 (on the next page), plot this firm's demand curve for workers.

Table 15.3

Number of Workers Demanded	Price of Labor (Wage)
1	
2	
3	
4	
5	
6	
7	

Figure 15.1

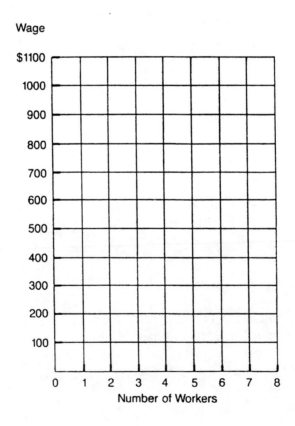

Labor Market Modifications

1. Answer questions a and b below based on Figure 15.2, which illustrates the labor market for a particular type of worker.

Figure 15.2

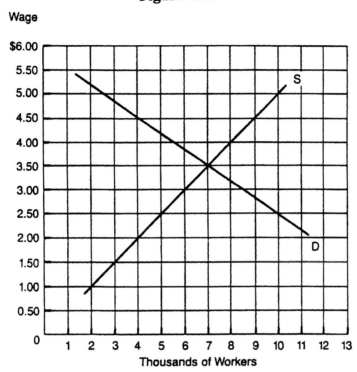

a. Assume that in this market the minimum wage is set at $4.50. At this minimum wage, the quantity of labor demanded is _____ workers and the quantity supplied is _____ workers, or a _____ (shortage or surplus) of _____ workers occurs.

b. If the minimum wage were set at $2.50, the wage paid in this market would be $_____, and there would be a shortage or surplus of _____ workers.

2.	Illustrate in Figure 15.3 the result of a craft union policy to restrict the number of union members in a particular occupation, and answer question a below the figure.

Figure 15.3

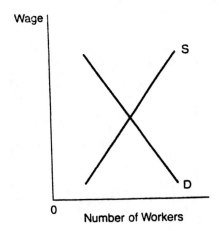

a.	After the restrictive policy, the wage will _____ (increase, decrease, remain unchanged) and the quantity of labor employed will _____ (increase, decrease, remain unchanged).

■ SAMPLE EXAMINATION QUESTIONS

Indicate the best answer to each question.

1.	Since the demand for factors of production depends on the demand for the products they produce, factors of production are said to have:
	a.	an ancillary demand.
	b.	a dependent demand.
	c.	a derived demand.
	d.	a secondary demand.

2.	The short-run demand for labor by a firm is affected by the:
	a.	behavior of the firm's product price as more units of output are sold.
	b.	behavior of the labor's marginal physical product as more workers are hired.
	c.	Law of Diminishing Returns.
	d.	all of the above.

The following table showing production conditions for a firm in the short-run applies to questions 3 through 5.

Number of Workers	Total Product	Product's Price per Unit
0	0	$1.40
1	200	1.20
2	360	1.00
3	480	0.80

3. The marginal physical product of the second worker is:
    a. 120.
    b. 160.
    c. 180.
    d. 360.

4. The marginal revenue product of the second worker is:
    a. $1.
    b. $72.
    c. $120.
    d. $360.

5. For this firm to hire three workers, the wage rate would have to be no more than:
    a. $0.80.
    b. $24.
    c. $126.
    d. $384.

6. An individual firm's demand curve for labor is derived from the:
    a. demand curve for the firm's product.
    b. firm's marginal revenue product of labor.
    c. firm's marginal physical product of labor.
    d. market demand curve for labor.

7. A decrease in the cost of an input that substitutes for labor would cause a firm to:
    a. decrease its demand for labor.
    b. decrease its quantity of labor demanded.
    c. increase its demand for labor.
    d. increase its quantity of labor demanded.

8. Which of the following would decrease the demand for professors of economics?
    a. A decrease in the popularity of economics courses.
    b. A decrease in tuition costs to students because of government-sponsored scholarship programs.
    c. An increase in the salaries paid to professors.
    d. An increase in the cost of teaching using computers and other self-directed learning programs.

9. Which of the following would cause suppliers of labor to move upward along a given labor supply curve?
    a. An improvement in the cleanliness and working conditions on a job.
    b. An increase in the possibility of long-term gains from holding a job.
    c. An increase in the psychic income that accompanies a job.
    d. An increase in the hourly wage for a job.

10. A decrease in the teenage population in an area would cause the equilibrium wage and quantity of labor for employers that typically hire teenagers to:
    a. decrease.
    b. increase.
    c. decrease and increase, respectively.
    d. increase and decrease, respectively.

11. Which of the following would create a surplus of workers in a labor market?
    a. An increase in the price of an input that can be used in place of this type of labor.
    b. Raising the minimum wage above the equilibrium wage rate.
    c. Rigidities that keep the wage rate from rising in response to decreases in the supply of labor.
    d. Stricter licensing and certification requirements for persons selling their services in this market.

12. Which of the following statements is true?
    a. A craft union seeks to represent all workers in a particular industry.
    b. A craft union attempts to increase the incomes of its members by restricting the supply of labor in a particular occupation.
    c. The A.F.L.-C.I.O. is a craft union.
    d. All of the above.

13. Which of the following statements about strikes is true?
    a. Management is generally unable to respond to a strike by assuming the tasks performed by union workers or by living off accumulated production inventories.
    b. There has been a great deal of labor time lost in recent years due to strikes.
    c. Employment in related industries can be affected when a striking union shuts down a firm's production.
    d. A strike is a riskless strategy for a union.

14. The National Labor Relations Board and right to work laws came into existence as a result of, respectively, the:
    a. Fair Employment Standards Act and the Taft-Hartley Act.
    b. Humphrey-Hawkins Act and the Employment Act of 1946.
    c. Wagner Act and the Taft-Hartley Act.
    d. Wagner Act and the Wage and Price Stability Act.

15. Currently in the United States:
    a. the poorest 20 percent of households receives about 1 percent of income, and the richest 20 percent receives about 90 percent.
    b. the poorest 20 percent of households receives about 4 percent of income, and the richest 20 percent receives about 50 percent.
    c. the poorest 20 percent of households receives about 15 percent of income, and the richest 20 percent receives about 30 percent.
    d. income is divided approximately evenly among households.

16. You would expect the return on a particular human capital investment to be:
    a. greater for a younger person than for an older person.
    b. limited to investments in formal education and on-the-job training.
    c. the same for anyone making the investment.
    d. unaffected by discrimination in housing, access to health care, or any other activity not directly involving a job.

17. In the United States, the minimum annual income that an individual or family can receive and not be included in the official definition of poverty is:
    a. is $4,581.
    b. lower than it was in the 1980s because of a downward revision in 1994.
    c. given by government-designated levels based primarily on family size.
    d. lower for households headed by a person under 65 years of age than for households headed by a person 65 years or older.

18. Poverty-level incomes:
    a. are income levels that must be earned to be considered not poor.
    b. have been attacked by some for being too low and not presenting a true measure of the extent of poverty in the United States.
    c. have been attacked by some for making the plight of the poor seem worse than it is because in-kind transfers are not included.
    d. all of the above.

19. Currently in the United States, the poverty population:
    a. is approximately 14 percent of the total population.
    b. is found more in male-headed than female-headed households.
    c. includes a larger percentage of elderly than children.
    d. all of the above.

20. The most likely source of government cash transfers to the poor is:
    a. public aid.
    b. unemployment compensation.
    c. Social Security payments.
    d. the United Way.

Correct answers to the Exercises and the Sample Examination Questions can be found at the end of the Study Guide.

Chapter 16
International Trade

■ *CHAPTER OBJECTIVES*

- To present an overview of U.S. international trade by highlighting major U.S. exports and imports, and countries with which the United States trades.
- To explain the principle of comparative advantage.
- To define free trade and discuss some arguments in its favor.
- To introduce the major tools for restricting trade: tariffs, quotas, and embargoes.
- To define protectionism and discuss some arguments in its favor.
- To discuss trade policies countries might adopt, and some measures for stimulating exports.
- To examine some key trade agreements.

■ *KEY TERMS AND CONCEPTS*

International trade

Export

Import

U.S. trading partners

Specialization

Comparative advantage

Free trade

Protectionism

Tariff

Quota

Embargo

Free trade arguments

Protectionist arguments

Infant industry

Trade subsidy

Dumping

International Monetary Fund (IMF)

General Agreement on Tariffs and Trade (GATT)

European Union (EU)

North American Free Trade Agreement (NAFTA)

World Trade Organization

■ STUDY ORGANIZER

1. Understand the effects of international trade on a nation's output, employment, and prices.

2. Know the magnitude of U.S. exporting and importing activity and how that activity has changed as a percentage of GDP over the years.

3. Identify the major imports, exports, and trading partners of the United States.

4. Explain the relationship between scarcity and specialization.

5. Explain the principle of comparative advantage and how it relates to opportunity cost.

6. Demonstrate, with an example, the overall benefits of trade based on comparative advantage.

7. Differentiate between free trade and protectionism and discuss the arguments for each.

8. Explain how tariffs, quotas, and embargoes restrict trade.

9. Explain how subsidies and dumping promote a country's exports.

10. Identify the basic functions of the International Monetary Fund and the General Agreement on Tariffs and Trade, and briefly describe the European Union and the North American Free Trade Agreement.

international

export

import

increased

capital goods

industrial

developed

Canada

Japan

European Union

1. The buying and selling of goods and services among different countries is _____ trade.

a. A good or service produced in the United States and sold in another country is a U.S. _____. A good or service bought in the United States but produced in another country is a U.S. _____.

b. Exports and imports as percentages of U.S. GDP generally _____ over the last few decades. The most important class of U.S. exports is _____ _____ and the most important import classes are capital goods and _____ supplies and materials.

c. The majority of U.S. trade is with _____ nations in North America, Europe, and Asia. The most important trading partners of the United States are _____, _____, and the countries that make up the _____ _____.

2. One way of reducing the basic problem of scarcity is to focus individual resources on a small range of tasks or on the production

311

of one or a few types of outputs. That is, scarcity can be reduced

specialized

if resources are used in a _____ manner.

more

a. Specialization reduces scarcity by allowing _____ goods

and services to be produced than would be the case if

not

resources were _____ specialized.

b. For specialization to work, individuals must be able to

sell, buy

_____ what they produce and _____ what they want and

markets

need, or it is necessary to have appropriate _____.

3. Specialization on an international level reduces the scarcity

problem when countries produce the goods and services in which

comparative
advantage

they have a _____ _____, and trade for other goods

and services. A country has a comparative advantage in a product

opportunity
cost

when it has a lower _____ _____ of producing that

product than does another country.

a. If country A can produce one unit of an item and give up

less of other goods and services than would country B

comparative

producing the same item, country A has a _____

advantage

_____ in the production of that good or service.

312

four

eight, A

ten

five

B

twenty, twelve

b.   With one unit of resources, Country A can produce ten tons of steel or four tons of rope. Country B can produce ten tons of steel or eight tons of rope with one unit of resources. The opportunity cost of producing ten tons of steel in Country A is _____ tons of rope, and the opportunity cost of producing ten tons of steel in Country B is _____ tons of rope, giving Country _____ the comparative advantage in the production of steel.

c.   According to the information in b, above, the opportunity cost of producing four tons of rope in Country A is _____ tons of steel, and the opportunity cost of producing four tons of rope in Country B is _____ tons of steel, giving Country _____ the comparative advantage in the production of rope.

d.   If Country A and Country B each had two units of resources, one devoted to the production of steel and the other to rope, a total of _____ tons of steel and _____ tons of rope would be produced.

e.   If Country A and Country B each had two units of resources and each specialized according to its comparative advantage,

twenty, sixteen	a total of _____ tons of steel and _____ tons of rope would be produced.
free trade	f. To receive the full benefits from production according to comparative advantage, there must be _____ _____ among nations.
protectionism	4. The philosophy that free trade is not in the best interest of a nation and that trade should be restricted is _____. There are several trade restricting policies.
tariff decrease	a. A tax placed on an import is a _____. This tax raises the price of the imported good, causing a _____ in the quantity of the import demanded.
quota, reduces	b. A limit imposed on the quantity of a good that can enter a country is a _____. This policy _____ the amount of a foreign product that can compete with domestic products in a market.
embargo	c. An outright ban on trade in a particular product with another nation is an _____.

5. There are several arguments for free trade and for protectionism.

a. The arguments in favor of free trade include: it allows the markets for products to grow, which in turn allows the resources producing those products to _____ and be utilized more _____; it allows _____ quantities of goods and services to be made available to buyers because of the absence of quotas; it allows buyers to pay _____ prices for imports because of the absence of tariffs; and it benefits the consumer because of increased _____ in markets. In each of these arguments the main beneficiary from free trade is the _____.

specialize

efficiently, larger

lower

competition

consumer

b. The arguments in favor of protectionism include: it allows newly developing domestic industries to be sheltered from competition from _____ rivals, or the _____ _____ argument; it supports domestic _____ and _____ by limiting foreign competition with domestic products; it allows a country to _____ its production so that it does not develop a major dependence on foreign-produced imported goods; and, in some markets, it is important for _____ security reasons.

foreign, infant

industry, output

employment

diversify

national

315

free	6. Most countries do not strictly follow a complete _____ trade or complete _____ policy, and a nation's trade policy will change as _____ and political conditions change.
protectionist	
economic	
	a. Sometimes a nation will adopt policies to stimulate its own exports. One method of carrying this out is to give producers a _____ for each unit exported, which helps producers _____ the prices on their products competing in foreign markets.
subsidy	
lower	
	b. The sale of a product in a foreign market at a price below its cost or at a price below its domestic price is _____.
dumping	
	c. Since World War II there has been greater cooperation in foreign trade and finance. The _____ _____ Fund has been providing financial assistance to countries, and the General Agreement on _____ and Trade, or GATT, has resulted in tariff rate reductions through several rounds of negotiations between countries. The responsibilities of GATT are to be taken over by the _____ _____ _____.
International Monetary	
Tariffs	
World Trade Organization	
	d. The goal of the European Union, or EU, is to create a _____ multi-country trading area within which there
single	

| barriers | are no national _____ to the movement of people, goods, or services. An agreement similar to the one creating the European Union was reached between the United States, Canada, and Mexico and is called the North |
| Free Trade | American _____ _____ Agreement, or NAFTA. |

■ EXERCISES

Comparative Advantage

1. With one unit of resources per country, the production possibilities given in Table 16.1 would occur. Answer questions a through e below on the basis of this table.

Table 16.1

Country	Production Possibilities
A	100 tons of iron ore or 5,000 pairs of shoes
B	10 tons of iron ore or 25,000 pairs of shoes

a.   The opportunity cost to country A of producing 100 tons of iron ore is _____ pairs of shoes, and the opportunity cost to country B of producing 100 tons of iron ore is _____ pairs of shoes. Because the opportunity cost of producing iron ore is lower in country _____, country _____ has the comparative advantage in iron ore.

b.   The opportunity cost to country A of producing 5,000 pairs of shoes is _____ tons of iron ore, and the opportunity cost to country B of producing 5,000 pairs of shoes is _____ tons of iron ore. Because the opportunity cost of producing shoes is lower in country _____, country _____ has the comparative advantage in shoes.

c. If each country had two units of resources, and if each country used one unit to produce iron ore and one unit to produce shoes, the production of iron ore would be _____ tons by country A and _____ tons by country B, or a total of _____ tons. The production of shoes would be _____ pairs by country A and _____ pairs by country B, or a total of _____ pairs.

d. Assume that country A and country B each decides to produce the item in which it has the comparative advantage, and to trade with the other country for the other item. If each country devotes two units of resources to the item in which it has the comparative advantage, country A will produce _____ _____ of _____ and country B will produce _____ _____ of _____ .

e. The benefits to these countries from utilizing the principle of comparative advantage can be seen by assessing the total production of each item with and without specialization and trade. When each country uses two units of resources without specialization and trade, a total of _____ tons of iron ore and _____ pairs of shoes can be produced. When each country uses two units of resources with specialization and trade, a total of _____ tons of iron ore and _____ pairs of shoes can be produced.

2. Answer question a below based on the assumption that, with one unit of resources each, Guatemala and Chile have the production possibilities given in Table 16.2.

Table 16.2

Country	Production Possibilities
Guatemala	50 tons of coffee or 1 ton of copper
Chile	10 tons of coffee or 100 tons of copper

a. Guatemala has the comparative advantage in _____ because _____
_____
_____, and Chile has the comparative advantage in
_____ because _____
_____   _____ .

3. Answer questions a and b below based on the assumption that the production possibilities in Table 16.3 exist for Gabon and Venezuela when one unit of resources is used by each country.

Table 16.3

Country	Production Possibilities
Gabon	2 million barrels of oil or 100,000 men's suits
Venezuela	2 million barrels of oil or 200,000 men's suits

    a. Would there be an advantage to specialization and trade in these goods between these countries? _____ Why?

    b. If comparative advantage works, which country should specialize in oil? _____ Which country should specialize in men's suits? _____

■ **SAMPLE EXAMINATION QUESTIONS**

Indicate the best answer to each question.

1. In recent years, the most important group of U.S. exports has been:
   a. automotive vehicles and parts.
   b. capital goods.
   c. foods, feeds, and beverages.
   d. industrial supplies.

2. The largest volume of international trade for the United States is carried on with:
   a. Canada.
   b. Japan.
   c. Mexico.
   d. The European Union.

3. International specialization according to the principle of comparative advantage:
   a. increases a country's dependence on markets and trade.
   b. increases the total output of goods and services available to the world economy.
   c. reduces the scarcity problem.
   d. all of the above.

4. When one country has a comparative advantage over another country in the production of a good, the country with the comparative advantage can:
   a. control the distribution of the good more than can the other country.
   b. earn a higher profit on the good than can the other country because of trade restrictions.
   c. provide the good at a lower opportunity cost than can the other country.
   d. supply the good to a wealthier group of buyers than can the other country.

5. Country A can produce 10 truck tires or 30 pairs of boots with one unit of resources. Country B can produce 15 truck tires or 30 pairs of boots with one unit of resources. Which of the following statements is true?
   a. Country A has a comparative advantage in the production of truck tires and boots.
   b. Country A has a comparative advantage in the production of truck tires, and Country B has a comparative advantage in the production of boots.
   c. Country A has a comparative advantage in the production of boots, and Country B has a comparative advantage in the production of truck tires.
   d. Country B has a comparative advantage in the production of truck tires and boots.

Answer questions 6 through 8 on the basis of the following table showing production possibilities for pizzas and birthday cakes from one unit of resources in Country C and Country D.

Country	Production Possibilities
C	24 pizzas or 18 birthday cakes
D	24 pizzas or 16 birthday cakes

6. On the basis of the information in the table, if these countries produce according to their comparative advantages, Country C should:
   a. produce pizzas.
   b. produce birthday cakes.
   c. produce both pizzas and birthday cakes.
   d. not produce pizzas or birthday cakes.

7.   If each country has two units of resources and specializes in the good for which it has a comparative advantage, the combined outputs of the two countries will be:
    a.   0 pizzas and 78 birthday cakes.
    b.   48 pizzas and 36 birthday cakes.
    c.   72 pizzas and 18 birthday cakes.
    d.   96 pizzas and 0 birthday cakes.

8.   The opportunity cost to Country D of producing one birthday cake is:
    a.   1/3 pizza.
    b.   2/3 pizza.
    c.   1 pizza.
    d.   1.5 pizzas.

Answer questions 9 through 11 on the basis of the following information.

Country E can produce 10 tons of coal or 2 tons of wheat with one unit of resources.
Country F can produce 10 tons of coal or 5 tons of wheat with one unit of resources.

---

9.   The opportunity cost of producing 2 tons of wheat in Country E is:
    a.   the same as the opportunity cost of producing 5 tons of wheat in Country F.
    b.   2.5 times as large as the opportunity cost of producing 5 tons of wheat in Country F.
    c.   only 40 percent as large as the opportunity cost of producing 5 tons of wheat in Country F.
    d.   zero, since Country E produces both wheat and coal.

10.   The opportunity costs of producing 1 ton of coal in Country E and in Country F are, respectively:
    a.   1/5 ton of wheat and 1/2 ton of wheat.
    b.   1/2 ton of wheat and 1/5 ton of wheat.
    c.   5 tons of wheat and 2 tons of wheat.
    d.   zero, since both countries produce coal and wheat.

11.   If the principle of comparative advantage is followed, Country E should:
    a.   buy all its coal from Country F.
    b.   buy all its wheat from Country F.
    c.   buy all its coal and wheat from Country F.
    d.   produce both coal and wheat, and not trade with Country F.

12. Which of the following statements is FALSE?
   a. A tariff is an example of a trade-restricting policy.
   b. Dumping or increasing a tariff by a country could result in a trade war with another country.
   c. International specialization can become more extensive as the markets in which trade occurs become larger.
   d. No one benefits from trade-restricting policies.

13. You would expect:
   a. businesses to benefit more than consumers from both free trade and protectionism.
   b. businesses to benefit more than consumers from free trade, and consumers to benefit more than businesses from protectionism.
   c. consumers to benefit more than businesses from both free trade and protectionism.
   d. consumers to benefit more than businesses from free trade, and businesses to benefit more than consumers from protectionism.

14. Suppose a country passes two laws. The first allows 10,000 units of a product to enter the country per year. The second allows the first 10,000 units per year of a different product to enter at a tax of $2.00 per unit, and all additional units to enter at a tax of $2.50 per unit. The first and second laws create, respectively:
   a. a tariff and an absolute quota.
   b. an absolute quota and a tariff-rate quota.
   c. a subsidy and a tariff.
   d. an embargo and a tariff.

15. A tax on imports of electronic equipment is an example of:
   a. an embargo.
   b. a free trade policy.
   c. a quota.
   d. a tariff.

16. The freer the trade between nations:
   a. the smaller the opportunity to increase the availability of goods and services and the smaller the opportunity to decrease the costs of production.
   b. the smaller the opportunity for specialization but the greater the opportunity for improved efficiency in production.
   c. the greater the opportunity for specialization and the greater the competition among sellers in a market.
   d. the greater the opportunity to use resources efficiently and the greater the opportunity for sellers to raise prices and restrict outputs.

17. Protectionism refers to the philosophy that:
    a. the U.S. should actively trade with less-developed countries to ensure their political stability.
    b. consumers should be protected from paying higher prices because of tariffs and quotas.
    c. free trade is not in the best interest of an economy and trade should be restricted.
    d. free trade should be protected at all costs.

18. The infant industry argument for protectionism is based on the concern that:
    a. firms in a newly developing domestic industry will have difficulty growing if they face strong competition from established foreign firms.
    b. foreign buyers will absorb all of the output of domestic producers in a growing industry unless trade restrictions are imposed.
    c. the growth of an industry that is new to a nation will be too rapid unless trade restrictions are imposed.
    d. firms in an economy will not grow unless the economy is highly diversified.

19. Which of the following policies would a government impose in an effort to encourage exports of its products to other countries?
    a. Absolute quotas.
    b. Embargoes.
    c. Percentage of value tariffs on products.
    d. Subsidies.

20. The trading area, formally creating in 1992, that is made up of a group of nations with a combined population and a combined GDP approximately equal to the population and GDP of the United States is the:
    a. European Union.
    b. North Atlantic Treaty Organization.
    c. Organization of American States.
    d. Pacific Rim Alliance.

Correct answers to the Exercises and the Sample Examination Questions can be found at the end of the Study Guide.

Chapter 17
International Finance

■ CHAPTER OBJECTIVES

- To define exchange rates and explain how they are determined under both fixed and flexible exchange rate systems.
- To introduce foreign exchange markets, and to identify some factors that affect the supply and demand of currencies in foreign exchange markets and cause exchange rates to fluctuate.
- To identify the major categories into which international financial transactions can be placed, and to understand how the various categories affect each other.
- To define balance of trade and balance of trade surplus and deficit, and to discuss the annual balance of trade for the United States for the past few decades.
- To introduce the debt crisis faced by some countries as a result of large-scale foreign borrowing, and problems in unifying the monetary systems of the countries in the European Union.

■ KEY TERMS AND CONCEPTS

Exchange rate

Fixed exchange rates

Devaluation

Flexible (floating) exchange rates

Foreign exchange market

Exchange rate determination

Current account

Balance of trade

Balance of trade deficit (surplus)

Current account deficit (surplus)

Capital account

324

External debt

Brady Plan

European Monetary System

Maastricht Treaty

▣ STUDY ORGANIZER

1. Understand how changes in exchange rates affect the amounts that buyers pay for imports and exports.

2. Differentiate between fixed and flexible exchange rates.

3. Explain devaluation and its effect on the amounts paid for the devaluing country's exports and imports.

4. Illustrate graphically how an exchange rate is determined by supply and demand.

5. Give some examples of factors that cause changes in the demand and/or supply of a country's money in a foreign exchange market, and show graphically how these changes affect the exchange rate.

6. Understand what is measured in the balance of trade, current account, and capital account.

7. Give some examples of international transactions that cause payment outflows and transactions that cause payment inflows.

8. Explain what is meant by a balance of trade deficit and surplus, and a current account deficit and surplus.

9. Understand why there should be a zero balance when the major international financial transactions categories are tallied for the United States.

10. Explain what is meant by an external debt and identify some costs to borrowing nations of repaying their external debts, and some costs to lending nations if those debts are not paid.

11. Explain the steps taken by the member nations of the European Union to integrate their monetary systems, and some obstacles to that integration.

exchange rate

100

100

gold

fixed

devalued

less

more

1. The number of units of a nation's money that is equal to one unit of another nation's money is the _____ _____ between those two monies.

   a. If the exchange rate between the dollar and the British pound were $2 equals one pound, a good priced at 50 pounds in England would cost a U.S. buyer $_____, and a U.S. good priced at $200 would cost someone in England _____ pounds.

   b. Until 1971, the exchange rates between the U.S. dollar and many other nations' monies were based mainly on the amount of _____ one unit of each nation's money would command, or the United States was on a _____ exchange rate system.

   c. When a nation on a fixed exchange rate system declared that one unit of its money would command less gold than previously, the nation _____ its money. Devaluation made the devaluing nation's goods and services _____ expensive for foreign buyers, and foreign goods and services _____ expensive for buyers within the devaluing nation.

flexible
   floating

foreign exchange

downward
   inverse

upward

direct

d. When exchange rates are set by the forces of supply and demand, nations are on a _____, or _____, exchange rate system. In this system currencies are traded in _____ _____ markets. In a foreign exchange market, the demand curve for a nation's money by foreigners is _____ sloping: there is an _____ relationship between the price of a money and the quantity demanded. The supply curve of a nation's money in a foreign exchange market is _____ sloping: there is a _____ relationship between the price of a money and the quantity supplied.

exchange rate
   amount

decrease

increase

more (less)

less (more)

expensive

e. A change in the demand and/or supply of a nation's money in a foreign exchange market results in a change in the money's _____ _____ and the _____ traded. For example, a shift of the supply curve to the right with no change in the demand curve for a nation's money in a foreign exchange market will cause the equilibrium price of the money to _____ and the equilibrium quantity supplied and demanded to _____. When an exchange rate changes, one country's money becomes worth _____ in terms of the other country's money, and one becomes worth _____. When a country's money becomes worth more, its goods and services become more _____ for cheaper | foreign buyers, and foreign goods and services become _____.

2. Several factors can cause a change in the demand and/or supply of a currency in a foreign exchange market, and change the

exchange rate

_____ _____ for that currency.

a. An increase in the demand for U.S. products by the English would shift the demand curve for dollars by those holding

right

pounds to the _____. As a result, the price of dollars

increase

to those holding pounds would _____, or the dollar

more

would become worth _____ in terms of the pound.

b. Inflation in the United States, but not in Germany, would

increase

_____ the U.S. demand for marks because German

less

goods and services would become relatively _____ expensive to U.S. importers and investors. Inflation in Germany, but not in the United States, would shift the demand curve for marks by U.S. importers and investors to

left

the _____.

c. If investors can earn a higher return on investment opportunities in another country than they can domestically, the demand for the currency of the other country will

increase	_____. Changes in the supply and demand of a currency can also be caused by a nation's government and
policies	central bank _____.

3. Account categories and statistics are maintained to keep track of the various financial transactions between the United States and other countries. The two major transactions categories are the

current capital	_____ account and the _____ account.

    a. When persons from the United States purchase foreign-made products or securities or travel abroad, money flows

from, to	_____ the United States _____ other countries. When persons from other countries purchase U.S.-made products or securities or travel in the United States, money flows
to, from	_____ the United States _____ other countries.

    b. The dollar values of exports and imports of merchandise, income from foreign investments, unilateral transfers, and

current	related items appear in the _____ account. When more U.S. dollars flow out of the United States for these items than foreign money flows in, there is a current
deficit	account _____, and when more flows into the United States for payments than flows out, there is a current
surplus	account _____.

c. Payment flows for the purchase and sale of real and financial assets are recorded in the _____ account. When the dollar value of U.S. assets purchased by foreign investors is greater than the dollar value of foreign assets purchased by U.S. investors, the capital account balance is _____. A positive balance in the capital account would likely occur if there were a _____ balance in the current account.

capital

positive

negative

d. A nation's balance of trade is equal to the value of its merchandise _____ minus the value of its merchandise _____. When the value of a nation's merchandise exports is less than the value of its imports, the nation experiences a balance of trade _____; and when the value of a nation's merchandise exports exceeds the value of its imports, there is a balance of trade _____. Prior to 1970, the United States primarily experienced balance of trade _____. Since 1970 the United States has primarily experienced balance of trade _____.

exports

imports

deficit

surplus

surpluses

deficits

e. When added together and adjusted for statistical discrepancies, the balances in the current account and the capital account should equal _____.

zero

external debt

interest

spending
recession
economic growth

commercial

monetary
fixed

differences
resource

4. Money owed by borrowers in one country to lenders in another country is _____ _____.

    a.   The external debts of some countries are so large that they have been unable to pay the _____ on their debts, much less the debts themselves.

    b.   To repay these loans, debtor nations need to cut back on _____, which could send a nation into a _____. Also, with less spending on investment goods, future _____ _____ could be hampered.

    c.   Failure by borrowing nations to meet their interest payments and other debt obligations creates problems and risks for lending institutions, especially _____ banks.

5. The countries that make up the European Union have signed treaties and taken other steps to integrate their _____ systems using, effectively, a _____ exchange rate mechanism.

    a.   There are several obstacles to European monetary integration, including _____ in the economic problems faced by member countries and _____ immobility.

Exchange Rates

1. Assume that the exchange rate between the British pound and the dollar is
    1 pound = $1.50.

    a. How much would someone in Detroit have to pay in dollars to acquire an English
        sweater priced at 80 pounds? $_____

    b. How much would someone in London have to pay in pounds to acquire an
        American automobile priced at $18,000? _____ pounds

2. Assume that the exchange rate between the pound and the dollar changes from
    1 pound = $1.50 to 1 pound = $2.00.

    a. An English scarf priced at 20 pounds would cost a U.S. buyer $_____
        at the old exchange rate and $_____ at the new exchange rate.

    b. A U.S. lawn mower priced at $360 would cost an English buyer _____
        pounds at the old exchange rate and _____ pounds at the new exchange
        rate.

3. Find a recent copy of an exchange rate table in a newspaper, such as *The Wall Street
    Journal*, to determine how many U.S. dollars a painting priced at 100,000 French francs
    would cost. (Note: Since exchange rates change continually, the dollar price would only
    be valid for the date indicated in the exchange rate table.)

4. Each of the following gives a factor that could change the demand or supply of dollars in a foreign exchange market. Illustrate each change graphically by making the appropriate shift of the demand or supply curve, and indicate the resulting change in the equilibrium price of dollars.

	EXAMPLE	GRAPHIC CHANGE	CHANGE IN EQUILIBRIUM PRICE

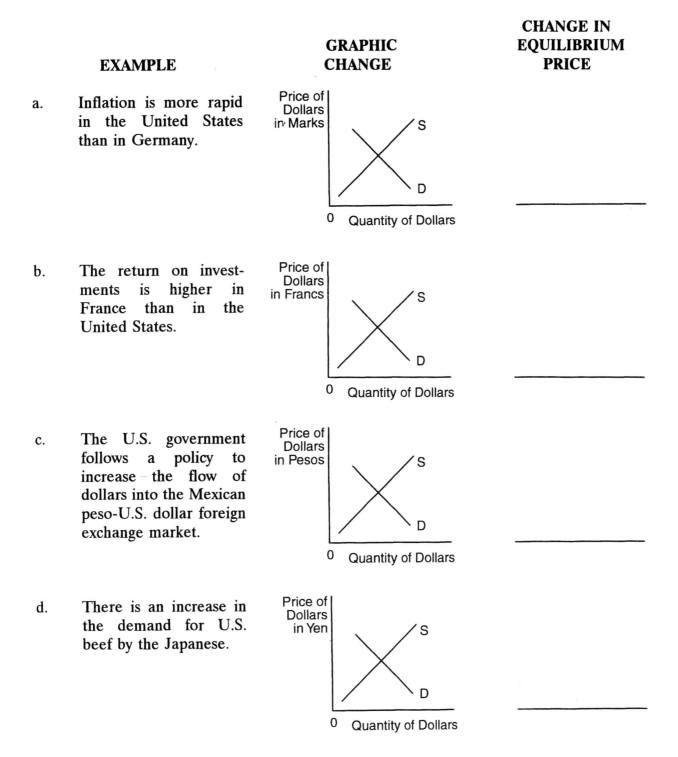

a. Inflation is more rapid in the United States than in Germany.

Price of Dollars in Marks

S

D

0   Quantity of Dollars

_____

b. The return on investments is higher in France than in the United States.

Price of Dollars in Francs

S

D

0   Quantity of Dollars

_____

c. The U.S. government follows a policy to increase the flow of dollars into the Mexican peso-U.S. dollar foreign exchange market.

Price of Dollars in Pesos

S

D

0   Quantity of Dollars

_____

d. There is an increase in the demand for U.S. beef by the Japanese.

Price of Dollars in Yen

S

D

0   Quantity of Dollars

_____

International Financial Transactions

1. Place each of the following transactions in a through e below into the correct international transactions category; that is, determine whether it belongs in the current account or the capital account.

   a. The purchase of Brazilian-made shoes by a U.S. shoe wholesaler.

   b. The purchase of U.S.-made candy by a hotel in Saudi Arabia.

   c. The purchase of an apartment complex in New Zealand by a U.S. manufacturer of plumbing equipment.

   d. A gift of $100 to a niece in Poland from an aunt in Pennsylvania.

   e. The purchase of 100,000 shares of General Motors stock by a businessperson in Hong Kong.

■ SAMPLE EXAMINATION QUESTIONS

Indicate the best answer to each question.

1. At an exchange rate of 12 Austrian schillings equals $1.00, a bottle of wine that costs 336 schillings could be purchased for the equivalent of:
   a. $28.
   b. $288.
   c. $376.32.
   d. $4032.

2. The United States:
   a. has been on a fixed exchange rate system since 1945.
   b. was on a fixed exchange rate system prior to 1971, but is now on a flexible exchange rate system.
   c. has been on a flexible exchange rate system since 1952.
   d. was on a flexible exchange rate system prior to 1983, but is now on a fixed exchange rate system.

3. If exchange rates are based on gold, and a nation devalues its money, goods from the devaluing country become:
    a. less expensive to foreign buyers, and foreign goods become less expensive in the devaluing country.
    b. less expensive to foreign buyers, and foreign goods become more expensive in the devaluing country.
    c. more expensive to foreign buyers, and foreign goods become more expensive in the devaluing country.
    d. more expensive to foreign buyers, and foreign goods become less expensive in the devaluing country.

4. Flexible, or floating, exchange rates are determined by:
    a. the Federal Reserve.
    b. International Monetary Fund agreements.
    c. changes in the price of gold.
    d. the forces of supply and demand.

5. If a good priced at 120 pounds in England can be acquired for $300.00, the exchange rate between the pound and the dollar is:
    a. 1.0 pound = $0.40.
    b. 1.0 pound = $2.00.
    c. 1.0 pound = $2.50.
    d. 2.5 pounds = $1.00.

6. A decrease in the dollar price of Mexican pesos makes Mexican goods:
    a. less expensive to U.S. buyers and leads to an increase in the quantity of pesos demanded by holders of U.S. dollars.
    b. less expensive to U.S. buyers and leads to an increase in the demand for pesos by holders of U.S. dollars.
    c. more expensive to U.S. buyers and leads to a decrease in the quantity of pesos demanded by holders of U.S. dollars.
    d. more expensive to U.S. buyers and leads to a decrease in the demand for pesos by holders of U.S. dollars.

7. If a good were priced at 15 marks in Germany when the exchange rate between the dollar and the mark went from 1.5 marks equal $1.00 to 2.0 marks equal $1.00, the price of that good in U.S. dollars would:
    a. increase by $0.50.
    b. increase by $7.50.
    c. decrease by $2.50.
    d. decrease by $3.75.

8. A decrease in the supply of Mexican pesos to holders of U.S. dollars would cause the dollar price:
    a. and equilibrium quantity of pesos to decrease.
    b. and equilibrium quantity of pesos to increase.
    c. of pesos to decrease and the equilibrium quantity to increase.
    d. of pesos to increase and the equilibrium quantity to decrease.

9. If nations were on a system of floating exchange rates and the demand for a country's exported products fell dramatically, there would be:
    a. a decrease in the demand for that country's money by foreigners.
    b. an increase in the demand for that country's money by foreigners.
    c. a decrease in the supply of that country's money.
    d. an increase in the quantity of that country's money demanded by foreigners.

10. Which of the following would cause a decrease in the demand for French francs by those holding U.S. dollars?
    a. An increase in the rate of return on investments in France above the rate of return on investments in the United States.
    b. Inflation in France, but not in the United States.
    c. Inflation in the United States, but not in France.
    d. None of the above.

11. Imports and exports of merchandise, and payment flows from the purchase and sale of assets between the United States and other nations are recorded in the:
    a. capital account.
    b. current account.
    c. capital account and current account, respectively.
    d. current account and capital account, respectively.

12. U.S. current account deficits:
    a. were a problem in the 1960s because of serious balance of trade deficits at that time.
    b. have disappeared in the 1980s and 1990s because of the federal government's tendency to run surplus budgets since the early 1980s.
    c. increase foreign holdings of U.S. dollars.
    d. none of the above.

13. The balance of trade is:
    a. a component of the current account.
    b. a component of the capital account.
    c. equal to the current account balance plus the capital account balance.
    d. equal to the current account balance minus the capital account balance.

14. A balance of trade of $75 billion indicates that exports of merchandise were:
    a. $75 billion.
    b. $75 billion less than imports of merchandise.
    c. $75 billion more than imports of merchandise.
    d. $75 billion more than income from foreign investments.

15. A $50 billion balance in the U.S. capital account indicates that, on net over the course of the year:
    a. $50 billion was spent by U.S. investors on foreign assets.
    b. U.S. investors spent $50 billion more on foreign assets than foreign investors spent on U.S. assets.
    c. foreign investors spent $50 billion more on U.S. assets than U.S. investors spent on foreign assets.
    d. there was a $50 billion increase in foreign indebtedness to the U.S. government.

16. When considering U.S. international transactions accounts, the current account balance plus the capital account balance should total to:
    a. a negative number if the U.S. is experiencing a capital account deficit.
    b. a positive number if the U.S. is experiencing a balance of trade surplus.
    c. a positive number if the current account balance is greater than the capital account balance.
    d. zero, once adjustments have been made for statistical discrepancies.

17. The external debt crisis refers to the fact that:
    a. few countries that want to take out loans are willing to support U.S. policies.
    b. many countries that borrowed from U.S. banks and other lenders are unable to pay off their loans.
    c. there is no mechanism through which potential lenders in one country can make contact with potential borrowers in another country.
    d. money is leaving the United States because interest rates on loans to foreign countries are higher than interest rates on loans to domestic borrowers.

18. The repayment of a debt to a foreign lender could create a recession in the borrowing country because:
    a. households and businesses in the borrowing country would have to cut their spending in order to pay back the lending country.
    b. part of the labor force in the borrowing country would have to be diverted to producing goods for export to the lending country.
    c. output in the borrowing country would increase faster than the labor force as production grew to meet debt obligations, resulting in too little unemployment.
    d. the general level of prices in the borrowing country would decrease as more goods and services were produced to pay off the debt.

19. The Brady Plan is designed to:
   a. ensure that the balances in the U.S. current account and capital account are equal.
   b. help countries restructure and reduce large external debts.
   c. protect U.S. interests abroad following the formation of the European Monetary System.
   d. none of the above.

20. The purpose of the Maastricht Treaty is to:
   a. bring an end to trade barriers between nations.
   b. prohibit lending to countries that restrict trade.
   c. reduce restrictions on international borrowing.
   d. unify the monetary systems of European nations.

Correct answers to the Exercises and the Sample Examination Questions can be found at the end of the Study Guide.

CHAPTER 1

EXERCISE ANSWERS
Graphing

1.   a-b

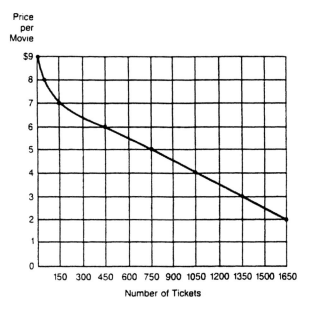

    c.   The line indicates an inverse relationship because it slopes downward, illustrating that as the price increases, the number of tickets sold decreases, and as the price decreases, the number of tickets sold increases.

2.   a-f

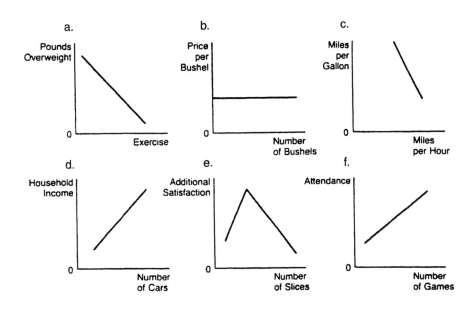

Production Possibilities

1. a. See accompanying figure.
    b. At point A, there would be no consumer goods produced and at point B there would be no capital goods produced. That is, at point A current needs would not be met, and at point B future needs would not be met.
    c. Where on the curve the economy should produce is a value judgment. If one values consumer goods more than capital goods the point will lie closer to B, and if one values capital goods more than consumer goods, it will lie closer to point A.
    d. Point U will lie inside, or to the left of the curve, and point U1 will lie to the left of, and below, point U.
    e. The curve will shift to the right as indicated by the dotted line in the accompanying figure.
    f. See the dashed line in the accompanying figure.
    g. 50 thousand units of capital goods; 40 thousand units of capital goods; 25 thousand units of consumer goods; 75 thousand units of consumer goods.

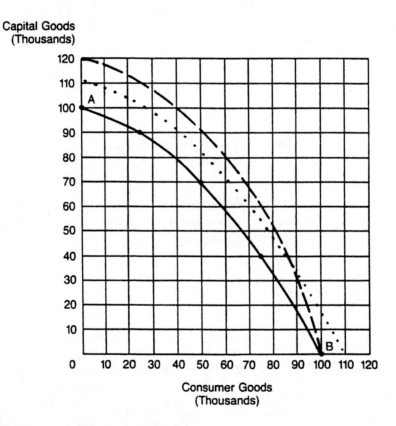

SAMPLE EXAMINATION QUESTION ANSWERS

1.c; 2.c; 3.d; 4.b; 5.d; 6.d; 7.c; 8.b; 9.d; 10.a; 11.d; 12.b; 13.a; 14.c; 15.d; 16.b; 17.d; 18.c; 19.a; 20.c.

CHAPTER 2

EXERCISE ANSWERS
The Circular Flow Model
1.

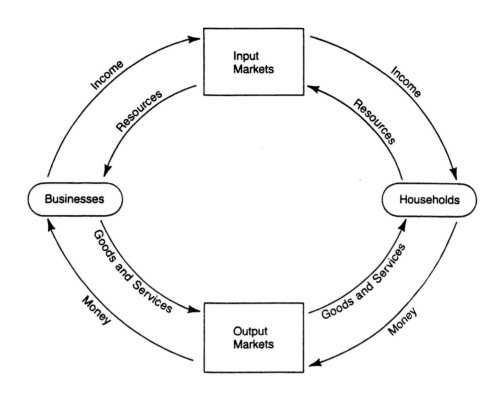

U.S. Economic Development
1.   Answer depends on the drawing, poem, or such that is selected.

SAMPLE EXAMINATION QUESTION ANSWERS
  1.c; 2.c; 3.d; 4.a; 5.c; 6.b; 7.b; 8.b; 9.d; 10.d; 11.c; 12.b; 13.b; 14.c; 15.d; 16.d; 17.a;
18.a; 19.d; 20.b.

CHAPTER 3

EXERCISE ANSWERS
Supply and Demand

1.a.

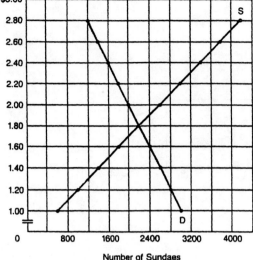

Price per Sundae

Number of Sundaes

b. Increase, decrease; decrease, increase.
c. $1.80, 2200.
d. Shortage, 1200, surplus, 1800, surplus, shortage.
e. A shortage of 600.
f. Price ceiling does not take effect--the equilibrium price results.
g. Since this is a resort town, there should be fewer buyers in the winter months. Also, ice cream is not as popular in the winter. Both of these cause the demand curve to shift to the left, which causes the equilibrium price and quantity to fall.

2.a.

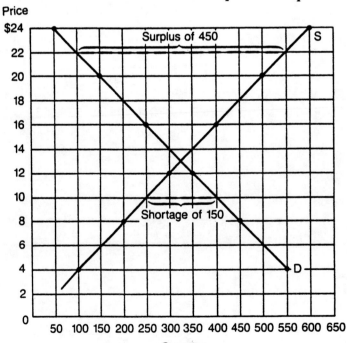

Price

Surplus of 450

Shortage of 150

Quantity

b. $13, 325.

c. Shortage, 150, surplus, 450.

Changes in Demand, Supply, and Equilibrium Versus Changes in Quantity Demanded and Quantity Supplied

1. a. Demand curve shifts to the right; equilibrium price and equilibrium quantity increase.

   b. Demand curve shifts to the left; equilibrium price and equilibrium quantity decrease.

   c. No shifts and no change in equilibrium.

   d. Supply curve shifts to the left; equilibrium price increases and equilibrium quantity decreases.

   e. Supply curve shifts to the left; equilibrium price increases and equilibrium quantity decreases.

   f. Demand curve shifts to the right; equilibrium price and equilibrium quantity increase.

   g. No shifts; market goes to equilibrium since floor is below the equilibrium.

   h. Demand curve shifts to the right; equilibrium price and equilibrium quantity increase.

   i. Supply curve shifts to the right; equilibrium price decreases and equilibrium quantity increases.

   j. No shifts and no change in equilibrium.

Price Ceilings and Floors

1. Market goes to equilibrium since price ceiling is above equilibrium; shortage of 10 million.

2. Surplus of 30 million; market goes to equilibrium since price floor is below equilibrium.

Elasticity

1. a. 1.25, elastic.

   b. 1.33, elastic.

   c. 0.67, inelastic.

   d. 0.75, inelastic.

2. a. 25%/10%, 2.5

   b. 12.5%/12.5%, 1.0

   c. 3%/5%, 0.6

   d. 50%/50%, 1.0

   e. 20%/15%, 1.33

SAMPLE EXAMINATION QUESTION ANSWERS

1.b; 2.c; 3.b; 4.c; 5.b; 6.c; 7.d; 8.a; 9.d; 10.a; 11.d; 12.a; 13.a; 14.c; 15.b; 16.d; 17.c; 18.c; 19.b; 20.c.

CHAPTER 4

EXERCISE ANSWERS

Unemployment, Inflation, and GDP Data

1. Answers can be located in any of the suggested sources.

2.
1994	87.5
1995	90.0
1996	100.0
1997	120.0
1998	130.0
1999	135.0

3.
1	$810
2	800
3	800
4	825
5	820

4.
$243,000	90.0	$270,000
$300,000	100.0	300,000
$360,000	120.0	300,000
$432,000	120.0	360,000
$448,500	130.0	345,000

SAMPLE EXAMINATION QUESTION ANSWERS

1.b; 2.d; 3.a; 4.c; 5.d; 6.d; 7.a; 8.a; 9.c; 10.c; 11.d; 12.c; 13.c; 14.d; 15.a; 16.d; 17.a; 18.c; 19.b; 20.a.

CHAPTER 5

EXERCISE ANSWERS
Total Spending and the Level of Economic Activity

1. a-d

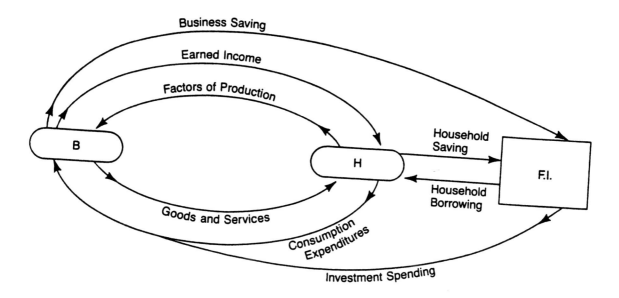

2. a-d

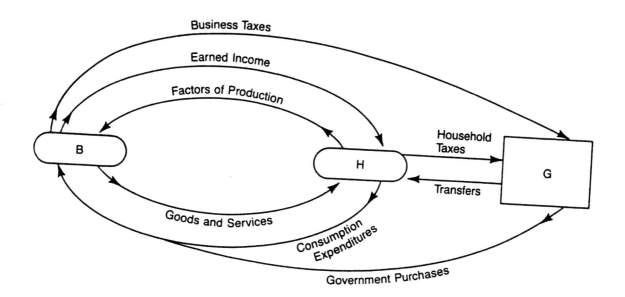

3.

Leakages	*Injections*
1. Household saving	1. Household spending from borrowing
2. Business saving	2. Household spending from transfers
3. Household taxes	3. Business investment spending
4. Business taxes	4. Government purchases
5. Spending on imports	5. Spending on exports

4. a. Decrease.
    b. Increase.
    c. Increase.
    d. Inflation.
    e. Decrease.

The multiplier
1. a. Increase of $24 billion.
    b. Decrease of $1.75 billion.
    c. Increase of $15 billion.
    d. Decrease of $133.3 billion.

SAMPLE EXAMINATION QUESTION ANSWERS
  1.c; 2.d; 3.b; 4.d; 5.b; 6.b; 7.c; 8.d; 9.d; 10.a; 11.c; 12.a; 13.b; 14.a; 15.c; 16.b; 17.d;
18.d; 19.b; 20.a.

CHAPTER 6

EXERCISE ANSWERS
Types of Taxes
  1. a. Regressive; b. Proportional; c. Progressive; d. Regressive; e. Regressive; f. Progressive.

Government's Impact on the Macroeconomy
1. a. Decrease output and employment.
    b. Increase prices.
    c. Decrease output and employment.
    d. Increase output and employment.
    e. Increase output and employment.

Federal Government Receipts, Outlays, Balances, and Debt
1. See source cited for data.
2. See source cited in number 1 for data to calculate this percentage.

SAMPLE EXAMINATION QUESTION ANSWERS
  1.a; 2.d; 3.b; 4.b; 5.a; 6.c; 7.c; 8.b; 9.c; 10.a; 11.a; 12.c; 13.b; 14.d; 15.d; 16.a; 17.c;
18.b; 19.d; 20.c.

CHAPTER 7

EXERCISE ANSWERS
Money Supply Data
1. See source cited for data.

Banking and the Federal Reserve
1. a-e Answers will differ depending upon the particular bank that is examined.

Changes in a Reserve Account
1. $ 6,375,000
2. $15,330,000
3. $10,045,000

SAMPLE EXAMINATION QUESTION ANSWERS
1.c; 2.a; 3.b; 4.a; 5.d; 6.d; 7.b; 8.c; 9.a; 10.c; 11.a; 12.b; 13.c; 14.c; 15.b; 16.b; 17.d; 18.d; 19.a; 20.b.

CHAPTER 8

EXERCISE ANSWERS
Reserves and Loans
1. $52.5 million; $32.5 million.
2. $20 million.
3. $43 million; $8.8 million; $34.2 million; $34.2 million.

Reserves and Monetary Policy Tools
1. $1.8 million.
2. $1.75 million.
3. $800,000.
4. $10 million.

Money Multiplier
1. 8; $560 million.
2. $1.75 billion.

Summary
1. $59.56 million.

SAMPLE EXAMINATION QUESTION ANSWERS
1d; 2.c; 3.b; 4.c; 5.a; 6.b; 7.a; 8.c; 9.d; 10.d; 11.b; 12.a; 13.d; 14.a; 15.b; 16.c; 17.c; 18.a; 19.c; 20.d.

CHAPTER 9

EXERCISE ANSWERS
Aggregate Demand - Aggregate Supply

1. a. The aggregate supply line is vertical at full employment GDP because the classical economists assumed that the economy would operate at full employment regardless of the level of wages and prices. In the new classical economics model, the long-run aggregate supply line is vertical at the natural rate of unemployment and the vertical axis focuses on prices.

    b. Aggregate demand slopes downward to indicate that households and businesses will buy more at lower prices and less at higher prices. The new classical economists provide three reasons: the interest rate, wealth, and foreign trade effects.

    c. An increase in aggregate demand means the AD curve shifts to the right and prices and wages increase; a decrease in aggregate demand shifts the AD curve to the left and prices and wages fall. In both cases, GDP stays at the full employment level. The effect is the same in the new classical economics long-run model, except that this model focuses on the natural rate of unemployment and uses prices on the vertical axis.

Equilibrium in the Macroeconomy

1. a, c.

Total Output	Total Spending	Injections Minus Leakages	Economic Condition
$ 0.00	$ 0.75	$0.75	expansion
0.50	1.00	0.50	expansion
1.00	1.25	0.25	expansion
1.50	1.50	0.00	equilibrium
2.00	1.75	- 0.25	contraction
2.50	2.00	- 0.50	contraction
3.00	2.25	- 0.75	contraction

    b. $1.5 trillion.
    d. Decrease, increase.
    e. Expansion occurs when injections are greater than leakages, and contraction occurs when leakages are greater than injections.

2.   a.

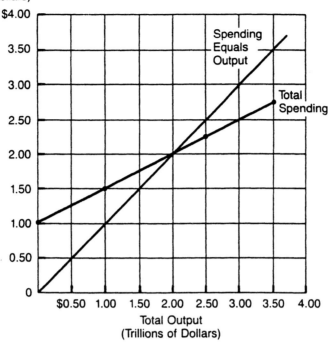

Total Spending
(Trillions of Dollars)

Total Output
(Trillions of Dollars)

b. $2.0, total spending equals total output.
c. $0.5; 0; -$0.5.

The Phillips Curve
1.   See cited source and place point(s) on Figure 9.4. The location of the point(s) answers
      the question about the shift of the Phillips curve.

SAMPLE EXAMINATION QUESTION ANSWERS
  1.b; 2.b; 3.a; 4.c; 5.c; 6.d; 7.c; 8.a; 9.a; 10.b; 11.d; 12.d; 13.c; 14.d; 15.c; 16.a; 17.a;
18.c; 19.b; 20.b.

CHAPTER 10

EXERCISE ANSWERS
Household Income
1.   See source cited for answers.

Maximizing Satisfaction
1.   Purchase the shirt and wallet. $60 spent on the pants adds 125 units of utility, whereas
      $60 spent on the shirt and wallet adds a total of 150 units of utility.

2. Spend all of the money to purchase a cola, a sandwich, and desert. The additional utility *per dollar* spent is highest for these three items, which add a total of 73 utility points. No other combination of spending all or part of $6 adds that many utility points.

Data Sources
1.
   a. General Electric's annual report; *Moody's Industrial Manual.*
   b. *F&S Index*; CD-ROM reference services.
   c. *Statistical Abstract of the United States.*
   d. Pacific Bell's annual report.
   e. *Statistical Abstract of the United States.*
   f. *Statistical Abstract of the United States.*
   g. General Motor's annual report; *Moody's Industrial Manual.*

SAMPLE EXAMINATION QUESTION ANSWERS

1.c; 2.d; 3.d; 4.b; 5.c; 6.d; 7.d; 8.a; 9.c; 10.b; 11.b; 12.a; 13.a; 14.c; 15.a; 16.c; 17.a; 18.c; 19.b; 20.a.

CHAPTER 11

EXERCISE ANSWERS
Maximizing by an Individual
1. a, b.

Number of Hours Studying	Marginal Cost	Total Cost	Marginal Benefit	Total Benefit	Net Benefit
0		0		0	0
	75		500		
1		75		500	425
	150		400		
2		225		900	675
	225		300		
3		450		1200	750
	300		200		
4		750		1400	650
	375		100		
5		1125		1500	375
	450		50		
6		1575		1550	-25

   c. 3; 750; less; rise; greater; fall.
   d. See accompanying figure.
   e. Total benefit exceeds total cost by the greatest amount; 3.

350

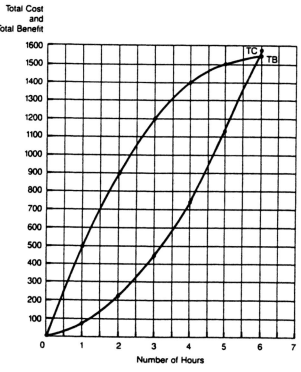

Total Cost and Total Benefit

Number of Hours

Maximizing by a Business

1.   a-c

Number of Units of Output	Total Cost	Marginal Cost	Price Per Unit	Total Revenue	Marginal Revenue	Profit
0	$ 50		$440	$ 0		$ -50
		$100			$420	
1	150		420	420		270
		150			380	
2	300		400	800		500
		200			340	
3	500		380	1140		640
		250			300	
4	750		360	1440		690
		300			260	
5	1050		340	1700		650
		350			220	
6	1400		320	1920		520
		400			180	
7	1800		300	2100		300
		450			140	
8	2250		280	2240		-10

d.   4; $360; $690.
e.   See figure on page 352.

351

SAMPLE EXAMINATION QUESTION ANSWERS

1.b; 2.a; 3.c; 4.c; 5.b; 6.a; 7.b; 8.c; 9.b; 10.c; 11.b; 12.a; 13.b; 14.c; 15.b; 16.d; 17.a; 18.d; 19.c; 20.d.

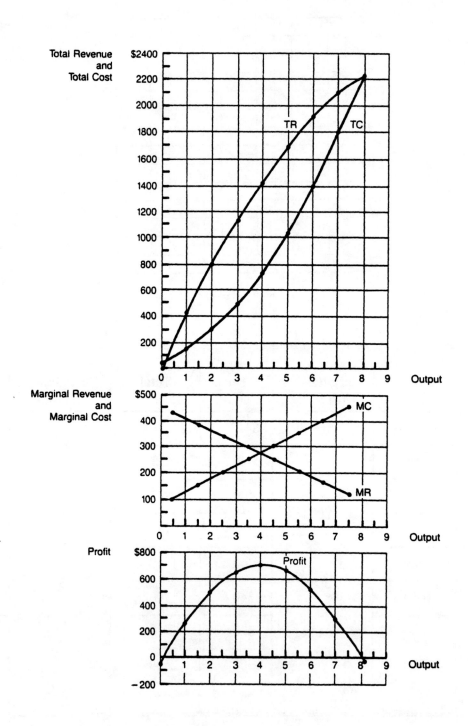

EXERCISE ANSWERS
Cost Determination
1.   a

Number of Cakes	Total Cost	Total Fixed Cost	Total Variable Cost	Average Total Cost	Marginal Cost
0	$ 25	$ 25	$ 0	----	
					$ 25
1	50	25	25	$ 50	
					10
2	60	25	35	30	
					15
3	75	25	50	25	
					25
4	100	25	75	25	
					35
5	135	25	110	27	
					45
6	180	25	155	30	
					65
7	245	25	220	35	
					91
8	336	25	311	42	

b.   At this higher level of output she needs to purchase more variable factors to compensate for the limitation of the fixed factors. Perhaps she will need to rent an additional oven, hire more help, purchase more pans, and such.

c.   She will produce and sell 5 cakes per days since this is her profit-maximizing level of output.

d.

Number of Cakes	Total Revenue	Total Cost	Total Profit	Marginal Revenue	Marginal Cost
0	$ 0	$ 25	$ -25		
				$40	$ 25
1	40	50	-10		
				40	10
2	80	60	20		
				40	15
3	120	75	45		
				40	25
4	160	100	60		
				40	35
5	200	135	65		
				40	45
6	240	180	60		
				40	65
7	280	245	35		
				40	91
8	320	336	-16		

e.

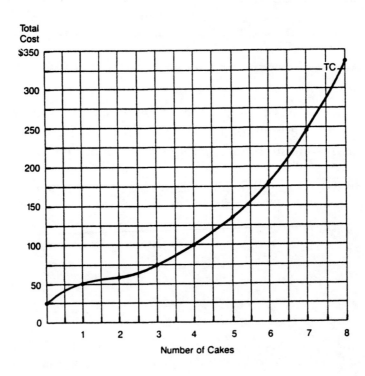

f. This pattern is the result of the interaction of fixed and variable factors as influenced by the Law of Diminishing Returns.

g.

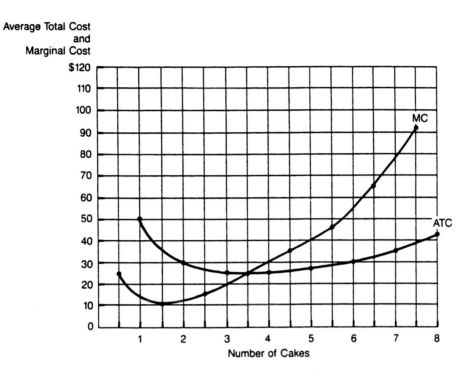

2. a.

Number of Children	Total Cost	Total Fixed Cost	Total Variable Cost	Average Total Cost	Marginal Cost
0	$ 15	$ 15	$ 0	----	$ 25
1	40	15	25	$ 40	
2	44	15	29	22	4
3	48	15	33	16	4
4	68	15	53	17	20
5	90	15	75	18	22

Number of Children	Average Fixed Cost	Average Variable Cost
0	-----	----
1	$15.00	$25.00
2	7.50	14.50
3	5.00	11.00
4	3.75	13.25
5	3.00	15.00

c.

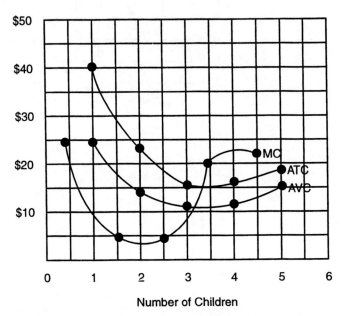

Average Total Cost Average Variable Cost, and Marginal Cost

Number of Children

d.   The distance between the average total cost curve and average variable cost curve narrows as the number of children in daycare increases because it represents average fixed cost, which decreases as the level of output increases.

e.   No production decision can be made on the basis of cost information alone. Marcia Deal needs to know what price can be charged for the daycare service in order to calculate total revenue. Profit is determined by assessing *both* cost and revenue information.

SAMPLE EXAMINATION QUESTION ANSWERS

1.a; 2.d; 3.b; 4.c; 5.c; 6.a; 7.b; 8.d; 9.c; 10.a; 11.c; 12.b; 13.b; 14.d; 15.a; 16.b; 17.a; 18.d; 19.a; 20.b.

CHAPTER 13

EXERCISE ANSWERS
Pure Competition
1. a.

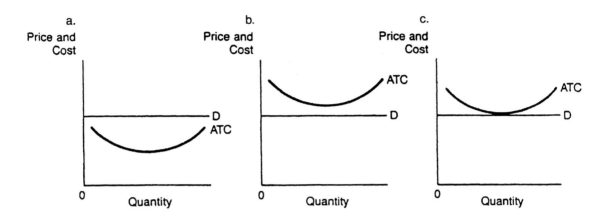

a.
Price and Cost

b.
Price and Cost

c.
Price and Cost

b. The market supply curve shifts to the right from S to S1, and the individual firm's demand curve shifts downward from D to D1.

2.

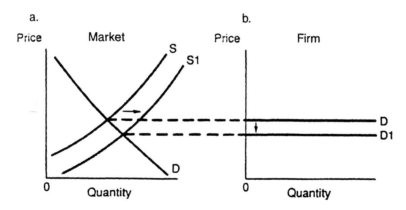

a.
Price Market

b.
Price Firm

3. You need to draw a U-shaped long-run average total cost curve that just touches the demand curve at its lowest point.
    a. The amount produced is determined by the output level where the long-run average total cost curve touches the demand curve. This amount will be sold for $5 per unit.

4.

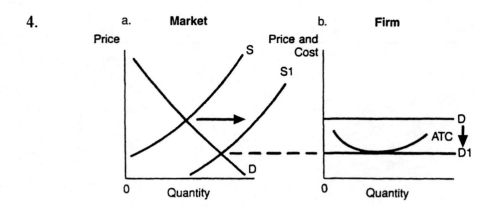

5.   a.   Profit; below.
        b.   9,000.
        c. $2.50; $3.50; $1.00.
        d. $9,000.

6.   a. $2.50; 6,000.
        b. $3.00; $1.50.
        c.   The firm would minimize its loss by operating. Since price is greater than average variable cost at the output where marginal cost equals marginal revenue, the firm is covering all of its variable costs and some of its fixed costs: Its loss is equal to the part of its fixed costs that is not covered by revenue. If the firm were to shut down its loss would be equal to all of its fixed costs.

Monopolistic Competition
1.   a.   150,000; $6; $0.
        b.   250,000; $5.

2.   a.   5,000; $3.00.
        b.   The long-run average total cost curve should be above the demand curve and just touch the demand curve at 5,000 units of output.

Oligopoly
1.

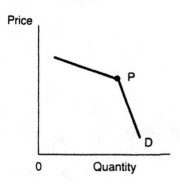

Monopoly
1.   a.   18,000.
        b. $16.
        c. $10; $16; $6; $108,000.

SAMPLE EXAMINATION QUESTION ANSWERS
  1.c; 2.c; 3.b; 4.a; 5.c; 6.d; 7.b; 8.a; 9.b; 10.b; 11.d; 12.c; 13.a; 14.a; 15.d; 16.a; 17.d; 18.c; 19.d; 20.b.

CHAPTER 14

EXERCISE ANSWERS

Antitrust
1.   This answer depends on the article that you locate.

Government Intervention
1.   a.

Units of Output	Long-Run Total Cost	Long-Run Average Total Cost
0	$ 0	-----
10,000	1,000,000	$100
20,000	1,600,000	80
30,000	1,950,000	65
40,000	2,200,000	55
50,000	2,500,000	50

        b.   The behavior of long-run average total cost suggests that this firm is a natural monopoly, making it more efficient to have one large regulated seller rather than several smaller competing sellers.

SAMPLE EXAMINATION QUESTION ANSWERS
  1.d; 2.a; 3.d; 4.b; 5.b; 6.c; 7.b; 8.c; 9.c; 10.d; 11.c; 12.a; 13.a; 14.c; 15.c; 16.d; 17.b; 18.d; 19.a; 20.b.

CHAPTER 15

EXERCISE ANSWERS
Demand for Labor
1.

Units of Labor	Total Product	Marginal Physical Product
0	0	
		480
1	480	
		460
2	940	
		420
3	1360	
		360
4	1720	
		240
5	1960	
		140
6	2100	
		20
7	2120	
		0
8	2120	

2. a-b

Number of Workers	Total Product	Price per Unit	Total Revenue	Marginal Revenue Product
0	0	$7.25	$ 0	
				$1050.00
1	150	7.00	1050.00	
				806.25
2	275	6.75	1856.25	
				581.25
3	375	6.50	2437.50	
				375.00
4	450	6.25	2812.50	
				187.50
5	500	6.00	3000.00	
				18.75
6	525	5.75	3018.75	
				0
7	525	5.75	3018.75	

c.   2; 4; 5; 5.

d.

Number of Workers Demanded	Price of Labor (Wage)
1	$1050.00
2	806.25
3	581.25
4	375.00
5	187.50
6	18.75
7	0

e.

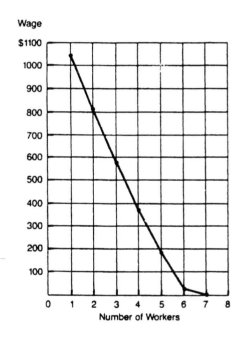

Labor Market Modifications
1. a. 4,000; 9,000; surplus; 5,000.
    b. $3.50; 0.

2.

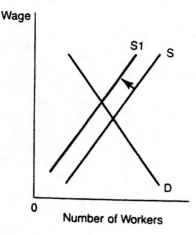

Wage

S1 S

D

0   Number of Workers

    a.   Increase; decrease.

SAMPLE EXAMINATION QUESTION ANSWERS
1.c; 2.d; 3.b; 4.c; 5.b; 6.b; 7.a; 8.a; 9.d; 10.d; 11.b; 12.b; 13.c; 14.c; 15.b; 16.a; 17.c; 18.d; 19.a; 20.a.

CHAPTER 16

EXERCISE ANSWERS
Comparative Advantage

1.   a.   5,000; 250,000; A; A.
        b.   100; 2; B; B.
        c.   100; 10; 110; 5,000; 25,000; 30,000.
        d.   200 tons of iron ore; 50,000 pairs of shoes.
        e.   110; 30,000; 200; 50,000.

2.   a.   Coffee because its opportunity cost of producing coffee is lower than Chile's (1 ton of copper is given up for 50 tons of coffee in Guatemala, compared to 500 tons of copper for 50 tons of coffee in Chile); copper because its opportunity cost of producing copper is lower than Guatemala's (10 tons of coffee are given up for 100 tons of copper in Chile, compared to 5,000 tons of coffee for 100 tons of copper in Guatemala).

3.   a.   Yes; with specialization according to the principle of comparative advantage the same amount of resources can produce as much oil, but more men's suits can be produced than before specialization.
        b.   Gabon; Venezuela.

CHAPTER 17

EXERCISE ANSWERS
Exchange Rates
1.   a. $120.
       b.   12,000 pounds.

2.   a. $30, $40.
       b.   240 pounds; 180 pounds.

3.   Locate source suggested; answer depends on exchange rate.

4.   a.   Demand shifts to the left; equilibrium price falls.
       b.   Demand shifts to the left; equilibrium price falls.
       c.   Supply shifts to the right; equilibrium price falls.
       d.   Demand shifts to the right; equilibrium price rises.

International Financial Transactions
1.   a.   Current account.
       b.   Current account.
       c.   Capital account.
       d.   Current account.
       e.   Capital account.

SAMPLE EXAMINATION QUESTION ANSWERS
1.a; 2.b; 3.b; 4.d; 5.c; 6.a; 7.c; 8.d; 9.a; 10.b; 11.d; 12.c; 13.a; 14.c; 15.c; 16.d; 17.b; 18.a; 19.b; 20.d.